£2.95

PUBLISHED BY

DISS PUBLISHING CO. LTD.,
40 MERE STREET, DISS, NORFOLK.

WAVENEY VALLEY STUDIES

Gleanings from Local History

by

ERIC PURSEHOUSE, B.Sc. (Lond.)

First Published in Great Britain
by Diss Publishing Co. Ltd.
1966

Reprinted 1983

Printed in Great Britain by
Richard Clay (The Chaucer Press) Ltd,
Bungay, Suffolk

Cover photograph of St. Mary's Church, Diss.
Kindly lent by Cyril Piper.

Biographical Note

THE LATE ERIC PURSEHOUSE, born in 1899 at Redgrave in North Suffolk, came of a teaching family. Both his parents were teachers, his brothers, his sister and he himself went into the same profession. During the first world war he served in the R.N.V.R. aboard a mine-sweeper; then transferred to the R.A.F., in which he was a flying cadet when the war ended. After this, he took a London B.Sc. extra-murally—"the hard way"—and eventually returned to East Anglia as headmaster of the same village school over which his parents had once reigned.

In 1929 he became geography master at Diss Grammar School, in 1952 he was appointed headmaster, in 1959 he retired because of ill health.

But he was not the man to vegetate in retirement. His whole life was based on the principle of service to any community in which he found himself, and already while still schoolmastering he had been taking part in the life of Diss as U.D. Councillor (he was chairman in 1948 and 1949). His heart-trouble caused him to put this work aside for a few years, but after retiring from the school he entered public office again, topping the poll in the 1960 and 1963 elections.

At the time of his death he was serving on more committees than would seem possible for a man who had retired on account of ill-health; and because he loved teaching, he continued this work part-time as well.

He was a valued singer in the choir of Diss Church: music was was one of his loves, and he was a founder-member of the Diss Music and Arts Society. In younger days he had played very good cricket and football, by way of contrast to his more learned interests. A full life. And though it was very largely a life of service to others, he enjoyed if fully.

He very greatly enjoyed the researches into local history which are recorded in this book. They involved him in much toil, and often in the exercise of great skill in deciphering the crabbed handwriting of ancient documents. The oddities he brought to light afforded him both amusement and instruction: he was one who never sat back and said "I need learn no more: I know enough". His continuous appetite for learning is shown by his long support of the W.E.A. and his founder-membership of the Diss Antiquarian Society. In his own line, he could be called one of the most active members of this Society, because by his original research he unearthed much which might otherwise never have been discovered and which would certainly never have been presented in coherent form.

His sudden death left many gaps in the life of his town and district. Nobody can take his place. None of us is indispensable ? That may be true, but it would take half a dozen ordinary men less versatile and devoted to add up to one Eric Pursehouse.

Preface

THESE PIECES were written for local newspapers. They appear here in their original form except where with a minimum of cutting I have run two consecutively because they complement each other. There is a little overlapping of subject-matter because parishes, districts and historical trends are not walled-off from one another. If Eric Pursehouse had lived to construct his own book, as he intended, he might have discarded the newspaper-article form: but it has seemed best to me, without his guidance, to make as little alteration as possible.

His friends feel that the perpetuation of his original researches in book form ought to be undertaken, not only for the pleasure of residents in Diss and district who recognise the names of people and places, but also for the benefit of students of social history, in Universities and Sixth Forms. Much of the material, for instance the pieces on Emigration, casts a light which extends beyond the immediate neighbourhood.

DOREEN WALLACE.

WORTHAM, DISS.

E. L. Button

Thanks for permission to reprint are due to the Editors of
THE DISS EXPRESS
THE SOUTH NORFOLK NEWS
THE EASTERN DAILY PRESS

Contents

DISS —

Names from the Past	1
That old liquor pit	4
The tragedy of Louie's Lane	7
Street names of Diss	10
Diss Mere	14
A freeze-up 300 years ago	19
Olde Cock Street Fair	23
The unsavoury history of Fair Green	26
Street naming in Diss 100 years ago	29
The workhouse on Diss Common	33
Proof of the pudding at the Workhouse	37
Diss Common	40
1814 Festival of Peace in Diss	43
Jubilee Year for Diss Waterworks	47
Significance of the New Town Sign	50
Diss — a wicked Town	53

AND DISTRICT —

These were the Roydon Riots	57
Roydon — in the days when you could be hanged for shooting a rabbit	66
Farm-workers were following in footsteps of the Luddites	69
Scholastic Academies a century ago	72
Schools for young ladies, 1862	75
Botesdale Grammar School	78

Leaves from a school log-book ...	82
Three Royalist Rectors	85
The Eye Anti-felon Society	88
Witnesses were paid 17/2d. for beer	92
Records rescued from the fire at Scole Church	95
Dickleburgh's 18th century Friendly Society	103
A highlight in the history of Dickleburgh	107
"Examinations for Settlement"	110
Hard times in Brockdish	115
A Palgrave house with a history	119
Tragedy in Gawdy wood	126

OLD CUSTOMS

Chalk-back day ...	130
Camp Ball	133
Beating the Bounds in Rogationtide	136
A system savouring of slavery	142
Help in distress — South Norfolk briefs	145
"Burial in Woollen"	149
Rustic sports of a century ago ...	153

OLD TRADES

Old Trades	156
South Norfolk crafts	158
Spinning in the school curriculum	162
Grow hemp or be fined ...	164
Woolcombers and worsted weavers	168

St. Blaize, Patron of woolcombers	173
Diss weavers	177
18th Century weavers of the Waveney Valley	182
The great days of Lopham linen	187
Costerton's flax factory at Scole	193
Diss corsets	196
The Diss Lace Association	201
Indentured apprentices	206

PEOPLE

A Diss family (Manning)	211
Bertie Harrison	215
Horse doctor	219
William Betts	222

GENERAL

Town topics a century ago	225
Emigration (1)	228
,, (2)	233
,, (3)	237
Some Norfolk bread doles	240
Charity at Christmas in bygone years	244
A Diss Petty Constable, 1649	247
The duties of a 17th century Petty Constable	250
The press gangs	254
Strangers in the gallery	258
Gallery singers and musicians	261
From hurdy-gurdy to finger organ	264

Parish registers — unusual entries	268
Whipping and burning in Merrie England	272
Corruption in high places 300 years ago	276
Diss Home Guard of 1640	280
Old Grog's victory	284
Devastating storms of yesteryear	288
In the dead of night	291
The great fire of Diss	295

Names from the past
(PUBLISHED AUGUST, 1961)

IN the annual accounts of St. Mary's, Diss, are two items which have appeared regularly since 1685, the rents of "Walcot Pightle" and "Penning's Green."

The word "pightle" used to indicate any irregularly shaped enclosure — hence "Calves' Pightle," "Willow Pightle" and "Hempland Pightle" appear in early maps.

But "Walcot Pightle" is special, for it was presented to the Hamlet of Walcote in 1620, so that its rent could meet the annual "leet fine" to the Manor of Diss. Later it became Town property, and the annual Vestry received, and still receives, the rent of this enclosure in Millway Lane.

Penning's Green was formerly part of a more extensive Westbrook Green. Accounts of 1685 state : "From time out of memory it has bin inclosed at May Day, and kept soe till Lammass ; he that is tenant to the house that stands by it allwayes have one halfe the cropp (i.e. hay) at 13s. 4d., the other halfe goes by turns to every house upon the Green at 13s. 4d."

The present owner still pays £1 6s. 8d. according to custom. Penning's Green was enclosed in 1816, but the origin of its name is lost in history.

There are many other picturesque names which have passed out of use. One is Listermere Way, now Mission Road, and Sandy Lane. Lister is a corruption of "litster" — old English for dyer. It appeared in old documents relating to the ancient linen and woollen industries of Diss.

The marshy lands near Frenze river contained meres or ponds where the dyers washed their fabrics. So "Listermere Way" led to the scene of the dyers' activities.

Leading north from Hill Farm, Burston, along the Heywood boundary was the mile-long Procession Way, the route which the Rector and townsmen followed in their annual "Perambulation" or "Beating the Bounds." Those who completed the exacting course were regaled with beer and cakes.

In 1688 "expenses for ye perambolation" amounted to £1, but in 1825, when the Rev. William Manning led the procession, they were £23 14s. 2d. Each man that went the bounds was allowed "1s. for his dinner, and 1s. to drink," while "the Music was allowed expenses for Dinner and Drink, and 30s. besides." Thirty completed the course, spurred on by outbursts from the band and prospects of cakes and ale.

Turning westward was Vagrants' Way which led into Rye's Lane, further north. Vagrants' Way was a rendezvous for "tramps" of bygone days who dossed among the scattered stacks and sheds.

Overseers' accounts from Elizabeth's reign onwards frequently refer to "poor walking men" (and even women and boys) who were given relief in the days of widespread vagrancy.

Rye's Lane was the haunt of Jimmy Rye, a notorious but colourful beggar of the early 19th century. His mother, the wife of a Fersfield farmer, died when Jimmy was seven. His father remarried, but Jimmy got little affection from the stepmother.

"A smack on the face for sitting too near the fire" was the first rebuke, followed by "so many kicks, cuffs and scratches that neighbours cried shame." Those were Jimmy's own words and he added, "Father took to drinking, and I to begging."

Jimmy maintained that the world was full of beggars—"The Parliament men 'beg' your votes; the young man 'begs' a smile from his mistress; boys 'beg' a shilling of their fathers, and the farmers are the cruellest beggars of all, for they 'beg' me to leave their premises." Such was the strange philosophy of this odd man who lived rough and "shacked" around with two stout sticks.

Diss Heywood excelled in unusual names. In Flexen Meadow the linen was spread to bleach. Fowle Slough was a low-lying, sticky clay field churned to a quagmire every winter. "The Spong" was a spongey, marshy meadow.

"Bootfield" adjoined the ancient "Tibenham Boot," while "Common Meadow" had been part of Heywood Common where the annual Diss Steeplechases were formerly held. Even today gorse and broom flourish by the roadside as witness of the old Common.

An almost oriental sounding name was "Upper Wong." It was derived from "wone," an abode or dwelling.

In Diss itself was "Pound Piece," now the site of the poultry packing factory. It was opposite the "Parish Pound" which was where the Church Hall now stands. Stray cattle were impounded here and had to be bailed out. Near by was "Hockle Hole," a low, marshy spot in what is now Park Road.

The overflow of the Mere trickled through Hockle Hole — so named from a species of hock or mallow growing there. In 1692 charges were recorded for "making ye arche and for four posts, four keyes and one rayle set at Hockle Hole."

"Pooley's Corner" and "Farthing Cross" are also names of the past. The first was the highest point in Diss, where Shelfanger Road and Sunnyside now meet. The name derived from a resident in one of the cluster of old houses which formerly formed almost a separate hamlet at that point.

"Farthing Cross" lay in the angle between the main Roydon road and the road to Brewers' Green. Farthing was formerly the word for a fourth of an acre. A wooden cross at the road junction marked the entry into Diss—hence Farthing Cross was the small enclosure by the Cross.

Many self-explanatory names also occur in documents and on old maps—"Barn Hempland," "Four Acres," "Mill Close," "Claypit Piece," "New-Broke-Up-Piece," "Stackyard Meadow" and "Sandfield" are just a few. They represent a more leisurely age and remind us that the husbandmen of earlier ages had a keen understanding of the subtle differences between their various fields.

That old liquor pit in a Diss lane
(PUBLISHED JUNE, 1960)

LOOK at a large-scale map of Diss, and you will see the words "Liquor Pit" placed beside a small stretch of water adjoining Croft Lane, on the western outskirts of the town.

Older residents will remember this lane, lined with French oaks, when it was bordered by open fields for its entire length. At all seasons, it was a favourite haunt for young couples ; and in spring and summer, the lane afforded a picturesque country walk for family groups.

But to walk down the lane by night, years ago, was a rather creepy experience, especially in winter. There was no lighting; in fact no services existed at all. The sudden rustle of leaves, as some animal scurried away, or the unexpected bound of a prowling cat, produced an eerie feeling in anyone who was timid of the dark.

And near the Liquor Pit there was an ivy-covered tree stump —harmless-looking by day, but by night, viewed from one special point, it loomed up like some shrouded monster ready to pounce on the unwary. A sigh of relief escaped when it was safely passed, with nothing untoward happening.

The Liquor Pit then, was surrounded by high and rank overhanging growth, almost eclipsing the pit itself, as if shielding some murky spot. Probing among and through the dense fringing hedge, it was possible to establish that this "pit" actually was an artificial pond, created by damming the south-east corner with a brick wall to impound water flowing in from neighbouring ditches and fields.

From the pond, water was led by pipes to various properties lower down in the town — notably Park House (now an hotel) and the Denmark Brewery. Pipes were discovered and removed only recently, but some still remain hidden below the surface of gardens, and one section, detached and secured to a tree, remains embedded in the tree.

The arrival of the town's piped water supply, in 1912, rendered this source of water no longer necessary. But as recently as 1946 one dweller in Croft Lane was served with a bill for 7s. 6d. for the use of a standpipe fed by water originating in the pit. The Brewery (as owners of the pit and surrounding land) tried to impose the charge, but failed.

It was difficult to establish with certainty if the water was ever actually used for brewing purposes—it may have been boiled to make it safe, or merely used for cleansing purposes, in former times. But its use for brewing, years ago, was highly probable. There were no scientific tests for ingredients in those days, as there are at every stage of the brewing process today. The public would not be so squeamish as to bother about such details as the source of water. It was the beer that counted !

I recall, as a boy, living in a house where the only water supply was from a scullery pump, which raised water direct from a pond where water rats, newts and frogs abounded. The water was boiled, and nobody took any harm—so why bother ?

But to return to the Liquor Pit, which 15 years ago was just a pond, almost invisible in its embracing foliage. Building land was scarce in Diss after the war—then, quite suddenly, land on both sides of Croft Lane was released for building plots. Two plots behind the pit hung fire for quite a time. Several prospective buyers looked pensively at them, but over and over again there was a reluctance "to live near that pit, with its unfortunate name, its past reputation, and possibly unsavoury smell."

Eventually, the plots were acquired, and two modern bungalows erected on them. The owners of the bungalows have shown great imagination in converting the pit from a mysterious dark object into an attractive ornamental pond.

Slashing down the high overgrowth to almost waist high, and opening up the surface to view, they have trimmed the overhanging trees, and developed colourful gardens on two sides. There is a constant, though small, flow of water through the pit, and the opening-up has helped to cleanse the surface. Dumping of refuse has ceased, and wild life has been attracted. In the first year of enlightenment, a moorhen built her nest among a group of rushes, and raised an attractive little brood. Even a heron was seen to rise from the pit early one morning—but only once.

In 1959 a pair of mandarin ducks from the Mere, after a preliminary reconnoitring flight, came to breed there. In a secluded spot among the undergrowth on the east bank near the road, and within a few feet of passers-by, the duck laid her clutch of 12 eggs. Though an errant dog devoured one of them, 11 were hatched.

It was a fascinating sight to see the proud parents lovingly steering and guarding their fluffy, multi-coloured offspring around, as they bobbed on the placid surface. Unfortunately, "Father" was unfaithful. The arrival of a second duck distracted his attention, and won his affection.

The deserted and broken-hearted mother had no appeal to the courts, so, under cover of night, she shepherded her diminutive family across country to a new abode—the Mere. And there they were the next morning, their journey wrapped in mystery. The ducklings could not fly, so the mother must have navigated them skilfully through gardens and across a busy road for nearly a quarter of a mile.

One last word—the trickle from the pit is cleverly used by one ingenious gardener further down the lane. He has converted the erstwhile "ditch" into a sunken garden, planted a colourful array of plants on its banks, with aquatic irises in the bed of the tiny stream. Passers-by pause to admire his work—a pleasant interlude in the long drag up the lane.

The tragedy of Louie's Lane
(PUBLISHED SEPTEMBER, 1960)

AN interesting old map—"Diss in 1830"—has recently come to light. It is about five feet square, drawn and tinted entirely by hand, on stout linen-backed paper. But its 130 years of life has had its effect, and it is grimed and wrinkled with age. Despite its signs of the passing years, it is most informative and the person who constructed it so beautifully and painstakingly must have been a real craftsman devoted to his work.

It covers the whole of Diss, from the bends of the Waveney in the South to the northern limits of the Heywood at Tibenham Long Row. The scale is approximately 25 inches to the mile so every tenement is shown, every enclosure named and its acreage given, the owners or occupier's name clearly printed on it.

At that time (1830) there was no railway, the Church Hall and the Church School had not been built, the old Guildhall was still standing in the churchyard, so too were the almshouses, nearby.

But to our subject—"Louie's Lane"!

What we now call Louie's Lane and Croft Lane were then just lonely lanes through which the townsfolk would take their Sunday afternoon rambles, or where the poachers would go to catch an occasional rabbit. From the Southern end (near the Denmark Arms) to where the waterworks now are—the only buildings were a chapel, a mill and a barn.

The present Roydon Road was called Cherry Tree Lane, and near the crossways stood Samuel Cornell's windmill—a wooden post-mill. Near it was a barn and then came a Baptist chapel (since demolished), adjoining the burial ground which remains to this day.

It was in Samuel Cornell's barn that dances took place after the Fairs associated with the Sessions in September and the Cock Street Market in November on Fair Green.

On the third Friday of September, 1829, when the Sessions Fair was over, Louie Bryant resorted to the Barn to wind up the jollifications of the day, dancing with her friends.

Louie lived in a small house at the top of Mount Street. She was described as "short-waisted and well dressed in the fashion of the period." Rumour branded her as a woman of ill-repute. Be that as it may, her husband had definitely left her for some years, and lived in London.

Dancing was in full swing, the time quite late, when a stranger entered the barn and inquired for "Louie Bryant." She was pointed out, he crossed the floor to her group, a very high spirited one, and engaged her in lively conversation. Suddenly without a word to anyone, she threw her cloak about her and disappeared from the barn into the darkness.

The dance continued as if nothing unusual had occurred. In the early hours of the next morning, Saturday, the bloodstained body of Louie Bryant was found lying in the lonely lane about 300 yards to the north of the Barn.

That lane has ever since been known as "Louie's Lane."

She had been brutally stabbed to death ; her assailant, who, on completing his foul deed, threw the offending knife into the adjoining field where it was later found, then fled from the scene to escape the results of his crime. Persons living at the time have recorded seeing three large holes in the soft surface of the lane—caused by the "death struggle" in which Louie must have put up a terrific resistance.

Diss was agog with horror, excitement and, of course, curiosity. The victim's clothes were exhibited as a sort of local "Madame Tussaud's." And it is on trustworthy record that they were kept for 40 years before being finally burnt. The one who recorded this said he had handled the knife and noted the many gashes in her clothes indicating the violence of the attack.

There were, inevitably, many suspects—but the knife proved of little value as evidence, there being no science of finger printing then and little to aid the investigators in their search.

The inquiry dragged on for six days, during which no less than 41 persons were scrutinised and minutely questioned — but without bringing anything definite to light. The "stranger" who entered the dance and seemingly enticed her away, was a suspect, but he proved to be merely a tool, carrying a message for a bribe, from some person unknown to him.

The former husband was also brought back for questioning. It was thought he might have been the culprit after hearing news of

Louie's undesirable associations. He had not been seen in the town or neighbourhood, but a local superstition said that if he was the murderer, then the pressure of his fingers on her body would cause blood to flow. He was subjected to this gruesome ordeal—but the "test" failed lamentably and he was acquitted.

Some years later a man who had been suspected at the time, but had cleared himself by an alibi, was committed to Norwich gaol for another crime. While in prison he contracted smallpox in the epidemic of 1872 and died. On his death bed he is said to have confessed to the crime, but "the confession was disbelieved."

So ended the tragic story of Louie Bryant, one of the many still on the long list of unsolved murders. The "lonely lane on the outskirts of Diss" has become an attractive and pleasant residential quarter of the town and we hope no ghostly apparitions will disturb its serenity.

Street names of Diss
(PUBLISHED OCTOBER, 1960)

THE names of most of the roads leading from Diss speak for themselves—Heywood Road, Roydon Road, Shelfanger Road, Frenze Road—while Church Street and Mere Street are equally obvious. But when we arrive in the heart of Diss the names are not so straight-forward. Why St. Nicholas Street, Market Hill or Pump Hill and Drapers' Alley?

These names enshrine the real history of Diss—its story covering more than a thousand years. When the Normans came to England, Sir Richard de Lucy was granted the Manor of Diss in the early part of the twelfth century. Then, men with foreign sounding names like de Veare and Champagne settled in Eastern England, bringing with them their skills and trades from the Continent.

Two trades which really flourished were the spinning and weaving of wool and linen—the latter from both hemp and flax fibres—for making coarse cloth and fine linen. By about the year 1200 these industries were firmly established in Diss.

The town became not only the centre for the actual industries, but also the accepted market for a wide area. Because of this a Charter was granted by the King in 1195 to hold a market every Friday, and a "Fair" on the feast of SS. Simon and Jude in October.

The two branches of the industry—linen and woollen—made such progress, and acquired such fame that they developed their own market as well as their guilds or friendly societies. The guilds regulated all aspects of their trades—wages, apprenticeships, standards, etc., and they had considerable funds for helping their less fortunate brethren in times of illness, depression, or loss of equipment by fire, and so on.

So prosperous were they, that they were able to add the chapels of St. Nicholas, and Corpus Christi to the parish church, which soared like a guardian above their workshops and their market.

The Guild of St. Nicholas had its own private chapel, too—standing where Aldiss & Hastings' shop now is. This chapel was dissolved and its funds were confiscated in the time of Edward VI when many religious foundations were suppressed. The chapel—according to Blomefield—was later sold when in a state of decay, to private citizens, much as a redundant chapel might be sold today.

St. Nicholas Street, then, was the narrow street trodden by the spinners and weavers of the guild when they joined in procession to the parish church for some special occasion, when all craftsmen of the town united to give thanks for delivery from plague or war.

The narrow alley from behind that chapel of St. Nicholas, which runs eastwards to the church, emerging alongside the White Horse, was also a scene of great activity in the Middle Ages, and even up to the early days of the nineteenth century. In the hey-day of the wool trade, the drapers sold their woollens by weight, and the spinners sold their wool in like manner, just as we buy wool by weight today.

In the heavily timbered attic of Brame's shop is the very hook from which the town scales (the standard scales) were suspended. Few, gazing at the fine range of modern radio and television sets, under the glare of neon lights, realise that behind the modern facade lie the beams of antiquity in rooms that reverberated with the babble of the voices of those anxious to have their wares weighed and conclude their sales. Diss was long famous for its knitted hosiery and the last woolstapler, Mr. Thomas Leech, of Market Hill, died in April, 1872. He was the last of five generations of woolstaplers in his family.

The other product of Diss and district was "linen," and the market for this was on "Market Hill," also in the spacious yard of the Greyhound Inn, and at the Weavers' Hall in the Saracen's Head yard. "Linen" covered a wide range of products; from the simplest of coarse materials for making smocks, to the most elaborate of damasks.

For the coarser goods, which also included shirting and sheeting, hemp fibre, locally grown and prepared, was used. It was introduced from the Continent and flourished in East Anglia, especially along the Waveney Valley. At one period every farm with 60 acres of arable land, or more, was legally bound to grow at least $\frac{1}{4}$ acre of hemp.

Even as recently as 1830 Diss had twelve enclosures called "Hemplands," and to this day part of North Lopham is "The Hemplands"—few realise why!

As part of his tithe the village parson used to receive the tenth sheffe of hempe. His wife would carry on the processing and spin and weave her own domestic needs, cloths, sheets and napkins—so picturesquely described in "The Betts of Wortham."

Diss is mentioned in history repeatedly for its "Hempen Cloth" and as late as 1839 not only were there 63 hands engaged in making huckaback, sheeting and shirting (in Mere Street), but there was a factory for spinning coarser yarns, set in motion by a windmill (in Victoria Road, now "Lincolns").

So Market Hill, Weavers' Hall and Greyhound Yard bustled with the linen trade until the early nineteenth century. Sales of fine linen, sacking, material for tilts and sails, ropes, twine, smocks, sheets and shirting were the principal items of trade in the town.

But Market Hill became also Pump Hill—though before that it was the scene of the barbarous "sport" of bull baiting. By the courtesy of the Rector I have seen the "Diss Towne Booke" which records that : "On 16 November, 1705, a piece of wood to put down the Bullringle, was purchased by the town. Later Bull baiting was removed to Cock Street Green, and a visitor about the middle of the eighteenth century expressed surprise that it was no longer on Market Hill."

Nearby was the parish well—later to become the site of the parish pump. The Towne Booke first mentions the well in 1703 when a bill was paid "To Jude Burdit for mending towne well (2s. 6d.)." Other references to the well are frequent, and water was then raised by chain, roller and bucket—with frequent repairs needed.

But, in 1742, an item appears : "Pd. Thos. Tokeby mende Towne Pump 5s.," which shows a pump had been installed. Thos. Tokeby seems to have been the first water engineer—his job was looking after the pump for which he received 3s. per annum— though he submitted frequent accounts for repairs.

In 1750 he deepened the well and fitted a new pump. So Market and Pump Hill became the chief source of town's water. Later we read in an old paper that "a lover of good water who lived at the top of Mount Street complained of having to go so far for her water."

The pump was frequently in dis-repair from repeated use. A letter was sent to the Board of Health on more than one occasion, complaining that it was "battered by urchins, stuck over with bills, its dingy wooden tunic rotten to the core, and its appearance ill-suited to its conspicuous position."

However, it had its day and served its many generations of Dysseans with water as well as being a rendezvous for all and sundry. Many among us remember its "passing" and recognise the slab of stone laid over its well when time, marching on, gave us the luxury of a "piped supply.'

It is good to see the recent introduction of the names of Wilbye and Skelton for street names. Wilbye Avenue perpetuates the famous madrigal composer, John Wilbye, son of a Diss "tanner" in the reign of Elizabeth I. Wherever good music is sung and appreciated the name Wilbye is revered.

John Skelton, tutor of Henry VIII and Poet Laureate, was Rector of Diss (1504-1529). He was described by the great Dutch scholar Erasmus as "the light and honour of English learning" and was also famous in his day for his oratory, wit and independence of spirit.

Let us hope the Council will select other names in the future from the illustrious citizens of the past—to remind us of our heritage.

Diss Mere

(PUBLISHED AUGUST, 1960)

AFTER being under the control of the Lord of the Manor for some hundreds of years, Diss Mere has recently become the property of the town of Diss. This change of ownership is not inappropriate, as the history of Diss, its crest, and even its name are intimately connected with the Mere.

Domesday Book of the 11th century records the name Dice or Disce as the Saxon word for a pool of standing water—the modern spelling has descended from this. It is no exaggeration to say "The Mere is Diss ; Diss is the Mere," and that occupations and social life have centred round it.

Many visitors have expressed both surprise and delight on first seeing the Mere and its surroundings. The view from the Mere's Mouth certainly is most attractive, especially if the vast array of colourful aquatic birds are preening, diving and chattering in the foreground, and the tints of the trees and brick and colour-washed buildings on the high ground above the Mere are enhanced by sunlight.

The view from the Arboretum in the south-west is equally beautiful, particularly if the sky is clear and the water of the Mere blue and unruffled. Then the church, with its tower stretching high to dominate the mass of buildings in the heart of the town, is reflected in the placid waters. Such a perfect picture this, that "The Field" used it as a coloured frontispiece but a few years since. Or, viewed from Upper Denmark Street, this time looking down on the Mere, the prospect is equally pleasing, the view extending over the town to Palgrave and Stuston.

The origin of the Mere has been a subject of considerable speculation. It was once considered to be bottomless, and, rather fancifully, to have been formed in the crater of an extinct volcano. Like crater lakes in other parts of the world it is certainly circular, but there the similarity ends. No records exist of volcanic action in East Anglia, nor are there any rock deposits to suggest it, in this most stable part of the country.

Less than 100 feet below the surface at Diss is an extensive layer of chalk some hundreds of feet thick. This layer is uneven and warped, so it is likely that the Mere occupies a clay-filled depression in this chalk, at one time forming an arm of the long lake or sea that filled what is now the Waveney Valley. Later this depression became detached, when the waters of the lake receded. Examine the dark soil in the lower levels of Bloom's nurseries towards the river, and you will discover myriads of marine shells incorporated in the soil, once the bed of the lake.

Whatever its origin, its area is known to be $5\frac{1}{2}$ acres, and its greatest depth about 20 feet, but there is evidence of a channel across its muddy bed from north-east to south-west—possibly the course of some ancient stream.

Many springs bubble up from the bed—the writer has actually felt them when swimming near the King's Head. The position of these springs is readily discernible if the Mere freezes, as only the thinnest of ice forms over them, if it forms at all.

The overflow is near the south-east corner. In olden days it was a "lete" or open ditch. In return for the manorial privilege of using Mere water in his tanning operations, the town tanner was bound to keep the channel clear, under penalty of being "amerced" (i.e., "fined," not "immersed" or thrown in the Mere). The obligation now rests on the U.D.C.

Interesting sidelights on the use of the Mere are mentioned in Blomefield's famous History of Norfolk. He quotes manorial records showing that in 1298 Robert Fitzwalter (Lord of the Manor) "sealed with his paternal coat, a grant made to Wm. Partekyn of Prilleston (now Billingford), for his homage and service and half a mark of silver in hand paid, two messuages in Disce, with liberty of washing his wool and cloaths in Disce Meer, whenever he would; with this reserve—that the gross dye should be first washed off, and that he should not suffer the drain of his dying office to run into the Meer."

It must have been the custom, too, to water animals at the Mere's Mouth and for a part to be railed off to prevent men and animals wading in too far. In 1639 the town was fined for not "keeping up the rails, for want of which a man, as he watered his horses, was drowned."

At about the same time—reign of Charles I—the Lords of the Manor "granted liberty of fishing to divers tenants, and that a

John Turner (and 5 other tenants named) have and maintain certain pits in their yards and grounds with inlets from them to the Mere." The pits were hemp pits, used for steeping the bundles of flax and hemp, then extensively grown in the district, and until about a century ago. The fibre obtained from the stems was used in the manufacture of "hempen home-spuns," and "retting" or soaking in water for some weeks, was the first process in a series of operations.

A great fire gutted Mere Street in 1640 and, "the wells and pumps being dry," the water from the Mere was the only means of controlling the conflagration, just as it was in the late thirties when that disastrous fire played such havoc with John Aldrich's shop and adjoining buildings.

The Mere continued to play its part in the life of Diss in an unusual way in 1669, when "there being a great scarcity of small change, and in defiance of laws and proclamations, many Diss farthings were coined and put into circulation locally." These counterfeit coins carried on one side the inscription "A Diss Farthing 1669," and on the other the crest of Diss—a shield with waves, indicative of the Mere, surmounted by the familiar anchor. Many such coins have survived as curios.

Blomefield was rector of Fersfield when he published his History of Norfolk in 1739, and it is almost certain that as a boy he was a pupil at the Diss Grammar School of those days, then housed in the Guildhall, which formerly stood in the S.E. corner of the churchyard. He would probably have ridden from his home in Fersfield on his pony, and stabled it for the day at the Star or the Bell—then standing in the market place.

We can imagine him, released from his studies at the end of the day, sauntering among the market stalls, which were then pitched the full length of Mere Street, until he came to the Mere's Mouth. He must have seen the Mere in all its moods, and his description is fascinating : "It being almost a standing lake, having only a small run or two into it, and only one out, and all the Filth of the Town centering here, besides the many conveniences that are placed over it, make the water very bad, and altogether useless, and so foul that when it purges itself, which it does once a year, it stinks exceedingly."

This purging has continued to the present day, but today we say "The Mere is sick." Certainly the revolting characteristics of former years have gone—but the Mere assumes a dark green colour, due to the rising from its oozy bed of a miniature aquatic weed. Blomefield noted this, because he recorded that when it purged itself "the fish rose in great numbers so thick that they were easily taken—chiefly roach and eels."

Older residents in Diss recall such occasions within fairly recent years. They describe how men with waders entered the shallower waters on the south side, armed with curious implements like wooden "shears," fitted with long nails along their "cutting edges." A sudden scissor-like jab with such an instrument and an eel was impaled and jerked out on to the grass verge.

A feasible explanation of this phenomenon of the rising fish and eels, is that they were rendered helpless by a surfeit of weed and a deficiency of oxygen. Apart from these periodic gluts of stupefied creatures, fishing must have been widely practised in the past. Manorial custom allowed people "to fish at their own staithes, and lay in bow nets, leaps, and eel poles, and other engines to catch fish without licence." But—without the leave of the Lord of the Manor "no man could keep a boat, or fish, except at his own stathe."

All but the youngest of us recall occasions when the Mere was frozen hard enough to make skating possible. Many will have watched hopefully the formation and thickening of the ice in a spell of cold weather, only to be denied their longed-for skating by a wind change from the south-west. During the early days of the first world war the ice was sufficiently thick to enable a moonlight dance to be held on it (with piano, too!), the ice having been intrepidly (or foolishly?) tested by riding a motor cycle combination across it.

Few freezings have occurred in recent years, but in one hard winter nearly 30 years ago, the whole town and district enjoyed a few days of skating. That occasion was marked by the appearance of an "old hand," suitably clad in long Victorian dress. cloak, muff and bonnet, reminiscent of the 'nineties. Though without practice for some years she sailed round gracefully with perfect balance and technique—hands in muff. She was no novice but had learned the art in the nursery of champions, the Fenlands.

The greatest event of all was in the winter of 1891—and what a winter it must have been, because skating went on for some 13 weeks. The highlight was a carnival on the ice when hundreds of skaters in fancy dress danced and made merry to the music of a band, 30 strong, in the middle of the Mere. There was no unemployment pay at that time. Men thrown out of work by the weather—from the building trade, farming and other occupations—were engaged to sweep the surface of the Mere clear of snow, after every fall. Payment was generously made by the Lord of the Manor of that time, Mr. Francis Taylor. Incidentally, the 30 or so springs were marked by inverted fish barrels, to prevent skaters from disappearing through the treacherously thin ice over them.

With the construction and extension of sewerage works in the 19th century, and the gradual elimination of the practice of dumping undesirable matter in the Mere, it has become progressively more salubrious.

A few adventurous spirits enjoyed a season or two of early morning swimming in the mid-thirties. Rowed out from his "staithe" by an elderly retired postman who had a special dispensation to keep a boat there, they took a refreshing plunge in the centre of the Mere. Enthusiasm ran high for a time with prospects of the Mere becoming a public swimming pool, but a "scare" followed a fatality attributed to the effects of Mere water. Swimming was banned.

The removal of the unsightly weighbridge and the beautifying of the Mere's mouth to mark Festival of Britain year have enabled townsfolk and visitors to see the Mere as Blomefield saw it—in all its moods and aspects throughout the year. One day—who knows?—a promenade may encircle it, but even as it is, it is already the showpiece of Diss.

Referred to by a London evacuee some years ago, rather patronisingly, as the "pond in the middle of the village," it really is the perfect setting for our thriving town—something unique in the county.

A freeze-up 300 years ago
(PUBLISHED APRIL, 1963)

THE intense, persistent, penetrating cold has gone. Frozen pipes have thawed out and spring is in the air. Perhaps all the discomforts of those bitter weeks have gone from our minds, but vivid memories linger of the scenes on the frozen Mere—of the skaters, the tractors, the illuminations and the barbecue. For it is more than 70 years since the Mere was the centre of winter activities on such a scale.

I found it interesting to turn to John Evelyn's diary of the grim winter of 1683-84. Here are some brief extracts :

23 Dec. 1683. The —— frozen, it being in England this year one of the severest frosts that has happened for many years.

1 Jan. 1684. The weather continuing intolerable severe, the air so very cold and thick, as of many years there has not been the like.

Jan. 6. The —— quite frozen. Jan. 9. I went across the —— on ice. Jan. 16. The —— was filled with people.

Jan. 24. The frost continued more and more severe. Fowls, fish, and birds, and our exotic plants and greens perished. Fuel was so dear there were great contributions to preserve the poor alive. Here was no water to be had from the pipes.

Feb. 5. It began to thaw, but froze again. Feb. 8. The weather was set in to an absolute thaw, and rain, but the —— still frozen.

In Evelyn's original diary the spaces I have left blank were occupied by "Thames"—but how well it would have fitted our own experiences in Diss in 1963, if we inserted "Mere" !

Of course, there was much more in that diary, for on the Thames were "booths and formal streets, shops furnished with commodities, a printing press, coaches plying in the streets, horse and coach races", all on the ice. In Evelyn's words, the weather was "a judgement on the land, the very seas so locked with ice, no vessel could stir in or out".

We have no account of conditions in Diss that winter—but

doubtless they were as severe as in London. The only hint we have is from surviving overseers' accounts, which mention unusually large quantities of fuel distributed to the poor owing to hard weather.

Not until 1827, when the Thames froze again and oxen were roasted on the ice, is there any clear record of past weather in Diss. Incidentally, John Doe, of Redgrave, now 87, clearly remembers his grand-mother, born in 1800 at Epping, saying she had eaten beef roasted on the Thames in 1827. What a span of years!

The Norfolk Chronicle of March 10, 1827, reported that "the continuance of the frost having occasioned that fine piece of water —Diss Mere—containing above 5 acres—to be safely frozen over, the 20 February was fixed for playing a match at cricket on the ice. which commenced at 10 in the forenoon, and was well contested all that day, concluding about 6 in the evening. There were also ten-pins, running, skating, sparring, and every other kind of appropriate 'Rustic-sports'. Stalls and booths were erected to supply all kinds of refreshments. At one, a card party sat till past 10 at night. No accident occurred, though it was computed that more than 1500 persons were present in the course of the day".

The scene on the Mere must have been similar to that on the Thames, depicted by Evelyn in 1684—for it was during the 1827 "freeze-up" that a cumbersome farm waggon, drawn by four cart-horses and belonging to Mr. Clarke of Stuston, crossed the Mere on the ice, without mishap.

Not for another 64 years—in January, 1891—were similar scenes to be witnessed, and on a highly-organized scale. The more adventurous spirits were skating from Boxing Day, 1890. By Saturday, January 3, 1891, the ice was safe enough for the Rifle Band to play a programme of music in the middle of the Mere.

The severe conditions persisting, plans were laid for a Grand Carnival and Fancy Dress Fete on Saturday, January 10 ("Jack Frost permitting"). But on January 5, after some thousands had given the ice adequate testing, a preliminary carnival was organized by some enterprising enthusiasts in case the weather should break before the 10th and frustrate their carefully planned scheme.

This hastily-improvised event was crowned with success. At 9 p.m. the flares from a host of torches, fixed in the barrels and arranged in a huge circle, lit up the arena. In the centre, another ring of gently swaying Chinese lanterns enclosed the Rifle Band.

High spirits prevailed—the profusion of colourful fancy costumes of the skaters—Father Christmas, Ally Sloper, Bogey Man, Buffalo Bill, Harlequin and a host of others carrying Roman candles transformed the Mere into a fairy land. Feathery flakes of gently falling snow enhanced the general effect.

The proceedings terminated at 10.30 p.m. with a procession of skaters round the fringe of the Mere with some 2,000 persons witnessing or participating in it. Great credit was accorded to Mr. Rowland Bobby as the leading organizer, and to Mr. Francis Taylor for engaging and paying many men—hard hit by unemployment in the severe weather—to sweep and improve the ice.

The prime object of the carnival arranged for Saturday, January 10, was to raise funds for relief of the distressed. Many familiar names appeared among the organizers—Burrage, Bobby, Rice, Tyrrell, Webb, Alger and Bryant—and how successfully they worked and were supported!

The weather remained ideal—almost windless, cold but sunny —and the ice was 7 inches thick.

Contemporary accounts mention the gaiety of the town, the masses of bunting, and the spirit of carnival which increased as the numerous visitors, with their skates, arrived by rail and road from distant places such as Ipswich and Woodbridge, "in all, not fewer than 5,000". Hundreds were in fancy costumes—colourful, gay, amusing or even grotesque.

A selected band of persuasive ladies and gentlemen wearing distinguishing sashes wove skilfully in and out among spectators and reaped a considerable harvest for the needy. At dusk a fire balloon was released, which, at a good height, discharged brilliant lights over the closing stages of the carnival.

So successful was this event that a "repeat" on an even grander scale was planned for Tuesday, January 20. But on that very morning a rapid thaw set in—which, by 3 p.m., had covered the ice with a film of water—just as the influx of visitors arrived. But despite the deteriorating conditions, the Mere once more became a blaze of colour. Most of the previous participants came again, their numbers swollen by new and exciting masked characters —including a comic double act—"two men from Eye, covered to represent an elephant".

The rapid thaw continued so the elaborate evening programme had to be abandoned ; and though a balloon was released it was whisked away by a strong upper current and its brilliant spectacle lost to Diss.

A torchlight procession through the town—led by the Rifle Band—concluded the day's events. The elephant, the clowns, mock policeman, and nigger minstrel group, with other "comic elements" delighted the jostling crowds in the Market Place. And a memorable day ended with the national anthem and the "orderly dispersal" of the spectators.

Many of our older friends actually experienced the winter of 1891 and took part in these celebrations. Among them was George Buckenham (now 87) who, with several friends, "made hay" by taking chairs to the Mere and offering a seat and help to many a skater in screwing on their skates "for a consideration".

There have been spells of skating on the Mere many times since 1891—but never for such a prolonged period until January, 1963. Certainly we had hard weather and much more snow in 1947. I remember that year so well—plodding one morning through a foot of snow on the Market Place, and asking a friend "How do you like this?" He must have been a student of John Evelyn, and certainly he was not enamoured of the then Government, for he retorted with considerable feeling—"It's a visitation on the country for putting in this Government."

Ye olde Cock Street Fair
(PUBLISHED DECEMBER, 1960)

COCK Street Green, or, as we know it, Fair Green or Denmark Green, is peaceful enough today. Only the occasional visit of a circus or travelling fair rouses it to a few days of glare, blare and excitement. But regularly, year after year, for nearly 700 years, it was the scene of tremendous bustle and activity in late October and early November, when the annual Cock Street Fair took place.

In fact when enclosure of the Greens and Moors of Diss took place in 1814, Cock Street Green was left, because, as the old document stated, "it was required for the Fair" whereas Westbrook Green, Walcot Green, Penning's Green and Diss Moor were enclosed.

As far back in history as the reign of Henry II, in 1185, Sir Walter Fitz-Walters then Lord of the Manor and Justice Itinerant of Norfolk and Suffolk, obtained a Charter to hold a Fair "on the eve, day and morrow after the feast of SS. Simon and Jude, and for three days following."

Sir Walter was the first of the long line of Fitzwalters, and father of the great Robert the Valiant who distinguished himself as leader of the Barons in the reign of King John. A further "Charter of Confirmation" of the Fair was given to Sir Walter's great grandson in 1295. The annual Stock and Pleasure Fair—as it came to be called—was held regularly until 1872, when by Act of Parliament it was suppressed.

The purpose of the Fair was not solely pleasure, though that was adequately catered for. The Lord of the Manor had dues to pay to the King ; retainers to equip and train ready to support the King in an emergency. He had many expenses also, in maintaining roads and bridges, manorial courts and buildings.

What better way of raising money than to hold a Fair ? Sales could be registered and taxed, stalls and booths paid for, and vehicles too.

The custom of the Manor of Diss in olden times was to charge 2d. for every tilted stall, 1d. for every untilted one—and no more."

Even down to our own time "a penny a wheel" has been the fee for a wheeled vehicle standing on the Green, though a composite fee is now charged for a whole Fair or Circus. Those engaged in entertainment paid rent for "space" and, as the years passed, the so called pleasure section with its bear pits, cock pits and bull rings, wrestling and boxing booths, became an important source of revenue.

Local shops were closed during the Fair in the early years. Shop-keepers had their stalls on the Green, which was railed off with improvised paling fence so that everyone paid for admission.

The Steward and Bailiff of the Manor had most responsible jobs at Fair time, and certainly not easy ones. The Steward presided over the "Court of Piepowder," as the English called it— they could not pronounce "pieds-poudreux." the French saying for dusty feet.

This referred to the dusty booted merchants and wayfarers who came to the Stewards' court to register complaints, or to settle disputes and differences which arose during such an exciting event as the Fair.

Much drink was consumed, for not only did the inns do great business in catering for visitors, but house-holders on the Green displayed oak branches from their upper windows to show that ale could be "purchased within" during the Fair.

To cope with the disorderly and irresponsible elements, the Bailiff recruited some of the tougher and more zealous citizens to help in maintaining order by inviting them to "take a halberd." Some, unwilling to face a brawl with unruly rustics, evaded the service by a "douceur" or bribe to the Bailiff, while others, armed with ribbon-bedecked halberds, took up their appointed stations as guardians of the law.

The Fair had quite small beginnings, but the woollen and linen industries were making great headway by 1400 and Diss was becoming noted for its wares, woollen hose, hempen cloth and even damask linen were among the chief articles sold at the Fair. Nets, baskets, clogs, leather goods, harness, produce of the joiner's and blacksmith's crafts, eels and fish from Waveney and Mere, were on sale.   So, too, were eggs and fruit and the peasants trundled in their small lots of wool, hemp and flax fibre to sell to the merchants and master weavers.

Entertainment, then, was of a simple kind. There was sparring and wrestling. The itinerant strong-man whose "man-eating" reputation had preceded him, came prepared to take on the local hopefuls. He issued his challenge by tossing his hat in the air, or by "trailing his coat"—inviting all-comers to try their luck. Great was the enthusiasm of the Diss supporters when their champion overcame the invader.

Punch and Judy shows were always popular ; soo too were the jugglers, the tumblers and the dancers who earned a precarious living by going from fair to fair. An ever popular item was "tilting at the Quintain," with a lance.

It drew the crowds, who roared with delight when a clumsy and inexperienced tilter tried his hand for the first time; missed the elusive target and was knocked flat by the swivelling sandbag.

Lastly, there was the stock section, where horses, ponies, donkeys, cattle, sheep and poultry were sold in increasing numbers.

Years passed, and the fame of Diss Fair was spread by pilgrims passing through, to and from the many shrines in East Anglia, and by travelling tinkers, merchants and salesmen. By the middle of the 18th Century it had expanded to fill the Green.

Fortunately, a visitor attending the Fair about 1750, left a fascinating account of it, when bull-baiting and cock fighting were still considered popular sports and legal entertainment.

The unsavoury history of Fair Green
(PUBLISHED NOVEMBER, 1962)

"**D**ENMARK GREEN" is a comparatively new name for that picturesque part of Diss. Until 1863 it was "Cock Street Green," for centuries the scene of one of the liveliest and most colourful events in the life of Diss—"The November Fair" or "Cock Street Fair," chartered by Henry II in 1185, for the "Eve, Day and Morrow of the Feast of S.S. Simon and Jude."

In Tudor and Stuart times the Green was famous, not only for its fair but as a training ground for the "Trained Bands" (the 16th century and 17th century equivalent of the Home Guard) and for the Militia in later periods.

Many references to Cock Street Green occur in the parish papers of villages around Diss. One is an order from the High Constable of the Hundred to the Constable of Gissing, in 1608, to give warning "to all trayned persons within The Towne of Gissinge personally to appear before Philip Gawdye, Esq.', Captayne of Ye Footemen in the Half Hundred of Diss, for trayneigne at Cockstreete grene".

The constable's expenses included 1s. "for my Jurny thather"; 6d. for "twoe pound of bulletes"; and 8d. for "twoe quarteres of pouder".

Later, in Napoleonic times, the Militia, and the Diss Volunteers, in their scarlet tunics and white pantaloons, trained on the Green, as well as on the Diss, Heywood, and Scole Commons.

Through the centuries the Annual Fair at Diss became noted as a market for local produce—especially wool, hemp, and hempen cloth brought by farmers, hecklers, spinners and weavers to sell to travelling merchants.

But it was perhaps more particularly noted for those barbaric sports, bull and bear baiting, and for cock fighting. The last named persisted well into the 19th century, until suppressed by law.

Cock Street derived its name from the gory spectacle of "fighting-cocks" being pitted against each other for huge wagers. Though the "cockings" are known to have attracted many visitors, accounts of them make unsavoury reading in this more enlightened age.

By the mid-19th century the fair had assumed a pattern—with a stock section at the Tottington end, the fun fair in the centre, and the stalls along the eastern fringe near the street.

The Green was filled to capacity 100 years ago, when 1,000 sheep were penned for sale, and 300 bullocks, cows, and calves, many horses and "droves of ponies"—not to mention scores of donkeys and mules—were on offer. A good donkey could be bought for "three half-crowns".

Nearby, Mr. Swootman, the Diss engineer who played such an important part in developing the plough and other agricultural implements, was there with a "Root Grater on a new principle", and a chaff-cutter "worked by steam, horse, or hand power, fitted with an appliance for throwing it out of gear instantly", in case of emergency.

The fun of the fair included the noisy cheap jacks and Gregory's "Exhibition of Mechanical Figures"; many shooting galleries ; the usual "shies" and swinging boats ; muscular "power-testers"; photographic galleries and the "turnabouts" with the then novel organ accompaniment.

Stalls stretched the whole front of the Green from Farrow's Brewery to Smedley's Academy (i.e., as far as Cock Street Bridge —for Smedley's school was across the bridge, where Mr. Hume now is).

There was a vast array of stalls selling such a variety of wares as to make one observer "apprehensive of serious disorders in the thousands of stomachs which might become receptacles of the many compounds prepared for the delectation of the public palate".

There were gingerbreads and toffee stalls ; roasted chestnuts for sale ; herrings "cooked" and herrings "raw"; hot sausages ; dumplings with treacle ; and rock in abundance—made behind the scenes under anything but hygienic conditions.

Lastly, the numerous drinking booths, with their accompaniment of heavy drinking and prevalent "the combined odours of tobacco, beer, hot sausages and bloaters anything but pleasant to his olfactory organs".

In 1862 there were rumblings of discontent over the state of Church Street and the Market Place, where cattle were indiscriminately herded for the Friday sale.

The ladies of Diss were even afraid to pass along the street— it was so filthy, and droves of cattle blocked the way.

Discussions were afoot about "making a market"—and soon Messrs. Elliott and Muskett were to begin a regular stock sale.

The Times demanded a change—a breakaway from the brawling and disorderly conduct generated by the Fairs.

A memorial from the Justices of the Diss Division, dated February 24, 1872, was submitted to the Home Office, saying that it would be "for the convenience and advantage of the public, that the fair should be abolished".

In spite of rumours of violent opposition by certain vested interests, no representations against abolition were made by the prescribed date.

Mr. H. H. Bruce, the Home Secretary, then ordered that "The Diss Cock Street Fair (Nov. 8) shall be abolished as from April 16, 1872".

And so the Green, which in 1816 had been saved from enclosure because it was "Wanted for the Fair", was no longer needed for that purpose. Scole, Thrandeston, Bury St. Edmunds, and many other fairs suffered the same fate at about that time.

Street naming in Diss 100 years ago
(PUBLISHED MARCH, 1964)

UNTIL just 100 years ago, St. Nicholas Street was known as "Half Moon Street." Where Mr. Cobb's cycle shop now stands, was the "Half Moon" Inn. From the "Crown" to the bridge over the Waveney was then "Cock Street," the bridge was "Cock St. Bridge," and the Green was "Cock Street Green." To many, the road from Mere Street to Frenze Bridge was still "The Common," though the adjoining land had been enclosed nearly 50 years. Some used the names "Norwich Road" or "Scole Road."

But in 1863 there were many changes. The dismal tolling of the Great Bell of St. Paul's on December 14, 1861, had conveyed the sad news of the death of Queen Victoria's Consort, Prince Albert, but before a year had elapsed came the happy tidings of the betrothal of Edward, Prince of Wales (later Edward VII) to Princess Alexandra of Denmark, on September 9, 1862.

The wedding was fixed for Tuesday, March 10, 1863, and Diss, like every hamlet, town and city in the land, prepared to celebrate the occasion in grand style. It proved to be as memorable a day as the Great Peace Festival in July, 1814, and the Coronation Festival of Queen Victoria in 1838.

The morning of March 10, 1863, was spent in ceremonial, as a preliminary to the feasting and fun that was to follow—for when the date of the royal wedding had been announced, the members of the local Board of Health—forerunners of the U.D.C.—had been officially requested "to take into consideration the propriety of altering the names of some of the streets and roads of the District on the 10th March, in commemoration of the marriage of H.R.H. the Prince of Wales, and as a memento to the late lamented Prince Albert".

The members of the Board met on February 26, "pursuant to such request", and decided that "The Common, extending from Mr. Cuthbert's Corner to Frenze Bridge, should thenceforward be called Albert Road" (this decision came after an amendment to call it "Prince's Road" had been defeated). The same meeting agreed that Cock Street, extending from Cock Street Bridge to Mr. Cooke's Corner (the "Crown") should be Denmark Street ; that Cock Street Green should henceforth be Fair Green ; that Half-Moon Street and Crown Street, from the "Crown" to the church should be St. Nicholas Street ; and that Market Hill should be Prince's Street.

In the days immediately following these decisions there was some rethinking, and, I imagine, much lobbying behind the scenes, concerning these changes. For when the Board met on March 7 the resolutions naming Albert Road and Prince's Street, were straightway rescinded on the casting vote of the chairman. It was then decided by a majority vote, to name The Common, "Victoria Road" and to plant a commemorative oak tree in Park Field, to be called "Prince's Oak". That oak, now a sturdy tree a century old, still flourishes.

Tuesday, March 10, arrived. The weather was propitious and the carefully-planned festivities were carried through in a spirited manner.

Diss was gay with colourful decorations—almost every house displayed patriotic favours, while numerous triumphal arches spanned the streets. The church bells pealed forth at an early hour and a Royal Salute reverberated through the early morning air to mark the opening of the day's proceedings.

By 9 a.m. Cock Street Green—bearing for the last time its ancient name, tarnished by association with the gory spectacle of cock-fighting in the past—was seething with activity as the members of all eight local friendly societies gathered to form a picturesque array, wearing their distinctive badges and carrying their colourful banners.

Headed by the Rifle Corps and Palgrave Bands, a gay and lively procession of the friendly societies' members and children of the British School (later the Board School) marched to the Market Place, where a volley was fired by the Rifle Corps, and the bands played the national anthem.

They then moved through garlanded Mere Street to the Rectory entrance (now Skelton Road) where the Rev. C. R. Manning officially proclaimed: "This road—now called The Common, shall in future, in commemoration of this day, be named Victoria Road."

Amid vociferous cheering and great excitement the parade then passed to Park Field, via Back Lane (there was no Park Road then), where, amid mounting enthusiasm and a further volley from the Corps, Mr. Heffill (deputising for Mr. T. L. Taylor) assisted by Miss Mary Taylor and Miss Taylor of Starston, planted and named "Prince's Oak".

It had been presented by Mr. Salter, of Attleborough, and was said to have been grown from an acorn of the Winfarthing Oak, that grand veteran of 1,500 years, reputed to have been 'old' when William the Conqueror landed in England in 1066.

Passing on through Chequers Lane to Cock Street Green, the Rector and Mr. Heffill jointly proclaimed Cock Street to be "Denmark Street" from thenceforward, and Cock Street Green to be "Fair Green". After exuberant applause and prolonged cheering the procession disbanded—with appetites whetted for the monster repast awaiting them.

Those who through sickness or infirmity were unable to attend the dinner or partake of the other festivities, received their dues on the 9th, but for the actual feast no less than 1,600 men, women and children were issued with tickets.

With the experience of organizing the 1814 and 1838 celebrations to fall back on for quantities and detailed preparations, the arrangements on this occasion appear to have been perfect. Those feasting, assembled in four different groups—one in the Old Corn Hall, one in a vast booth erected in the Market Place, and the remainder (some 300 country members of friendly societies) at the "Crown".

They were regaled with lashings of cold beef (boiled or roast), bread, and plum pudding, while beer flowed freely. Three-hundred children, under nine years of age, too young to dine with the adults, enjoyed a feast of buns, nuts and oranges, in Miss Simpson's buildings in Mount Street (now "The Grove").

After these very satisfying repasts, everyone resorted to the newly-named "Fair Green" to engage in what were described as "rural sports and rustic amusements". The programme was reported to be "laughable"—doubtless there were many somewhat unsteady participants who had over indulged in the liberal fare at dinner.

However, these "sports" were really to fill the gap until dusk, when a torchlight procession, with bands playing, made its way through the town (now gay with fairy-like Chinese lanterns and coloured lamps swaying in the gentle wind), to what we used to call "Anness's Meadow" (now Uplands Way). There a gigantic bonfire was lighted—and coloured flares on the church tower flickered in the western sky.

The fire died down, the flares burnt out, and the day's excitements closed with a display of fireworks such as had never before been seen in Diss.

The aftermath! There was such a surplus of meat, bread, pudding and beer that the organizing caterers—Messrs. Leathers and Chase—offered "Cheap Dinners at 6d. a Head" on the following day. No less than 629 availed themselves of the opportunity.

Such a day as March 10 was not to be repeated until the Jubilee of 1887. For the record, the Board of Health of 1863 consisted of Messrs. Gostling (chemist), Cuthbert (brewer and maltster), Burrows (brewery manager), Quadling (coal merchant), Bunyan (saddler), Broad (brushmaker), Ellis (farmer) and Eglinton (gentleman).

The Workhouse on Diss Common
(PUBLISHED NOVEMBER 1962)

THE Almshouses—a familiar Diss landmark for well over a century—became a heap of rubble under the bulldozer's onslaught in 1961. They had been "created" out of the old Workhouse in 1838 and that in turn had been created from an earlier terrace of almshouses in 1728.

The earliest reference to town buildings on Diss Common occurred in 1690, when repairs were made to "The Towne House" there (not to be confused with the Guildhall, near the church). Accounts for such items as "sweeping 12 chimneys" and "for brick and for work done to the Pumpe at Almeshouses on the Common" occurred frequently up to 1728, when the word "Workhouse" first appeared.

The earliest buildings of which we can be certain were just "homes for the impotent poor", erected in the 17th century under the great Poor Law Act of 1601. There was no provision of work in these homes, as there was in workhouses later.

The first workhouse was built at Bristol in 1695, by special Act of Parliament, providing both accommodation and work. Others followed—also by special Acts—at Colchester, Sudbury, Worcester, etc., and then at Norwich, in 1711. A "General Act" (1722-3) authorized church-wardens and overseers to purchase or hire buildings and to "contract with some person to lodge, keep, maintain, and employ the poor".

Thus, in 1728, the major part of the old almshouses on the Common was adapted as a workhouse—two units only being retained for their original use.

What was the Workhouse like? Externally, much as we remember the almshouses in 1961. For its internal arrangements a detailed description has survived in "An Inventory of Diss Workhouse", prepared by Henry Calver, auctioneer and appraiser.

A study of this conjures up memories of Oliver Twist and recalls some poignant lines of the Suffolk poet Crabbe, who, after his experiences as a doctor's apprentice and later as a curate at

Aldeburgh, noted among the workhouse inmates :—
"Heart broken matrons on their joyless bed,
Forsaken wives, and mothers never wed,
Dejected widows with unheeded tears
And crippled age with more than childhood fears."
The inventory helps us to picture the place and visualise the stark conditions and spartan life "in the house". No insurance against sickness or unemployment existed then—the only relief in distress came from private charity or parish relief.

The workhouse had 29 named rooms or compartments, including four 'out-door'. A Master administered it—not a trained social worker, but one who "contracted" to run it under an agreement with the churchwardens and overseers who formed the nucleus of the house committee.

He had his "study", with its "book case and shelves" containing personal records of inmates, vagrants, casuals, and those receiving out relief. He had his "Keeping Room", or parlour, equipped with a "30-hour clock, range and coal shoot", but he also enjoyed the use of the large committee room, with its "12 hollow seated elm chairs, two elbow chairs, oval table with green baize cloth, and stove".

Here the wardens, overseers, doctors and constables held their monthly deliberations and settled "Requests at the House"—the multitude of applications for out relief, which reflect the poverty of the age.

For obstreperous customers, there was a "Dark Room" for temporary confinement and cooling off (no furniture in this) and for the really tough a prison containing just a straw bed, but fitted with padlock and key.

The Master's deputy was quartered in the Page's Room—with "stump bedstead, mattress and chair".

Feeding was communal—in a large "Dining Room" sparsely furnished with "four tables, eight forms, 23 earthenpans, 22 wooden dishes, a Dutch oven, a coal range and Brass Boiler".

Workhouse fare consisted of three meals—for breakfast, bread with either gruel, meat broth or pease pottage ; for dinner, meat with suet or plain puddings, or dumplings, bread and small beer ; or, for variation, milk broth and bread, or pease pottage and small beer ; and for supper just bread, cheese, and small beer, every night.

This delightful and varied food was prepared in the "kitchen"

(with broth ladle, dumpling stirer, three coppers, lids and furnaces)
—the "Baking Office" (with kneading trough, meal hutch, bushel
and strike, and scales)—the "Soup House" (with soup copper, lid
and furnace, and even a swill-tub).

For idling away their time the inmates had three day rooms—
"The Middle Room", for general use, with "benches, chairs and
stools"; the men's "Low Room", with "old men's settle"; and the
"Widow's Room", with seven chairs, candlesticks and a tinder-box.

Sleeping accommodation was provided for 29 in five "wards"
and sick-ward—the women's ward with its seven bedsteads, one
chair, five coverlets, ten blankets and ten sheets, being the largest.

Under his contract the Master could use his inmates profitably
—hence the "Taylor's shop" with "Taylor's Board, Goose, and
sundry old pieces of clothes" for repairs—and the "Laundry" with
mangle, ironing boards, box and flat irons—and the "Weaving
shop" with two looms, winding wheel and warping bar—where
hemp was spun and hempen cloth woven. (26 bundles of hemp
were in store).

Thirty spinning wheels were stored in the "attics"—for loan
to outpatients on request. "Slops" and boys' jackets were also
stored there in profusion.

The contents of the store room reflected both the contemporary
clothing materials of the poor, and the products of local industry—
40 yards of shirt and shift cloth, 37 yards of sheeting, 70 sheets and
shifts, five yards of stay-stuff (all of course hempen cloth)—with
22 yards of Duffield, 80 yards Wolsey, 43 old Wolsey dresses, 12
pairs women's and 12 of men's stockings, 26 flannel petty-coats
and 18 yards flannel. (All coarse woollen materials).

Wool spinning, weaving, and the making of hosiery still
lingered in Diss—and many "wool wheels" were out on loan from
the Workhouse.

No reference is made in the inventory to washing or bathing
facilities—apart from coppers. Life was hard and certainly un-
hygienic. One Norfolk workhouse of this period even recorded its
own process for "debugging" old clothes, to pass on to new inmates.

However, at the time of the inventory (1834), the erection of
the Union Workhouse at Pulham was about to begin. It was
completed 1836-7, to accommodate 500 inmates, with provision for
employment of the able-bodied. It was then that Diss Workhouse
was reconverted to the Almshouses as we knew them. The bill

for "making the late workhouse into almshouses" in 1838 amounted to over £276—and the sale of contents of the 'House' provided about one third of it.

The recent sale of these Almshouses—together with the accumulated proceeds of a number of charities—has made the erection of two old people's bungalows possible—one of them being occupied by the last occupant of an almshouse.

Today a modern hatchery has arisen on the site where for 300 years the poor were accommodated.

Proof of the pudding at the workhouse!
(PUBLISHED NOVEMBER 1962)

SINCE I mentioned here recently the 18th century Association for the Prosecution of Felons in Roydon, and the acute poverty of that time which literally drove hungry men to acts of petty theft, I have been asked, "Was there really such widespread poverty then?"

There is adequate proof of it.

In 1714, the sponsors of the Charity School in Diss, when drafting an appeal for funds, stated : "We have endeavoured to plant a Charity Schoole here for ladds, but finde most of their Parents so very poore and indigent that they cannot provide even their cloathes and comon necessaryes."

Later, when funds were forthcoming, they taught—and clothed completely—30 boys.

In 1761 there were food riots in Diss on a large scale. The Justices read the Riot Act, and the militia helped to maintain order. Again, when Napoleon fled to Elba in 1814 and there were rejoicings throughout England—feasts and entertainments "for the poor"—in Diss, 1,600 poor persons, almost half the population, were regaled with roast beef, plum pudding and strong beer. Then, at Queen Victoria's Coronation, no less than 1,700 of "the poorer sort" were again feasted.

Study the state of things in Diss as the Overseers of the Poor recorded them, month by month, when receiving "Requests at The House" from a constant stream of poor people, literally begging at the Workhouse door for work, money, clothes, bedding, fuel or tools.

Such requests were considered each month by the churchwardens, overseers and others of the Workhouse Committee in the committee room at "The House". Three books of requests have survived, covering 1809-1819, and containing nearly 8,000 requests, an average of about 70 per month.

Apart from those for work, they were mainly for money for rents, sickness or unemployment, to repay debts or equip apprentices ; for footwear, clothing, and materials—shoes, highlows, flannel, shirts, shifts, petticoats, breeches, coats, slops, etc.; for bedding—mattresses, ticks, quilts, pickling, coverlets, blankets, sheets ; for "firing"; for tools ; and for "miscellaneous requirements".

Here, to illustrate the widespread poverty of the period, is a selection of requests just as the overseers recorded them—with the committee's decision in brackets :

Money requests—Sam Sandy wants more weekly, being able to do but littel (Not Granted) ; Robt. Parr want to be excused rates (He is to pay rates, but to be paid for tolling the Bell on Thursday) ; Susan Shibly want releif being afflicted with ye evil (10s.) ; Jno Elsey request small sum of money to put his son apprentice to shoemaker (40s. if bound properly) ; Joseph Norman want Releif till get better and peice of flanel to wear next him (Granted) ; Jas. Cattermole a littel extra releif, being incapabel of work, wife having ye ague (Enquire) ; John Nobel bad with a wind rupture, beg a truss (Truss) ; Jno. Leather want a nurse for wife and midwife, being near her time, and a trifel for ye child when born : 8 children oldest 16 (Enquire) ; John Sterlin want 6d a week more, his wife being incapabel of dressing or undressing herself (Granted) ; Sarah Thurlow want weekly pay with her illeg. child by Sam Capes, he being absconded (1s. 6d.) ; Wid. Rudd request pay as usuall, very littell outdoor work (Enquire) ; Sam Woodrd want assistance towards discharging a debt 4£ (Not Granted).

For clothes and materials—Ed. Page want pair shoes and stockens, shirt, hat, slop, and pr. trowsers, going to business (Part) ; Thos. Potter request pr. of Buskens (Not Granted) ; John Everson, 2 shirts, pr. Highlows and slops for boy (Part) ; Sarah Avis, a bed gouen (G.) ; Henry Batley want a few yards clorth for 3 children, and bedding (G. materials) ; Mary Hines, clorth for shift, under petticoat, and more weekly (Shift) ; Robt. Woodrd want clorth Highlow for daughter afflicktid with ye evil in her ancle (G.) ; Girl Bond at Mr. Pyms, being going to continue, want an outside coat, shift, and 2 Handkercheifs (Half of them).

For bedding—Mariah Midson want picklin for bed teck, having no work (N.G.) ; Beck Howe—something to lay on (G.) ; Wid. Cornell—a sheet (seem to be much wanted) (G) ; John Peak, a slop and blankets (Slop only) ; Geo. Thurlow's wife want child Bed linen and shift, being near her time : 7 chn. (Part G.) ; Charles

Feak want a pr. sheets and coverlid, 7 chn. at home (N.G.) ; Wm. Cattermole, Highlows and Bed Tick (G.).

For fuel and firing—Wid. Henley an undercoat and something for coal (2s. for coal) ; Wid. Mills request to be allowed ye Turf money (G.) ; Jno. Lock 8s. towards ¼ chaldron coal (G.) (Note— "Chaldron" was 36 bushels) ; Wid. Algar 3s. to purchase some furze now clearing away on Stuston Common, and shoes mended (G.) ; Rich. Crisp, littell for fireing and Extra Releif, child being bad with Hooping Cough (5s.).

For tools and work—Thos. Potter want a spade (Give spade, take off 1s. week) ; Abr. Hall—a woll wheel (Enquire) ; Sam Woodrow—a shirt and a scuppett having lost his in ye pitts (Half) ; Abr. Scott want a Hook and Shirt (Hook) ; Jno. Lords wife want a Tow wheel for learning Boy, and mentel for herself (Wheel) ; Roper—a spinning wheel (Enquire) ; Jno. Sadd want assistance, having no employ, or Give him a horse to enabel him to be employed carting brick (Enquire).

Other requests—Jas. Dack beg assistance towards ye loss of a sow and pigs, as appear by his petition (10s.) ; Wm. Barber beg 2 days lost time for refusing to pound two asses when ordered by his Master, and a pr. shoes (N.G.) ; Francis Ready had ye misfortune to loose a poney, Beg a little assistance towards ye loss (1£) ; Wid. Rudd exceeding sorry for offending ye overseer, Hopes ye Committee will be so kind as to re-allow her 6d. weekly (N.G.).

But when Elij. Wragg begged "to have Wm. Clark removed from his quarters in consequence of bad behaviour and swearing", the committee decided it was "not our business". Nor did they take action when John Sadd complained "for self and others" that "they have no water without going to Stuston".

Diss Common
(PUBLISHED AUGUST 1962)

INTEREST in local history has undoubtedly been stimulated by the exhibits in "The Shambles." That name is most appropriate for the museum of our Antiquarian Society, for "Shambles" is a very old word—meaning a "flesh market." And centuries ago, the meat market was on that very spot. In 1597, Bishop Redman, visiting Diss, ex-communicated Roger Foulser and six others for "selling meate openly in the Markett on Sabaoth dayes, in tyme of devine service."

One very interesting exhibit is the Diss map of 1830. A keen observer may notice that on it are two meadows (now part of Pleasure Farm) named "Common Meadow". They were formerly part of Diss Common (or Moor), an open space resembling Wortham Ling, and enclosed by authority of Parliament in 1816.

That Common commenced where the Picture House now stands. The "Cottage" (Dr. Woodhead's) was on the edge of it, too. The northern fringe ran from The Cottage, south of the Old Rectory, behind the almshouses, past Pleasure Farm, Vince's Lane, the Court, and Mill Cottages to Frenze River.

The southern edge was the Waveney, bordered by otter haunted swamps. Triangular in shape, 90 acres in extent, the Common was a mile long, and 600 yards across at its widest. Through the centre ran a rough dirt road, rudely repaired with stones for the potholes, and faggots for the ruts.

Copyhold tenants had "right of Commonage for Great Beasts" —but sheep grazing was forbidden. In 1693, a John Cracknell was charged with having put "seaventene sheep on the Comon called Diss Moore". He was fined 2s. 6d. for "trespass and damage done".

Princess Mary Tudor often crossed the Common, journeying from Kenninghall Palace to Framlingham, where the Dukes of Norfolk lived. When Thomas, Duke of Norfolk, died, his body was borne from Framlingham to Thetford Priory for burial. The clergy and choir of each parish escorted the cortege through their villages.

It was late on June 22, 1524, that the great cavalcade trundled across Diss Moor from Stuston Bridge. What an unforgettable spectacle, as 400 men with staves and flaming torches, 900 horsemen in rich trappings, with three coaches of Friars, accompanied the chariot and mourners to Diss Church. After an early mass on the following day, the slow progress to Thetford continued.

Diss was the centre of an unsuccessful insurrection against Queen Mary in 1556. A Diss school-master, Cleber, planned to join his collaborators at a wedding feast at Yaxley (or so the chronicler says), to which each was pledged to bring "one hundred horsse". He set his servant to watch near the Common for the approach of horsemen—at which time he was to warn Cleber.

After dusk, "Certeine men riding through that lane about their businesse, came about such an hour as Cleber had appointed, upon which the servant told Cleber his friends had come". Not realizing that the alarm was false, Cleber galloped over the Common to Yaxley. But someone had "played false"—Cleber was ambushed by the Queen's supporters, pursued, and "tooke at Eye, in Suffolke".

He paid the penalty—being hanged, drawn and quartered at Bury, with three accomplices.

But the most gruesome scene on the Common was the public execution of Robert Carleton, a Diss tailor, on April 5, 1742. His assistant, Lincoln, was in love with a Mary Frost. Carleton, afraid of losing Lincoln's services, forbade their marriage, under violent threats. They defied him and then one day he seemed to "come round", and invited Mary to dinner. He entreated her to eat heartily of the boiled mutton, himself helping her to salt.

But mixed with the salt was the deadly poison, corrosive sublimate. Mary suffered an agonising death. Carleton was arrested, tried at Thetford Assizes, and sentenced to be hanged in chains on Diss Common.

Brought from Castle Gaol on Saturday, April 3, he was placed in his customary seat in the church on the following day in the hope that he would confess to the crime. He denied his guilt—then on Monday evening the sentence was carried out, on a gibbet at the corner of Stuston Road.

The event—the last public execution in Diss—aroused intense local interest (not unusual in those harsh times), for 5,000 people gathered for the occasion.

(I cannot refrain from adding that when I told this story to a "Canary" fan, he retorted : "My word—that was a good gate !")

In an old diary I note that much damage was done to the Common in the late 18th century, ending in a notice signed by many of the leading townsmen, threatening prosecution of anyone who "cut, dug, or took away flags of turf, sand, gravel, or any dung or manure thereon".

The ancient rights of "stubbing furze and digging turfs" had been abused, and the Common was in an appalling state.

However, it was used during the Napoleonic wars for training the Diss Militia, a band of 160 men fitted out with red jackets, white pantaloons and black gaiters (all locally made), and armed with flint-lock guns.

They manoeuvred among the bushes in preparation for the defence of the country against possible invasion. Active service came in 1803 when they performed garrison duty at Great Yarmouth Marching away across the Common on Saturday, December 17, to the cheers of hundreds of people, they were billeted at Harleston for two nights, moved to Beccles on the Monday, and arrived at Yarmouth on December 20, wet through and grimed with mud from the churned-up dirt tracks they had traversed.

But they paraded spick and span the next day and fulfilled their spell of duty with great credit.

In 1814, a year before Waterloo, a petition "to enclose the Greens and Commons of Diss", was presented to Parliament. It was favourably received, and John Josselyn, of Sproughton, was appointed Commissioner to carry through the involved procedure of enclosure.

Its completion was proclaimed by Robert Parr, Sexton and town crier, in the Parish Church on August 11, 1816, in accordance with the law. Incidentally, Robert Parr was Bertie Harrison's great-great-grandfather.

So disappeared Diss Common—later to be traversed by the railway, and gradually "developed" for housing and factories, depots and garages. Today all evidence of the Common has been obliterated—though the old tower of the Mill off Waveney Road stood "on the Common", and many of the older houses and cottages indicate its original limits.

The 1814 festival of peace in Diss
(PUBLISHED DECEMBER 1963)

THE Summer of 1814 was a period of great rejoicings throughout the length and breadth of Britain, for Napoleon had abdicated, and the dreary, exacting years of war and privation were over at last. Every city, town, village and institution organized its "Festival of Peace" to mark the downfall of the tyrant who had bedevilled Europe for more than 20 years.

For months the Allied armies had been closing in on Napoleon. Paris capitulated on March 30, 1814 ; six days later Marshal Mormont surrendered with 12,000 picked troops ; and for Napoleon the game was up. On April 11, on the advice of his remaining senior marshals, he fled to Elba.

Relief that hostilities were concluded was followed by a frenzy of excitement and rejoicing, which found expression in a succession of festivals throughout the country. Bells pealed out, bands played martial music, elaborate feasts were arranged for the poor, processions depicted the victorious Allies and the defeated Napoleon, while sports and displays of fireworks gave delight to every community.

It is not surprising, then, that the inhabitants of the respectable and loyal town of Diss celebrated the occasion "in a style not inferior to any in the County of Norfolk".

Events in Diss followed the general national pattern : The regaling of the poor with roast beef, plum pudding and strong beer, followed by loyal toasts, and "lots of fun" on the Common.

Tuesday, June 21, was the appointed day for the Diss Festival. It was brilliantly fine and elaborate preparations had been made to feed 1,600 poor people. Fortunately details of these preparations have survived. A president and vice-president were appointed for each of the 32 tables, with instructions to provide "3 persons as waiters, 3 pitchers to hold a gallon each, 8 salt cellars, 2 carving knives and forks, table cloth 13 yards long, dishes and pudding bags."

On the preceding Monday morning, each president and vice-president was requested to send for "15 lbs. flour, 10 lbs. raisins, 5 lbs. suet and 10 pints of milk, to be made into 13 puddings, to be boiled for 5 hours (the raisins to be chopped)"; to send for $3\frac{1}{2}$ st. of beef to be baked at Mr. —— ; and to apply for 52 penny loaves (1 for each person at the table), 1 lb. salt, 12 pipes and 12 half-ounces of tobacco".

On Tuesday, the 32 tables, each seating 50 poor persons and the president and vice-president, were arranged on Market Hill, "extending a furlong in length and decorated with triumphal arches, garlands, colours and ingenious devices". The occasion was "graced by the Presence of the Rector, the Rev. Wm. Manning, the magistrates and respectable inhabitants who presided, with suitable assistants for each table, and attended by a good band of music and the ringing of bells".

Precisely at 1.30 the First Bugle called the participants to their allotted seats. The Second Bugle, at a quarter before two, warned the waiters to take up the provisions, ready to carry them to the tables at the Third Bugle, at 2 p.m. sharp.

Grace was followed by the "set-to", appetites were satisfied, stomachs extended, spirits enlivened. It is hardly surprising that after dinner His Majesty's health was drunk "with rapturous applause" while "God Save the King" was "sung and chorused by all".

Yet "the utmost decorum was preserved, and universal harmony prevailed", we are informed.

Dinner over, the spectators were entertained by the passage through the town of "a grand pageant depicting the Allied powers and the defeat of Bonaparte, personified by some of the spirited townsmen".

All roads now led to the "Common"—then a wide open space of some 90 acres—where an arena was roped off (and surrounded by carts and waggons to act as grand-stands) for the "rustic sports" which were to follow. These provided entertainment and generated high spirits among the 10,000 spectators who had come from far and wide to witness the occasion.

The sports over, the figure of "The Usurper" was borne high round the ring to the mocks and jeers of the onlookers, then hoisted high on a 60ft. pyre surmounted by five tar barrels. And as dusk fell the effigy of Napoleon was consumed in the flames of the furiously-burning pyre, and the happy day was concluded.

Similar celebrations were held in almost every place in 1814—at Bungay, 1,800 persons sat down to dinner, the tables extending "from near the town pump in Earsham Street to the front of St. Mary's Church". Then followed "a procession representing Bonaparte accompanied by a Don Cossack", and rustic sports on Bungay Common—the grand finale being a display of fireworks and a large bonfire surmounted by "The Tyrant in Chains."

At Beccles, 2,300 poor persons were feasted at 23 tables in the Market Square ; at Halesworth 1,000 ; at Hingham 700 ; at Earsham 500 ; and at Pulham Market 640.

These, and similar figures for all other places, represent a staggering proportion of the population of each place as "poor persons".

Official parish returns for Diss in 1800 show a population of 2,246, reduced to just over 2,000 when boarders at schools, academies and young ladies seminaries were deducted. I could scarcely believe there were 1,600 poor among a population of 2,000—but Overseers' accounts confirm this.

In 1814 public relief was being dispensed to a very large section of the town. Sixty-nine families were so poor that the parish paid their rents in whole or in part. An average of 30 families received a weekly allowance for subsistence, some 1s. a week, others up to 5s. where there were larger families.

And there was a continuous flow of "Requests at the House" from poverty-stricken individuals too poor to purchase even the barest necessities. No fewer than 1,500 items were approved by the "House Committee" at their monthly meetings in 1814, for such items as highlows, pattens, shifts, shirts, slops, bed-ticks, spades, scuppets, and firing, or a small sum of money "to go in search of work". That figure of 1,600 poor persons regaled on Market Hill is no flight of imagination.

There is little doubt that there were "extremes" in society—to be depicted later (1845) by Benjamin Disraeli in his novel *Sybil* or *The Two Nations*—the rich and the poor. And did not President Roosevelt refer to the "depressed third" of the U.S.A. when he became President in 1933 ?

That division of society seems to come through in the report of Tibenham's Festival, where "the rustic enjoyments were enlivened by the company of the benefactors of the poor, whose cheerful condescension and attention greatly contributed to the general happiness of the day"; or at Coltishall, where "the ladies and gentlemen of the parish vied with each other in attendance on their neighbours, and the partakers of the feast in their turn as gratefully acknowledged it".

The summer of 1814, with its feasts, pageants and rejoicings, faded into autumn and winter. France drifted into upheaval and discord as the Bourbons regained influence while Allied statesmen haggled at the Congress of Vienna over the redistribution of territories recovered from France.

Then, in the spring of 1815, Napoleon escaped from Elba, reached France and was welcomed by Marshal Ney and vast numbers of the disbanded French Army. He arrived in Paris on March 20, 1815—not a shot having been fired. The war flared up again while memories of those Festivals of Peace still lingered.

But the Allies forgot their bickerings and reunited for the final effort to overthrow Napoleon for good—at Waterloo on June 18, 1815. This time he was banished to the distant St. Helena to end his days.

Beyond "paying the Ringers 2£, 1s. for a form of Thanksgiving Service, and 1s. for a notice to collect for the wounded at the Battle of Waterloo", there were no public celebrations in 1815.

There were however, many private dinners to mark "The Second Peace", and one such dinner at the "King's Head" is said to have prompted these lines by H. Ward :

"At Diss there was a sound of revelry by night.
Wine was poured out freely—both red and white,
For Bonaparte had been defeated in the fight."

The bottoms of the wine bottles were later used to decorate the flint cottages at Waterloo, Scole. There they are today, a permanent reminder of the final battle against The Tyrant, fought nearly 150 years ago.

It's jubilee year for Diss waterworks
(PUBLISHED NOVEMBER 1962)

THE YEAR 1962—the "Jubilee" of the Water Works—must not pass without a thought for those whose persistence and perseverance brought a piped supply of pure water within reach of every Diss household in 1912. Many will remember the old pumps, and doubtless have used them—especially the Town Pump on Market Hill, that at Mere's Mouth, and the one on the Mount Street pavement. Until 1912 wells and pumps provided the only available supplies of drinking water, though at the Heywood even ponds were used.

In 1739 Francis Blomefield described Diss as "a neat, compact village with a large basin of water, but all the filth of the town centering there, besides the many conveniences placed over it, make the water altogether useless—so foul, it stinks exceedingly".

So the Mere, in spite of its strong springs, afforded no supply.

Three hundred years ago the Churchwardens' Accounts show payment "for a rope for the Guildhall well", and "a Buckett for the Towne well". In 1700 they appointed Jude Birdit to "fye the well". He was the first known water engineer in Diss, and he was followed by Tom Tokely, who received 3s. p.ann. "for maintaining the Towne Pump".

Though the breweries later developed their deep bores in the 19th century, wells and pumps remained the only sources of drinking water until 1912. (The Denmark Brewery was connected to the liquor pit until 1948).

The publication of the *Diss Express* in 1864 enabled public grievances to be aired in its correspondence columns. A letter in 1865 complained of "scarcity of pure water" and of residents "at the top of Mount Street having to fetch water from Market Hill" (often finding the pump dry !). Later a well and pump were placed on the 'canser'—the spot is detectable today, and particularly noticeable during snowy periods, as the snow always melts on the slab over that well.

An outbreak of choleraic diarrhoea in 1866 caused widespread concern. Doctors Amyot, Rose, Stewart and Ward, at the request of the Board of Health, reported "The town is very badly supplied with wholesome drinking water. Pigsties and collections of putrid filth exist in close proximity to many doors and wells of the humbler classes, poisoning the water they drink and the air they breathe". They recommended urgent attention to "this evil".

The Board called in a Mr. West to report on town drainage, but no attempt was made to develop a water supply. The cholera scare passed—after the distribution of 250 copies of "Mr. Samson's Precautions Against Cholera", ten gallons of carbolic acid for flushing sewers, and two gallons of Condy's fluid.

For some years attention was focused on improving the sewage system, and the general sanitary state of the town. A curious order was made that "all privies must be diverted from the Waveney and Mere, and must be emptied in the week next preceding every full moon".

Then in 1871, another fright! At Waterloo, Scole, 50 were taken ill and six died from drinking water contaminated by a cesspool.

This 'scare' created a demand in Diss to provide water, under pressure, for flushing sewers. In 1878—note the date—the Local Government Board called for a water supply for the district, but the Diss Board of Health, staggered by the possible cost, did nothing. In 1880 the School Board complained of pollution of the school well. In 1885, at a Diss inquest, the Coroner's verdict of "death from typhoid caused by drinking tainted water due to neglect of drains" generated further anxiety—but matters drifted once again.

In 1896 Mr. Cocks recalled an earlier proposal to construct two large reservoirs for surface and rain water on the high Bury Road at Palgrave—33ft. higher than the highest point in Diss—to provide a gravity supply for the town.

This won no support—but the local council (now the U.D.C.) was obviously conscious of having to do something, for in 1897 they inquired of Messrs. Lacon if they would sell their artesian well, pump and engine in Shelfanger Road, and at what price?

In March, 1898, hearing the price was £3,941, the Council decided to take no action—"a new Council would shortly be elected ; let them decide !". They too did nothing—the town had a low death rate, and there were no epidemics due to impure water.

But the public was not happy. Letters to the *Diss Express* emphasized the danger of "drifting", and the disgrace to the town of making people walk up to half a mile to fetch water. The Medical Officer of Health reported on the discoloured and foul smelling water in the lower parts of the town, and the Local Government Board again asked "What are you going to do?"

In October, 1902, J. P. Albright and R. A. Bryant joined the Council and these two in particular persevered until a public supply became an accomplished fact. Twice—in 1903 and in 1905—they were outvoted in Council when proposing the construction of a water works, their opponents maintaining that "such an expense would ruin the town".

However, when, in 1907, a private company sought permission to provide a piped supply, the whole Council voted against such an intrusion by a private concern. This decision naturally sparked off violent protests in the Press, and Dr. Whitaker and others assured the Council that the town would willingly bear the additional expense of a water works in order to have a pure supply.

And at last they became convinced that a piped supply was not an expensive luxury, but a vital necessity.

A Mr. W. H. Booth, an eminent water engineer, was called in in 1908, the preliminaries were ironed out, and by April, 1910, Duke and Ockenden's estimate for a trial bore in Louie's Lane was accepted, and a loan of £400 negotiated with the Loyal Nelson Lodge of Oddfellows. That bore proved successful—producing 150,000 gallons per day, with continuous pumping.

The stage was now set—final approvement for a complete water works, with all equipment, at a cost of £8,000 was given in January, 1912. Mr. R. A. Bryant was appointed the first chairman of the Water Works Committee and 1912 was a year of feverish activity in building the works, laying mains and making connections.

All honour to that Council of 1911-12—and, in particular, to those persistent and enlightened members who overcame the procrastinations and evasions of earlier years, to provide Diss with pure water, 34 years after the Local Government Board had asked in 1878, "What are you going to do about it?"

By 1922 some 12 million gallons a year were provided. In 1962 it is 90 millions, with a new bore and a new tower to mark the "Jubilee".

The significance of the new town sign
(PUBLISHED JUNE 1962)

VISITORS winding their way through narrow Mere Street, to the centre of Diss have a grand view of the imposing 13th century Parish Church, towering above the Market Place. In future an added attraction will greet them—the colourful town sign—that has been erected at the Mere's Mouth.

It is the most recent creation of that superb artist and craftsman, Mr. Harry Carter, of Swaffham, and generously commissioned by the Diss Chamber of Trade to mark the completion of the redecoration of Mere Street in Magdalen Street style.

Mr. Carter has selected the themes for the two main panels, and for the angle decorations, from a wealth of material from the history of Diss through the centuries. His choice has been beyond praise, and the result is a delightful sequence of carvings covering many aspects of the story of Diss from medieval to modern times.

For one panel the artist has gone back 750 years, when Robert Fitz-Walter, the "Valiant", was Lord of the Manor in King John's reign. The story was quoted by Blomefield from the *Book of Dunmow*. It concerns Robert's daughter, the Fair Matilda, "whom the King unlawfully loved, but could he not obtain her, nor her father's consent".

The King thereupon banished the valiant Robert, "which being done, he sent a messenger unto Matilda about his old suit in love". Again his advances were scorned, so the messenger "poisoned a potched egg, against she was hungry, and gave it to her, whereof she died, in 1213". Matilda's remains rest in the priory Church of Little Dunmow.

Mr. Carter has depicted the King's messenger offering the ill-omened egg to the guileless girl.

The other panel shows John Skelton, Rector of Diss 1504-1529, instructing the young Prince Henry (later Henry VIII) and his sisters Margaret and Mary.

Skelton may be the most famous figure in the town's history—he is certainly the most controversial. Born in 1460, he graduated at Cambridge in 1484. Both Universities of Oxford and Cambridge conferred on him the title of "Poet Laureate"—an academic honour for distinction in rhetoric and poetry.

Skelton composed many tributes to members of the Royal family, and so caught the eye of Henry VII, who appointed him tutor to the young Prince Henry. He taught the Prince to spell, and introduced him to the "Muses Nine". A treatise on "the demeanour of a prince" was addressed to the young pupil, and one wonders how far Henry's later conduct was influenced by the contents of that document.

Skelton was reprimanded by Bishop Nix for "living irregularly" while at Diss, whose parishioners complained to the Bishop that Skelton was the father of a boy recently born in his house. Skelton confessed the fact openly from his pulpit. Exhibiting the naked infant, he silenced his critics by saying "It is as fair as is the best of yours".

A contemporary described him as "more fit for the stage than for the pew or pulpit", yet the great scholar Erasmus called him "a light and ornament to British Literature".

His name is already perpetuated in the old people's estate, Skelton Close, and Mr. Carter has selected for the town sign one of the indisputable and non-controversial episodes of the famous Rector's life.

The upper corners of the panels are buttressed with reproductions of an ancient carving at least 500 years old, but still well preserved on the corner post of the Diss Publishing Company's shop. The figure, with outstretched wings, bearing the Star of David on its breast, has religious significance, for the building it adorns was once the house of a Guild Priest.

The carving is thought to represent the Christmas Angel, looking over the ancient market place to the church beyond. One lower corner of the panel carries replicas of the sides of a Diss Farthing. In the reign of Charles II, when there was an acute shortage of small change, counterfeit coins were minted here in defiance of laws and proclamations. "Diss Farthing, 1669" appeared on one side, and the "Shield Wavy" on the other.

Several such coins still exist today, as do similar coins for other towns. Quite recently a "King's Lyn Farthing, 1668" was discovered at Swaffham.

The remaining corner is embellished with a spinning wheel on one side, ears of corn on the other. The former represents the staple Diss industries from Tudor times—the spinning and weaving of flax, hemp and wool.

The church chest contains hundreds of "civil papers" recording the occupations of former inhabitants and leaves no doubt about the number of linen and worstead weavers, woolcombers, spinners, hecklers, flax and hemp dressers in Diss and district.

The wheel symbolises their crafts, which endured until a century ago and are now carried on by mat-weavers in a different medium.

The ears of corn emphasise an important aspect of the town's modern prosperity.—its corn market, malting and milling industries. The railway of 1849 enabled Norfolk barley to be sent far and wide, while the Corn Hall of 1854 provided—and still provides—a spacious market with diffused northern light where farmers and merchants can examine their barley samples and haggle over prices.

Finally, the town emblem, the "Shield Wavy", bearing a hint of the ripples on the Mere from which Diss took its site and its name. 'Dic' meant a ditch, dyke, moat or embankment, and Dis, Disce, Dysse, or Diss arose on the northern slopes of its "moat".

It is not inappropriate that the sign "Diss" should be erected at the "Mere's Mouth", opening on a pleasant vista of the Mere with the town's earliest settlements on the hill beyond.

Diss—a wicked town
(PUBLISHED FEBRUARY 1964)

A WEATHERED and tilted headstone in Diss Churchyard, mid-way between the Tower and the Saracen's Head, bears this inscription—"Beneath are deposited the mortal remains of George Taylor, late of this Town. By his side are interred the remains of Eleanor Taylor, his beloved wife and companion in the Kingdom of Jesus Christ . . . "

George Taylor was born in November, 1762, and became a pioneer of Methodism in Diss. It seems fitting, when the building of a new, modern church is proceeding, to look back to the early struggles and endeavours of John Wesley's followers to establish their cause in this town.

Methodism had reached North Lopham in 1770 when one Thomas Glover came to reside there. Supported by friends from Norwich, he preached in the open air under an old ash tree near King's Head Lane, before being offered the use of Mr. Gooch's kitchen in Tan's Lane. It was probably through Thomas Glover that the Revd. Thos. Lee visited Diss in 1770, and attempted to hold a meeting in the Market Place. But he met with great hostility—his words were drowned by the clashing of church bells, while he himself was ridiculed, and drenched when the local fire engine was brought into use against him.

George Taylor, then a boy of seven, not only witnessed these degrading scenes—he even joined in pelting Lee with missiles. Lee, after further abortive efforts to speak, left the town, never to return. Shortly afterwards Taylor moved to Bath—but remained indifferent to any religious call, until, when 20 years of age, he became deeply impressed and influenced by a Capt. Thomas Webb whose forceful preaching at Bath made him (Taylor) acutely aware of his own shortcomings.

Capt. Webb had fought under Wolfe in the Seven Years War, losing his right eye at the siege of Louisberg, and being wounded in his right arm when taking part in the attack on the City of Quebec. He became a Methodist in 1765 and thereafter devoted his material assets, and his talents as a preacher, to the cause he had embraced. He was one of the Lay Evangelists to plant Methodism in America—forming a class in a sail loft in Philadelphia in 1768.

From Bath, Taylor moved to London, where he joined a Methodist Society at Lambeth Marsh. There he seized the opportunity of hearing many of the great exponents of Methodism then preaching in London. From them "he perceived a clear idea of the Divine Truth", and developed his own personal religion. While in the capital he married Eleanor Betts, who shared his convictions and became the perfect partner in his subsequent work.

After occasional visits to Diss to see his mother, Taylor and his wife came to Diss in 1785 at the behest of John Wesley himself. He exhorted them to labour in what he termed "one of the most wicked towns in the Kingdom"—for gambling, gaming and cock-fighting were rife in Diss, supported by powerful vested interests. It was from this section that violent opposition came, and George Taylor, in his attempts to reform the town, met with even greater hostility and suffered even greater indignities than Thomas Lee had experienced 15 years earlier.

But slowly the "infant cause" blossomed, as opposition was worn down with the aid of persuasive and eloquent visiting ministers. It was at this time that invaluable support came from George Hey and his wife—Governor and Governess of the Workhouse on Diss Common. They were in constant touch with the genuinely poor, as well as with many who had abused and wrecked their lives by self-indulgence. Taylor and his supporters fought hard through the Methodist Society to arrest the general decline in moral standards.

It was, in fact, Mrs. Hey who obtained the promise of the site on which the first chapel was erected shortly before John Wesley came to Diss in person. Her husband, as Workhouse Master and Overseer, was in daily touch with the Rector, William Manning—a liaison which enabled him to request the use of the Parish Church when John Wesley preached in Diss in 1790. Mr. Manning gladly sought the approval of Bishop Horne, who readily consented, adding his famous reply, "Mr. Wesley is a Brother."

This gesture by Bishop and Rector added strength to the Methodist cause. The labours of its adherents prospered, a Circuit was formed, with George Hey, Henry Calver, Edward Scales,

George Taylor and Charles Reeve as trustees of the Chapel.

George Taylor remained a Methodist member for nearly 40 years, holding the offices of Leader, Steward and Trustee for the greater part. His son, also George Taylor, wrote of him—"He never grew weary in well doing, never shrunk from reproach or turned aside into folly." He died after seven weeks of acute suffering, borne with patience and fortitude.

The Baptisms of the Taylors' children are recorded in the Diss Parish Registers. One of their descendants, a grandson Dennis, was apprenticed to Thomas Gostling, a watchmaker in Mere St., and later he took over the business in 1848. Older Dysseans will remember Dennis Taylor, and many more will have known John Taylor, his son, who was in the same business until his death in 1931. (The shop is now Olivia's). John's brother George Henry (born 1853) learned the watchmaker's skills from his father Dennis, but when 24 he emigrated to Charlottetown, capital of the Province of Prince Edward Isle off the east coast of Canada's mainland. There he acquired a small shop from a jeweller's declining business, and now "Taylors—Jewellers for five generations" is blazoned across the shop's extended facia. George Henry was followed by his son Reginald (b. 1882), he in turn by his son Roland (b. 1915) who is now assisted by his own son. They own the largest jewellery business in the city.

When 'George Henry' emigrated in 1877 he was engaged to May Robinson, daughter of John Robinson, draper, of London House in the Market Place (now Gipson's, the fruiterers). Mrs. Mary Gooderham, who died at a great age in the summer of 1963, was an apprentice with John Robinson in 1878, and remembered May's departure for her marriage in Canada. In her last letter to me in April, 1963, Mrs. Gooderham recalled seeing May's baggage standing in the shop ready for despatch to Canada—while her father, John Robinson, paced the shop trying hard to suppress his emotions at the prospect of his daughter's impending departure.

Roland Taylor, the present head of the Charlottetown business visited Diss in March, 1963, to see the town from which his grandfather emigrated nearly 90 years ago. He asked for information about his ancestors, and with the help of the Registers, and many friends, it has been possible to piece together the Taylor story and draw the family "tree". George Henry carried the family's traditional affiliation to Methodism, with him to the New World. He became an active member of the Church there, served as a Lay Preacher for some years until a throat infection forced him to retire from preaching. His family, however, has continued to support the cause embraced by "George Taylor—the Methodist Hero"—first commissioned to come to Diss in 1785 by John Wesley himself.

NOTE—"Historical Sketches of Diss", published by Lusher's in 1932 contained details of Thomas Lee's visit to Diss in 1770, and of George Taylor's return to Diss in 1785. When I first read these I was dubious of their authenticity, feeling reluctant to believe that the hostile excesses perpetrated in Diss really took place. Having read George Taylor's obituary notice on his father (by permission of Mr. W. A. Green of the Wesley Historical Society) my doubts were dispelled. And in the past 30 years have not our eyes been opened to the barbarities men will practise in the name of race and religion ?—E.P.

These were the "Roydon Riots"

(PUBLISHED AUGUST 1960)

IT was on August 7, 1893, that the first incident occurred to spark off the series of events known as "The Roydon Riots." Though normally peaceable, the villagers of Roydon had been uneasy for some time. They resented the autocratic ways of the Lord of the Manor. Common land at the "Doit" had been arbitrarily enclosed, so depriving them of certain rights of pasturage which they and their forbears had enjoyed. Continuous carting of stone from the pits along the roads known as Fen Street and Sandy Lane (now Tottington Lane) had reduced them to a chaotic state, barely allowing access to the houses on the edge of the Fen.

A row of young trees had also been planted in Brewers' Green, lining the road from Manor Farm towards the Friary. This was regarded ominously as a further attempt to enclose common land, first the trees, then a connecting fence, and enclosure for private use.

It had already happened on the Doit.

Brewers' Green had always been an "open" green, with ponies, donkeys and geese grazing on it regularly by "law of custom" centuries old—the inalienable right of the cottagers and tenants, so they thought. In addition to Brewers' Green, there was also grazing on "Freezen Hills", a stretch of manorial waste between the Doit Road and Bressingham.

This was reserved for the copyholders of the estate, who, in return for payment of their dues to the Lord of the Manor, were entitled to pasture animals on strips marked out for them, and to have the right of cutting sedge on the fen lowland by the River Waveney.

Unfortunately, certain people who were not copyholders, or even residents of Roydon, were in the habit of turning their ponies on Freezen Hills, thus committing a trespass. And in the rather tense atmosphere that existed, the Lord of the Manor and his agent decided to take drastic action against the owners of the ponies.

Early in August a warning notice was circulated by the Pinder stating that any animals found unlawfully grazing on the Manorial waste after August 7, would be impounded for trespassing. This notice was ignored, and the animals continued to graze peacefully.

On August 7 the Pinder (Fredk. Culling) assisted by estate workers, seized and impounded "three head of horse stock" belonging to Henry Youngman, Wm. French (both of Roydon) and Chas. Lines (of Wortham) for "unlawfully grazing on Freezen Hill", belonging to Manor of Roydon Hall and Tufts. At the same time five head of geese grazing on Brewers' Green were also impounded. The village pound adjoined the "White Hart"—there the stock were placed in custody.

Printed notices were next posted, stating that the animals had been legally impounded for trespass and that they could be reclaimed on payment of the customary fees, i.e. a fine, added to the cost of keep. The owners were advised not to pay any costs. No attempt was made to reclaim, so, according to law, after seven days had elapsed a further notice was posted intimating that as the animals had not been claimed, they would be sold in open market on August 18.

The days between August 7 and 18 were busy ones. Secret meetings were held and careful plans of action laid for the day of sale. But the police had an inkling of what was to happen, so on the day of sale three police officers went to Roydon Pound to escort the animals and geese to Diss, to prevent possible interference.

In the middle of that Friday afternoon the three horses emerged from the pound, each haltered and led by an estate worker, followed by a tumbril containing the geese, covered by a pig-net.

Villagers by the score thronged round the procession. There was considerable interference. Whips and sticks were used to excite the horses—they were tickled with hands and twigs, to force them out of control.

In spite of this they slowly but surely made their way to Diss ; at the "Crown" Corner the already-agitated caravan was met by a boisterous mob of townsmen, and others in for the weekly market. Shop assistants and customers poured into the street to swell the throng. Seething and weaving it made its way down Pump Hill to the Market Place.

It was an odd journey for Culling and the geese. He said later that sometimes he was facing the horses, and sometimes they were behind him. Eventually, with several hundred people shouting and jostling around, they reached the Shambles, where in the confusion, the halters were surreptitiously slipped off the horses, releasing them to gallop away, amid great jubilation, through avenues made by the crowd.

Meanwhile the tumbril was so assailed from all sides that Culling lost control—the net was removed, and the geese returned in triumph to their rightful owners. Excitement then abated, after this deliberate frustation of the due course of law. At 4 p.m. nothing was left for the auctioneer to sell.

So ended the first round in the fight for rights.

On the surface at least, peace was restored to Roydon—and there was a certain satisfaction in having defeated the designs of the Lord of the Manor, his Agent, and the Pinder.

But on August 25 notice was given that the triennial election of members of the School Board would be held on September 7, and asking for nominations. The list would be published on August 26 ; withdrawals could take place up to August 30.

There were ten nominations for five places, including Mr. Todd, the agent, who lived at the Friary. But he and another, "Bleacher" Thurlow, withdrew their nominations, hoping to avoid an election and possible 'scenes'. However, eight candidates remained on the list, so voting had to take place on September 7 as notified.

In the meantime an act of vandalism was committed on Brewers' Green. During the night of August 28 between 80 and 90 of the young trees planted across the green were either uprooted or ruthlessly slashed and damaged, and their protective palisading knocked down. The green presented a scene of desolation the following morning, as if it had been struck by a tornado. The *Diss Express*, commenting on this action, mentioned that there was strong feeling among Roydon people against what was considered an encroachment on their rights, and that the time was gone for public rights to be arbitrarily interfered with. But, it continued in a diplomatic and conciliatory leader, "would it not have been better to have vented the grievance at a public meeting, rather than resort to such barbarous methods, which would surely recoil on the perpetrators ?"

This act of desecration widened the gulf between village and hall and to quote the *Express*, "added no small amount of fuel to the smouldering fire."

The day of the election of the School Board, September 7, arrived. The contest was keenly fought and the voting heavy, but a lighter touch was introduced by the appearance of posters—one asking people to "Vote for Scott, the Geese's Friend," suggesting the part played by Scott, a shopkeeper, on the release of the geese on August 18. In spite of this he was defeated.

Voting continued until 8 p.m. in the old Schoolroom, which still adjoins the Roydon "Hart", and the result was declared at 9 p.m.

It had obviously been decided to make the election an occasion for a demonstration against the Agent of the Estate, Mr. Todd. Rightly or wrongly, as the executive officer for the Lord of the Manor, he was regarded as the prime mover in the restrictive acts curtailing the parishioners' rights.

During the evening of the poll, and after the declaration, the "White Hart" had been the scene of secret preparations ; and of very considerable drinking, too. By 10 o'clock feelings ran high and tongues were loosed. In the words of the police, "there was a room full of men shouting, holloaing and drinking."

At 10 p.m. an effigy of Mr. Todd was carried out of the "White Hart," with the obvious intention of burning it ceremoniously on the space outside. But a police force of 13 (Supt. Tuddenham, Sgt. Rix and 11 constables) was in the vicinity—some hidden among the trees. The superintendent prevented the burning of the effigy, and amid drunken shouts of abuse, it was torn to pieces.

This frustration of their designs seems to have incensed the excited mob. The shout went up : "To Snow Street." Armed with sticks, the angry crowd made its way along the dark avenue from the "Hart" to the Friary, where Mr. Todd lived. Some of the police went ahead to make preparations for defence of the building, others pleaded with the mob to act with moderation—but to no purpose. They were bent on destruction.

It was a moonless night and they reached the Friary in almost pitch darkness—a darkness made even more black and ominous by the trees in that area—then, of course, still in leaf. Several assaults were made on the house—windows were smashed by sticks and stones. Sgt. Rix was knocked insensible by a blow on the jaw from a stone ; P.c. Brighton sustained injuries to the scalp ; and five police helmets were smashed.

The so-called demonstration had developed into a riot of wanton destruction and the police were outnumbered by more than ten to one. The running battle went on until nearly midnight. Stones were brought up in relays from the roadside heaps—figures darted to and fro in the darkness—until Supt. Tuddenham, after a final appeal to refrain from damage, ordered his depleted force to use their staves.

Many rioters had gradually slunk away to avoid possible recognition and the exhausted remnants eventually retired, wreaking the final vengance by smashing down 30 to 40 trees on the Green. Mr. Todd is variously reported to have sought refuge in a cellar ; in a large 'brick-oven'; in a shed. But wherever he had been, he emerged in a state of great fright, asking "Are they gone ? I'm afraid of my life"! Well might he feel so under the circumstances.

No arrests had been made during the disturbance, but the police officers had recognised several of those who appeared to be the ring-leaders, by their voices or by close contact. Seven men were subsequently arrested and brought up in custody at the Petty Sessions in Diss on September 13.

As the time for the Court arrived, several hundred people thronged St. Nicholas Street and the approach to the Magistrates' Room. This was packed to capacity.

Further disturbances were expected, so the Deputy Chief Constable of Norfolk attended, with a strong force of police. Their arrival was the signal for much hooting, but they were kept in the background, and were not called upon to act.

The seven defendants arrived in custody, to a tremendous reception from the crowd. The charge preferred against them was that they "unlawfully and riotously did assemble to disturb the public peace, and they did make a great riot and disturbance to the terror and alarm of Her Majesty's subjects."

Supt. Tuddenham prosecuted and outlined in detail the proceedings on the night of September 7, mentioning the abuse, provocation and threats the police had endured and the serious injuries to Sgt. Rix and P.c. Ducker, which prevented them from attending. He was quite convinced that the defendants were the principal instigators of the affair and asked for an adjournment to enable the wounded officers to appear and give evidence.

One of the defendants was released, as he was known to have been so drunk as to have to be helped home directly from the "White Hart." He was never in the vicinity of the Friary. The remaining six were remanded on bail.

At the conclusion of the Court, Mr. Frere, the Lord of the

Manor, who had actually sat on the Bench, met with much hostility and many uncomplimentary remarks as he left. The other magistrates, Revd. Brandreth, Mr. Francis Taylor and Mr. R. W. Crawshay, were cheered—so, too, were the defendants, who left amid great excitement and cheering, intensified by the throwing of small brown loaves into the air, said to symbolise "prison fare."

At the adjourned hearing, on September 20, Mr. Frere was present, but retired from the Bench when the hearing started. The Bench consisted of Revd. Brandreth, Mr. Francis Taylor and Mr. Edward Mann.

Further evidence was given by the police to supplement that previously given. P.c. Ducker was present, but Sgt. Rix was still unable to attend.

Mr. Chittock defended, and brought forward a number of witnesses, one of whom caused a titter by saying he thought the crowd had gone "to serenade Mr. Todd"; he went "to hear the music—though he didn't understand the songs they sang."

The evidence on both sides was inconclusive and confusing, as well it might be considering the blackness of the night. Mr. Chittock relied on "mistaken identity." One man had proved beyond all doubt to have been at home drunk and incapable of taking part.

With 150 present under such conditions it was impossible to be certain who were the culprits—"other mistakes might well be made"—but the Bench decided there was a case to answer and committed the six defendants on bail to the Quarter Sessions at Norwich on October 18.

The magistrates were again cheered as they left but the strong force of 30 police, held in reserve against possible contingencies, departed amid further "hoots and groans."

Seven men appeared before the magistrates the following week, on September 27, charged with being concerned in a "pound breach." Three were involved in "the forcible release of horses" and four in connection with the release of the geese on August 18. The adjourned cases were heard by the Rev. C. R. Manning, the Rev. Brandreth, Mr. Francis Taylor and Mr. Edward Mann.

It appeared from the legal argument put forward that once the animals were impounded, they were protected by law until the necessary fees had been paid to reclaim them. No fees were paid for horses or geese, so their forcible release before the sale was an illegal act—a "pound breach".

Mr. Blofield, prosecuting, maintained that only the copyholders of the estate had the right to depasture animals on Freezen Hill and Brewers' Green. While he granted that all and sundry had for years been in the habit of turning on whatever stock they liked, the time had come for the copyholders' privileges to be upheld. The men involved in this case were not copyholders—one was not even a Roydon man, he said.

The Steward of the Manor stated that he held the deeds showing who were the copyholders and what were their rights. Mr. Blofield then outlined the events of August 18—with supporting evidence from the Pinder, the three men who led the horses to Diss, and the police officers who formed the escort. There was much confusion again, as one might expect when 800 excited people crowded round and jostled the frightened animals and geese cart.

Mr. Wild, defending, cross-examined the Pinder and his three assistants and their vague and halting evidence brought no conclusive proof that the accused had actually released the horses or the geese. He agreed they had interfered, but there was no proof that they had actually freed the animals.

The Bench, however, were satisfied that a bona fide case had to be answered, and the first three defendants were committed, on bail, to the Quarter Sessions at Norwich on October 18.

Mr. J. T. Frere then intervened and stopped the proceedings with regard to the geese. He said he was satisfied that as three men had been sent for trial, the rights of the copyholders would eventually be upheld, and he had no desire to press the case for "pound breach" relating to the freeing of the geese.

Before dealing with the final episode in these protracted proceedings, it is interesting to note that accounts of these events in a Norfolk village had by now become national news, and were the subject of comment in weekly journals such as *The Spectator* and *Truth*.

It may be stretching things too far to say that events in Roydon had affected legislation in Parliament—but who knows? *The Spectator* in September, 1893, mentioned the passing of an Act of Parliament which "virtually closed the last doors by which commons could be enclosed". Recourse to the "Statute of Merton" of 1235 on which many Lords of the Manor relied, would no longer be available to them as an excuse for enclosing common land. It was now a dead letter under the new Act. The Roydon outbursts may have played a part in this.

An editorial in *Truth* (September 27, 1893) criticised the court proceedings of September 13, when Mr. J. T. Frere was a member of the Bench hearing the case against the seven rioters. Its comment was a pertinent one : "It seems scandalously wrong for Mr. Frere, who is apparently the cause of the trouble, to sit on the Bench while a case is being heard in which he is the de facto prosecutor." Mr. Frere, though present in Court, was not on the Bench for the adjourned and subsequent hearings.

On October 18, Mr. J. B. R. Bulwer, Q.C., sitting at Norwich Quarter Sessions with a jury, first heard the case committed from September 20. Six defendants surrendered to their bail, charged with "riotously assembling with divers other persons to the number of 50 or more, to disturb the public peace at Roydon on September 7." Mr. Blofield again prosecuted ; Mr. E. E. Wild defended.

Mr. Blofield outlined in detail the events of September 7 and called police evidence in support of the case against the various defendants for leading the riot, for inciting others to acts of destruction, or for the actual smashing of windows.

Mr. Wild called nine witnesses for the defence and their evidence, if accepted, would have exonerated all the defendants from any blame. They were all obviously in sympathy with the rioters and even showed great relish when describing their experiences.

Like the prosecution, Mr. Wild could produce nothing really conclusive. Every bit of evidence either way seemed only to emphasize the confusion that existed on that very dark night.

After the summing up by the learned chairman—a very fair one indeed—the jury retired. On their return their verdict was one of "guilty, with a recommendation to mercy." The two undoubted ring leaders were sentenced to six months imprisonment, the remainder to one month.

Then followed the final episode in this sorry village squabble. Three men were charged with "pound breach" on August 18. The actual charge read "forcibly releasing three horses lawfully impounded at Diss on August 18.." They pleaded guilty.

Mr. Blofield again appeared for the prosecution. After stressing that it was the duty of Mr. Frere, as Lord of the Manor, to protect the copyholders' grazing rights, he said he was instructed not to press this case. By admitting their guilt the accused had actually established the case of the copyholders and for them alone.

The learned chairman, after severely reproving the three men for their "intolerable and grossly illegal acts," bound them over in their own recognisances on their undertaking not to commit further similar misdemeanours. He concluded by saying he was glad to hear that Mr. Frere "was desirous to live in peace with everybody there."

So ended this prolonged and unfortunate chapter in the history of Roydon.

ACKNOWLEDGEMENT—The author is indebted to the following for their personal reminiscences and confirmation of the sequence of events he has described :

Mr. E. Hose (whose father was Rector of Roydon at the time and who knew most of the characters involved) ; Mr. Dick Nunn (who was present at the turning out of the high-spirited rioters from the "White Hart" with the effigy) ; Mr. Fred Nunn (who knew very well several of the characters involved) ; Mr. Walter Howard of Bressingham (to whose house opposite the Friary the injured police were taken for treatment) ; Mr. Will Cracknell (who then lived at the Manor House) ; Mr. George Prentice and Mr. W. Cooper.

Roydon in the days when you could be hanged for shooting a rabbit
(PUBLISHED OCTOBER 1962)

THE other morning the B.B.C. broadcast in its "Today" programme a recorded interview with the secretary of the Tamworth and Arden Society for the Apprehension and Prosecution of Felons. Founded about 1780, the society originally consisted of a group of men who mutually agreed to share the expense of bringing to justice those who committed theft, destroyed trees, caused fire, damaged bridges, etc. and so on. Now, in 1962, it has become mainly a social club, holding an annual dinner, but still functioning in accordance with its original purpose. This year it has distributed rewards for information leading to the conviction of four felons.

This programme was of special interest to me, because only the previous day, through the kindness of the Rector and Churchwardens of Roydon, Mr. Copeman and I had discovered a parchment relating to just such a society in Roydon, but founded much earlier, in 1748.

In spite of all the provisions of the Welfare State, we are, alas, all too frequently informed of wanton damage and petty theft by irresponsible people—and of organized raids on business and private premises, resulting in huge hauls of loot. Such acts are a blot on our affluent 20th century society ; but in the 18th century the causes were somewhat different.

There were, of course, racketeers and thieves scooping in big "prizes", as today, but much of the petty crime was the result of desperation and sheer need, especially in rural areas.

In *England in the 18th Century*, J. H. Plumb wrote : "The agricultural labourer had formerly eked out a precarious living by using his small allotment and his common rights, but with "enclosure" these rights disappeared, and the consequence was a growth in rural poverty. Hungry men will snare and poach. In lean years the despair of the poor became unendurable ; food riots, burning, looting and mob violence, born of despair, were a commonplace. The militia suppressed them, and hangings and transportations followed."

It was against this background, and in the absence of a police force, that we must see the reason for the existence of such a society as the one organized in 1748.

Roydon then had just a parish constable—unpaid and unpopular, nominated by the Vestry to serve his year, approved and sworn in by the Justices at Long Stratton Sessions. He served reluctantly and did little to prevent crime. He would hope for the co-operation of other parishioners to track down a thief when a hue and cry was raised, but his beat ended at the parish boundary.

The Roydon Society was founded on September 17, 1748, with 19 members, each of whom paid 2s. 6d. "to provide a fund for carrying out its purposes". These were : "To sustain and bear in equal shares the costs, charges and expenses attending all prosecutions which shall be commenced against any person or persons whomsoever for ffelonies, Burglaries, Robberies, Larcenies or Thefts committed within the precincts of the Parish of Roydon upon or against any of our Persons, Houses, Goods, or Chattells."

Care was taken that no proceedings were to be initiated by any member without the consent of two others ; that the expense of each prosecution should be laid before two or more subscribers who would "tax and settle the same, and adjudge what each subscriber should pay".

There were other rules governing removal, refusal to pay subscription, or to share expenses, and for admission of new members.

The parchment records many renewals of subscriptions from 1748 to 1820, and several familiar names in the history of Roydon and Diss—Frere, Mattholie, Hart, Fincham, Eaton, Punchard, Muskett. Edward Chappelow, the Rector who initiated the scheme, and became its first treasurer, had been curate at Diss and headmaster of the Grammar School there, and had married Francis Blomefield's sister.

Several actual cases are recorded on the document :

"Apprehending and conveying Marth M— and Frances M— to Windham Bridewell, and Expences, for Stealing Wood from Mr. Elliott . . . £1 4s. 6d."

"Apprehending and Committment, Conveying and Expences to Windham, Thomas S— for Stealing Wood from the Rt. Hon. J. H. Frere . . . £1 2s. 6d."

"Mr. Freeman's Expenses for Prosecuting James C— for Stealing a Fat Hog . . . £1 7s. 6d."

James C— was apparently not sent to Wymondham Bridewell (later to become the police station). He might have been hanged for such a crime, but was probably transported. At that time such offences as shoplifting, cutting down trees, shooting rabbits, or stealing linen from a bleachfield were punishable by hanging.

A strong liberal element in Parliament was then pioneering for reform of these harsh laws, and the fate of James C— may have weighed on the consciences of those Roydon parishioners whose society brought him to book.

At all events, the subscribers dwindled to five, and the last entry, on November 5, 1821, showed that the funds were exhausted after paying 16s. for apprehending two brothers and conveying them to Windham.

Twenty years were still to elapse before the County Rural Police Force was established.

Farm-workers were following in footsteps of the Luddites
(PUBLISHED AUGUST 1962)

MANY of the older residents of South Norfolk remember the "Roydon Riots" of 1893. They were purely local, and far less violent than the widespread riots some 70 years before, for the 19th Century opened none too happily for the rural population in this area. The Napoleonic Wars had drawn many a father and brother from the family circle. The year 1801 was one of very high prices and acute shortages. Parish overseers were distributing relief to increasing numbers, and, in some villages, rationing supplies to avoid starvation, recent enclosures of common land had deprived villagers of grazing rights and of the chance of gathering fuel.

Penal laws, too, were savage—for sheep stealing the penalty was death by hanging ; a pickpocket could be transported for life ; and "netting of rabbit" could mean transporation for seven years. Unemployment and distress were rife.

When, in 1804, an engineer named Ball invented, and successfully demonstrated a "threshing machine on a new principle," agricultural workers envisaged further unemployment. No longer would they be needed to "whirl the lashing flail," for Ball's machine could thresh "30 sacks of corn in less than an hour." As mechanized threshing became more widespread, so resentment and discontent increased, finally bursting in a wave of machine-wrecking, just as the Luddites had wrecked factory equipment in the past.

The first "wrecking" was at Hockham in 1816, after which four ringleaders of a group of 100 were convicted for "riotous assembly," two being sentenced to 12 months in the Castle Gaol. At Downham, the following day, there were more disturbances, following the farmers' refusal to increase wages. The Justices were insulted, and the Upwell Yeomanry called out to support the helpless constables. Two of those apprehended were hanged. One, Thody, after first displaying great fortitude, "sank under the agony of grief and terror, at the recollection of his wife and children, and the horror of immediate death." Such was the savagery of the law.

In February, 1822, unrest came to a head in the extreme south of Norfolk. At first the protests were mild enough. The hungry unemployed of Shimpling protested en masse against the use of machines, by dragging a threshing machine into Burston, and leaving it there, undamaged, on the Green. About the same time the poor of Winfarthing removed a machine to Shelfanger, whose inhabitants then hauled it to Diss, leaving it stranded at Westbrook Green.

This "mildness" was shortlived, however, for shortly after, a hostile crowd prevented the removal of a 'thresher' from Burston to Shimpling by blocking the road. The farmer's appeals, and threats, were unavailing, and after unhitching the horses, the mob destroyed the machine with hatchets, hooks and pickaxes, and left it beyond repair.

Six of the 50 rioters were summoned to appear before the Justice at the "King's Head". The whole of Shimpling must have escorted them to Diss Market Place, for some 200 angry protesting villagers assembled, bent on preventing the six being taken into custody.

In this situation the "Riot Act" was read, and those summoned then presented themselves for the hearing. They were released on bail. At the next Quarter Sessions Robert Chatton and James Goddard were sentenced to 12 months imprisonment, the remainder committed to "Aylsham Bridewell."

So deepseated and general was the unrest that these sentences failed to abate the seething discontent in Winfarthing, where, on February 28, a group of Winfarthing-Bressingham-Shelfanger men wrecked two machines. Seven men were named in the subsequent warrant issued to the Petty Constables of Winfarthing.

There were no trained Police then, and doubtless those Petty Constables had many uneasy moments at the prospect of apprehending the rioters—for the villagers were openly hostile. But events took an unexpected turn . . . .

The 16th Lancers, after a spell of duty at Norwich, were returning via Scole, to Romford. It was not just coincidence that they broke their journey at Diss, for, on this occasion "the Civil Power availed itself of the assistance of the Military."

At dawn on the 18th, just as horsemen and cowmen, with their frails, were going to work, the Lancers rounded up the offenders,

and brought them to Diss to appear before the Justices.
They were 'bailed', to appear later at the Quarter Sessions.

I have seen the actual warrant directed to the Constables—on it is written, "Lieut. Crosley with Troop of 16th Lancers in full marching order, arms and accoutrements executed this warrant. Though much tumult and resistance had been threatened none was made."

The villagers had hardly expected such a move, though the military had already been used in other parts of the county under similar circumstances.

At Thetford the ringleader, William Baker, of Bressingham, Robert Dixon and William Ellsey, of Winfarthing, and Richard Coleman, of Shelfanger, were sentenced for "riot and misdemeanour" —Baker to 18 months, and the others to 12 months in the Castle Gaol. This district was but one of many areas of discontent where—in the words of the late G. M. Trevelyan—"rick-burning and rioting gave expression to the sense of hopeless misery, and owing to the absence of an effective police force, resort had to be made to the soldiers to repress the mobs".

The question of agricultural depression in South Norfolk was discussed in Parliament, and without doubt these outbursts, however regrettable, played a part in initiating reforms that gradually came later.

Today, the attitude to machinery has changed, and every invention that takes the "hard grind" out of work is a welcome innovation.

The scholastic academies of a century ago
(PUBLISHED DECEMBER 1962)

THE National, or Church, School, celebrates its centenary this year, having begun a new phase in 1862 in what were then described as "noble and commodious buildings in the Parson's Entry." It had outgrown its original home of 1847—the schoolroom in the north-east corner of the St. Mary's Churchyard, later adapted for the Young Men's Friendly Society.

In Diss there was also the undenominational counterpart of the National School—the British School, erected in 1860 beside the Causeway and attended by some 150 children.

But what of the older schools—those offering education beyond the elementary stage? For boys there were two in Diss and one just over the river, in Palgrave, all advertising themselves in glowing terms, competing for the support of potential patrons.

The *Agricultural Gazette*, in 1862, referred to the lack of good schools in Norfolk where farmers' sons could obtain a sound education at moderate cost, complaining that "the schools, mainly supported by tenant farmers, were of a low type, conducted by men in many respects inferior to the certificated national schoolmasters."

But, happily, the Diss schools were emphatically excluded from such a charge.

Was not "Dunlop's Academy for Young Gentlemen" offering a sound classical, commercial and agricultural education? There, in the Entry, Messrs. Dunlop conducted their scholastic establishment at what was later to be called The Wilderness.

William Grear, formerly an assistant at the Guildhall Grammar School, had first founded a school on the Market Terrace, but in the early 1820s he had acquired the house in the Entry from Mr. Wiseman. He added a large classroom, with dormitory above, and moved his school there.

It was when he retired to Islington that his school eventually came to the brothers Dunlop, remaining in their proprietorship until 1872, when the surviving brother sold up and retired. Mr. Cupiss bought the premises in 1873 and named them The Wilderness.

The master's desk used by Grear and the Dunlops still remains —the underside of its lid scored deep with names and initials, while the old school cupboards now bulge with printer's equipment.

Dunlop's Academy was a private boarding grammar school, patronized by well-known local families whose sons played many a thrilling cricket match on the Rectory Field against their principal rivals, Maling's Academy and Palgrave Place Academy.

The daughter of one of Mr. Dunlop's pupils told me this authentic story : Her father and his fellow-pupils were hard at their lessons in the schoolroom when a shapely leg suddenly crashed through the ceiling, littering boys and desks with plaster and dust. The dormitory floor had given way as the maid made the beds.

Mr. Dunlop hastily ascended the narrow stairway to help the maid in her distress, while the excited boys tenaciously clung to the protruding limb, until Mr. Dunlop's voice, thundering above, persuaded them it would be wiser to discontinue their tug-of-war, to avoid severe consequences.

Opposite the "Two Brewers", in what now are business offices, was "Mr. Maling's Middle Class Day and Boarding Academy for Young Gentlemen". Mr. Maling lived at St. Mary's Terrace, but "respectfully solicited patronage and recommendation from Gentlemen who attended Diss Market", so his school was in St. Nicholas Street, where his "farmer patrons would find it convenient for weekly boarders".

Mr. Maling was a great publicist and followed the usual practice of holding his internal school examinations in the Corn Hall, under the very eyes of parents and patrons ! The hall was filled to capacity in 1862, when the little victims were doubtless on their toes for such an awe-inspiring occasion.

Persistent in his efforts to attract all types of pupils—and to ensure payment of fees—he offered "three prices, according to education required", and "20 per cent discount on fees for payment in advance"; while "a plain English course at moderate terms" was available, or "mnemonics and short-hand taught privately".

His time was fully occupied, to be sure, for he added to his school advertisement : "Tradesmen's Books posted up" and "Orders for pianoforte tuning attended to promptly".

Whereas Mr. Dunlop announced his new term in a friendly "will be pleased to meet his pupils on Monday next", Mr. Maling's was somewhat forbidding : "Mr. Maling will be ready to meet his pupils at the usual hour", as if a battle was imminent.

However, from the glowing testimonials he received (and published) he must have instilled a sound education, and, in fact, he eschewed "corporal punishment".

Just across Denmark Bridge was Palgrave Place Academy (now Mr. Hume's), under Daniel Thynne, offering, like Mr. Dunlop, "A classical and commercial education at moderate terms", with "references of the first respectability".

He engaged to instruct young gentlemen carefully in all branches of a sound and liberal education, and stole a march on his rivals by providing "convenience in the premises for ponies and conveyances of pupils from the country". Many in those days travelled miles by pony or trap to attend school from outlying villages.

Other similar schools within easy reach were Eye Grammar School, Botesdale and Banham Commercial Schools, under Mr. Laker and Mr. Cole respectively (both to attain Grammar School status later), and "Hill House Academy" at Eye (where the Yaxley Road joins Lambseth Street.)

The last named provided courses for "Mercantile, Agricultural and Professional Pursuits" with an array of subjects, including surveying, navigation and "natural and experimental philosophy", a curriculum which a modern Grammar School might envy. But how much was window dressing ?

In this academy a Mr. Bevis attended to the "mental improvement and domestic comfort of his pupils with anxious solicitude, while inculcating correct moral and religious principles".

But this academy, like the others, passed away—their premises converted to other uses. Banham Grammar School was absorbed many years later by Thetford Grammar School, Botesdale Grammar School survives in spirit in the form of "Bacon Exhibitions", and Eye Grammar School alone remains, awaiting the day of amalgamation with its counterpart over the border.

Schools for the young ladies, 1862
(PUBLISHED DECEMBER 1964)

THIS year (1962) a Norfolk girls' school announced its Easter term in these words : "Recognized by the Ministry of Education—School for Girls and Kindergarten, to G.C.E.—Newly-Built Gymnasium and Swimming Pool—Next term, Jan 16th." How concise, yet comprehensive, and how different from the glowing advertisement, for "Mrs. Hart's Establishment for Young Ladies, Mount Street, Diss" of a century ago, which offered "Board Instruction in English, A. and M. History, General Literature, Geography, Writing, Arithmetic, Elements of Astronomy, Plain and Ornamental Needlework, the French, Latin, German and Italian Languages—with the pianoforte, singing, dancing (each one guinea per quarter extra) and the Use of the Globes" ($\frac{1}{2}$ gn. per quarter extra). Terms for young ladies above 14, 25 gns. per annum, Parlour Boarders 30 gns."

Mrs. Hart's was then the fashionable school in Diss, conducted in a large room at the Laurels, adjoining the Cedars. How the staff for 25 pupils of varied ages could provide for such a range of subjects in those restricted quarters is quite amazing. Most intriguing, however, are "The Use of Globes", and the possible privileges the parlour boarders enjoyed for their extra guineas—with thoughts for the non-parlour young ladies, and the menial chores they were expected to perform.

Mrs. Hart had recently transferred her school from Barbauld House, Palgrave, which had been "Palgrave School" from Queen Elizabeth's reign, apart from a spell when occupied by the famous antiquary, Tom Martin.

The challenge to Mrs. Hart's supremacy came from the Misses Robinson (Mere Street), Mrs. Ann Rush (Grasmere House, later Haddon Lodge), the Misses Blagrove (of The Terrace), the formidable Miss Dix (Mere Street) and Miss Elizabeth Legood (Cock Street).

Mary and Ann Robinson opened school in a small way in 1851, but by 1862 were "gratefully acknowledging the liberal patronage received, soliciting a continuance thereof, and assuring their friends that no effort would be spared to render the intellectual and moral culture of those entrusted to them, efficient and satisfactory (at moderate terms)".

Mary lived to a great age, later following Miss Hart at the Laurels, Mount Street, to complete well over 50 years as a schoolmarm. The Misses Warne, pupils in her later years, remember her and her "back-board with grips", a rather stringent corrective for round shoulders, as she made a feature of lady-like deportment.

She had a passion for cats too—their basket occupied a privileged place near the Tortoise stove during lessons, as one of the Miss Warnes has good reason to remember. Miss R. became unpunctual with advancing years, and Miss Warne, anxious to begin her lessons, inquired when they would start—Miss R. meanwhile fussing over the cats. A sharp "cuff" was the response, and Miss Warne landed in the cat basket !

Nevertheless, Miss Robinson was a kindly, charitable soul. Her annual Christmas tree, ornamented with useful and attractive articles made by her pupils, for sale (in aid of destitute children), was supported by a large and responsive patronage.

The best situated of all the young ladies' establishments was that of Mrs. Rush, of Grasmere House, opened 1862 in a large handsome stone mansion built in 1855, overlooking the Mere.

Mrs. Rush courted her patrons with the usual ambitious curriculum, but her speciality was "drawing", with an open-day exhibition in view. In 1862 the young ladies' efforts were so good that they drew forth "the encomiums of the spectators", giving great satisfaction to Mrs. Rush, who was soon to move to Osmond House, Botesdale, to accommodate her increasing number of boarders. Grasmere House later became a hospital, and is now the headquarters of the British Legion.

Miss Eliza Legood's seminary was in Cock Street, in a private house adjoining the Tabernacle. Here were taught "Grammar and Composition in English and French". Miss Legood asked for no entrance money, but acquired an extra half-guinea per quarter for each of arithmetic and writing—which one would have expected to be essential parts of the normal routine, and not extras, as were also "the Use of the Globes" and "the use of astronomical and celestial maps (15s.)".

These last items implied a certain degree of competence in the early teaching of geography—but were really added for prestige purposes.

This school was attended by some 20 pupils—among whom at this time was Miss Alice Cattermole's mother.

Competing strongly for the honour of being the "most select" establishment was the Misses Blagrove's School on The Terrace, where the English and French tongues were "taught grammatically, also plain work in the neatest manner, and fine embroidery in the newest state".

But the Blagrove's greatest baits to attract young ladies were the weekly lesson given by an "able dancing master" in their commodious premises, and the added attraction of a resident Parisian governess.

Miss Dix, of Mere Street, was the martinet of the period, and appears to have deserved her reputation as a battleaxe. She advertised little except to announce she would be "happy to resume her duties". She ruled strictly, simply by admonition.

Her pupils staged a musical evening each Christmas, with pianoforte duets as a feature. For this an additional piano was hired, and the charge for this, in 1862, Miss Dix thought excessive. She tried to compromise but the owner took the case to Court, claiming £1 10s. and informing the Judge that Miss Dix had already "sworne" him out of 16s. "You are not equal to Miss Dix", remarked the Judge. "No, Sir!" he replied, "But there are many who would like to be!"

A century ago there were several minor kindergartens in Diss where a few pupils were taught in private houses for 2d. a week, and a peripatetic lady, "experienced in tuition, and willing to attend upon pupils in their homes", on the lines of an itinerant music teacher I remember years ago who gave lessons for "6d. and her lunch".

One final reference to this period. At "The Hollies" (Redgrave) the Misses Reeve gave a very sound all-round education to only seven pupils—two of whom I knew in their later years. They were certainly a fine testimony to the training given in some Dame schools.

Botesdale grammar school
(PUBLISHED SEPTEMBER 1962)

CROWNING the hill in Botesdale Street is a 15th century Chapel of Ease bearing an ancient Latin inscription. It was built by and for the people of "St. Botolph's Dale"—a hamlet within the parish of Redgrave—because the parent church was so distant. Early in the 16th century the Chapel was endowed as a Chantry by John Sheriff—with income to support a priest to pray for his and his wife's souls.

When Chantries were suppressed and endowments confiscated by Edward VI, the Chapel fell into decay. In this state it was granted by Queen Elizabeth to Sir Nicholas Bacon, of Redgrave Hall, to found "a free Grammar School" for the education of poor local boys.

The school opened in the early 1560s. In 1571 the first scholar went up to Cambridge, followed by a steady stream of others. In 1576 Sir Nicholas, finding his venture a success, made provision for the future. In a lengthy document which survives, he laid a charge of £30 per annum on his "Mannors of Studdy and Burningham in Norfolk", to secure "for ever" £20 per annum for the Master of the School, £8 for the Usher and £2 for repairs.

He also endowed six scholarships to "Benet" College, Cambridge (his old college),—for boys from his "Free School in Botesdale". Benet College, now Corpus Christi, still receives that annuity of £20, I am informed by the Master, Sir James Thomson.

Sir Nicholas ordained that "two honest inhabitants of Redgrave and Botesdale" should be appointed Governors for one year. They were to meet each All Saints' Day to appoint successors—"this changing of Governors to be kept yerely perpetually". He reserved for himself the appointment of the Master—a graduate of Corpus Christi.

Alas! those Governors had little authority beyond spending £2 for repairs, for the Master could literally snap his fingers at them, later he did, when the Bacons left Redgrave Hall. For long periods there were no Governors—no one would undertake this thankless and powerless office.

In all Grammar Schools of that time—Eye, Bury, Thetford, Bungay—school hours were "6 a.m. to 11" and "1 p.m. to 5", on Saturdays to 3 p.m. The curriculum included "learning by heart all such things as concern the Christian Faith, in the Latin and English tongues." (No maths or science then !).

Each day began with a long prayer for the Founder, repeated every Sunday in Redgrave Church, where the Master, Usher and Scholars were to attend "from the beginning of morning and evening service till the ending of them". The 'Chapel of Ease' was then the Schoolroom).

School equipment included "candles for winter"—"a bow, three shafts, a bowstring, shooting gloves and a bracer, to exercise shooting".

For a century the school was a great success. It reached its capacity of 60 scholars—many of whom went up to Cambridge. Then came a period of decline.

The arrival of King William III in 1688 to succeed the deposed James II was not popular in the Botesdale district. The Rector of Wortham-Jarvis (Thomas Thurlow), the citizens of Eye and Samuel Leeds (headmaster of the school) were among the supporters of King James. Many of them gathered at a seditious meeting on Botesdale Market Place and drank "Confusion to King William", Leeds was sacked by Sir Edmund Bacon, and "pilloried" at Bury.

His usher took charge of the school, only to be dismissed for impropriety, and what today would be called "flogging school property". He even brought an unsuccessful action against Sir Edmund for wrongful dismissal, and the "depositions" of the case taken at the "Crown" coaching inn by a Commission, make most entertaining reading.

This unfortunate though intriguing period brought the school to a low ebb. There were but ten boys when Samuel Mabourn became head in 1698. A man of tremendous personailty and vigour, and teaching ability, he raised the school to such a pitch that it ranked among the finest in East Anglia.

His scholastic successes were exceptional. The Bacons moved from Redgrave in 1706, and Mr. Mabourn, disregarding all the Founder's "ordinances", filled his school with paying boarders from far and wide, to the exclusion of "poor local boys". His usher, Price, succeeded him and continued the practice.

Feeling ran high locally. The disgruntled parishioners of Botesdale—their boys excluded—sought Counsel's opinion on the school organisation, this resulting in six "free scholars" being once again admitted.

Masters came and went—but the departure of Rev. John Cole Galloway to Thetford School in 1774 was a turning point. The Rev. Mr. Smith followed, but finding his £20 per annum totally inadequate for the task undertaken, he became quite indifferent about his school. The locals clamoured for his removal—twice protesting to the Earl of Buckinghamshire (to whom power of appointment had passed) before events took a turn for the better.

The Rev. William Hepworth became head in 1791. He ran the school as the Founder had prescribed, and was referred to as "dear old Hepworth—a scholar and a gentleman—good and kind hearted, yet stern in school, though not relying on the terrors of the rod." He revived the great days of Mr. Mabourn, bringing in clever boys from afar, while taking his quota of "free scholars".

In his day cricket was played in Barley Birch, that spacious home of good cricket played in the finest English spirit—until the exigences of the Second World War demanded its use for food production. The coaches, too, stopped at the "Crown"—bringing news of the Napoleonic wars. Mrs. Hepworth also restored the Chapel for parochial use.

Then in 1822, an ageing sick man, he suddenly decided "no more boarders". The six "free" boys were sent to a recently opened Commercial School under the Rev. Mr. Haddock (not 100 yards away, where Simonds Garage now is). Mr. Hepworth virtually "shut up shop"—but lived in the school house free and drew the combined Master's and Usher's salaries until he died, aged 82, in 1841. His body rests in Wattisfield Church.

Into this sinecure stepped his son, who held office until he died in 1869, "having never taught the boys personally". Such were the disastrous results of not having an effective Governing Body.

Meanwhile the Commercial School had gained in prestige and efficiency. The Marquis of Lothian, who now had power of appointment, resolved an awkward situation by making Mr. Laker of the Commercial School, headmaster—and allowing his establishment to be called "Botesdale Grammar School, founded by Sir Nicholas Bacon".

This school too "had its day"—flourishing until 1878—but on Mr. Laker's death, it closed.

The Charity Commissioners stepped in at last. After much negotiation a "Bacon Exhibitions Endowment Scheme" was approved by Queen Victoria in 1881. The Chapel, built 400 years before, was restored to the parish by Mr. G. H. Wilson—the house was sold, and for many years was a successful Girls' Private School —now, in 1962, the residence of Dr. Cordeaux.

The proceeds of sale and the annual charge of £30 provided and continue to provide help in their school and university education for boys living in Redgrave, Botesdale, and contiguous parishes —in a manner I am sure the Founder would approve.

I knew two friends who remembered the last days of Mr. Laker's school, which, incidentially, was attended by the father of one of the present trustees, Mr. R. H. Rash. An original Elizabethan desk remains—gouged deep with the initials of generations of boys pondering over their Latin in the flickering candlelight.

The school bell—bearing the Bacon crest of 'Boar passant'— which once called boys to school, called modern generations to public worship, until it was taken down two years ago.

Of the old boys of this defunct school—"Phiz" (Hablot Browne) illustrated Dickens, Edward Law became Lord Ellenborough and a Chief Justice of King's Bench, Richard Fisher became Master of Caius College, John Fenn published the Paston Letters—and many became Fellows, Rectors, Barristers and Recorders—surely a school with a proud though varied history.

Leaves from a school log-book
(PUBLISHED OCTOBER 1962)

IN 1872 the Special Committee of H.M. Privy Council responsible for education, ordered grant-aided schools to keep a log-book, with daily entries of "ordinary progress," but adding that "the zealous teacher will not be at a loss to add other details." Many schools already kept log-books or diaries of school events, and one of these, commencing in 1862, was retrieved from a waste paper collection in 1940. It had been inadvertently (or patriotically?) discarded to help the war effort, but was recovered. Its preservation has given us a glimpse of school life a century ago.

Attendance was not compulsory then and the struggle to establish education as part of national life, in the face of parental indifference, of irregularity of attendance, lack of competent staff and equipment, etc., are vividly portrayed in the log entries.

The village squire figured prominently—often helpfully, as when "The Squire's keeper called with an otter, just shot in the river. I gave an object lesson while he stayed..." or... "Through the kindness of the Squire, soup dinners will be supplied at 1d. per week."

At other times he entered the school and "threatened to punish any boy who broke down the shrubbery fence"; "ordered eight girls to be punished for bad behaviour on Sunday". And he even desired the Master "to seize all catapults".

The Rector, too, had much influence, for the squire and he were pioneers of this National School, and supplied any deficiency in the cost of running it not met by the pitifully-small Government grant. One day "The Rector spoke severely to Charles B—, and removed him from the choir for six weeks for stealing a book from the Curate's house".

The lack of even simple equipment was most apparent, though the Rectory helped out in needlework, for "Girls put needlework to practical account today, by darning and mending worn linen from the Rectory"... "The finished work was sent to the Rectory; one chemise was returned to be re made; several towels to be picked out and re-numbered".

An examination was due, but in the log, "Insufficient paper for scholars—no examinations !" Two days later, "A quire of foolscap sent from the Rectory".

The Master, trained and qualified, conducted his school of 138 pupils with the help of his wife (unqualified) and a monitor (aged 14). Little wonder difficulties arose ! "Albert C— commenced as paid Monitor at 1s. per week for three months, when his father thinks of apprenticing him as a harness-maker"; while "Mrs. B— sent word that Mary was not to be taught by a monitor, she would teach her herself".

Then those large classes ! "The Mistress has 70 girls for sewing ; very trying and difficult work, single handed".

After the master's wife had had a baby the Mistress was absent. "We have no servant, and it has been too cold to have the baby at school . . . "

A persistent bar to progress was frequently absence for seasonal work to add a few pence to the low family income. Among typical entries : "More than half the children dropping wheat and potatoes and stone picking" (March) ; "Several away bird-keeping" (Apr.) ; "Many absent in haysel" (June) ; "Small school, many thinning turnips and gathering currants (Jly.) ; "56 absent ; they will return when potato picking and gleaning end" (Sept.) ; "Many away seed dropping and gathering acorns at 1s. a bushel" (Oct.) ; and "Several boys brushing for the Squire's shoot" (Dec.).

Weather, too, was a hindrance to attendance : "Snow, very cold in school, children few, huddled round stove" (Feb.) ; "Mon. and Tues. bad days, wet and cold, small school"; "Parents will not send children rest of the week—not worth paying 2d. for three days".

Then many awkward situations were noted : "Mr. L— beat the Monitor because his boy was kept in"; "Herbert P— struck Alice W— and made her nose bleed. They had mobbed each other and she kicked him in the leg"; "Two boys cheated at marbles ; I spoke about honesty in play"; "Punished Arthur C— for eating his brother's and sister's dinners, after he had eaten his own"; "Seventeen children excluded from the Rectory for stealing peas as they came from Church"; "Sent Emily H— home, head in a very dirty condition (sixth time)"; "Julia C— came to be re-admitted, but was sent home. Had not recovered from the itch".

Truanting was common, too. "Ernest H— truanted to see the foxhounds, his father punished him severely". Another boy truanted persistently, making but 36 attendances out of possible 428, and at last the exasperated father brought him to school secured by a halter, and bundling him into the porch exclaimed, "Do what you like with him".

"Julia W— was absent. She had been chained to the bedpost for telling a falsehood ; poor child only released by the intervention of the Rector".

It is not surprising that when H.M. Inspector conducted the annual examination to assess Government grant, only 90 of the 138 qualified by attendance to be examined. Of these, 55 passed in writing, 52 in reading, 50 in arithmetic.

This was disappointing enough, but when the Diocesan Religious Inspector suggested in his report "More scripture might be learned by heart", the affronted Master wrote in his log : "Considering the children had 'got up' the Catechism, 6 Hymns, the Canticles, 20 Texts, and six Parables, I don't know how much the Revd. Inspector really does require".

These and a host of other extracts indicate the constant struggle to make education an essential part of a child's life a century ago. One can share the Master's relief at the end of a trying week when he wrote : "Coughing of children so distracting, I am glad it is Friday".

But there was compensation at the end of the year. After hearing from the Inspector that "In future the Master's salary as Church Organist should not be included in the accounts submitted to their Lordships", he received his share of the Government Grant with gratitude, and his wife and he "were presented with a silver cruet and an egg stand, subscribed for by scholars, parents and friends".

That indeed was some consolation for his efforts, and buoyed him up for the New Year . . .

Three Royalist Rectors
(PUBLISHED SEPTEMBER 1962)

KING CHARLES I presented the living of Fersfield to the Rev. Arthur Womack in 1642, just as the rift between King and Parliament had reached an acute stage. In spite of his manifest Royalist inclinations, he contrived to hold the living through the Cromwellian period—though always under the watchful eye of his influential neighbour, Sir John Holland, of Quidenham, a staunch supporter of Cromwell

This is rather remarkable, for there is evidence in the Diss Petty Constable's book that Womack committed (at least twice) one of the offences for which many Royalist Rectors were dispossessed of their livings—for alleged "tipling and alehouse-haunting".

On January 25th, 1649, the constable noted, "Tepling · at Turnars between 8 an 9 at night Parson Womacke, Henry ffoulser, John Peedock, Gorg. Cresp, som other". They were not, like some others, "veri fre in words"—but in Puritan eyes the fact of "tipling" was enough to warrant summary removal.

Because of his jovial personality and popularity Womack survived, aided by his friendship with Thomas Sheriffe, a local magistrate who had been commissioned under Charles I and continued to hold office under the "anti-royalists".

Womack's warden, John Piddock (the Peedock of the Constable's book) removed the King's Arms from the church before the Rebels broke in "to deface the pew-ends, reave the brasses, smash the windows and pull down the Altar rails.', but, with the Rector and Robert Howckin, he was eventually brought before Thomas Sheriffe on the "information" of Henry Clark, of Diss, and George Francis and Robert Skurle, of Fersfield.

They were charged with harbouring malignants (Royalists) in their houses, endeavouring to provide a "Horse and Man" for the King, at their own cost—but, above all, for drinking a "Health unto His Majesty" and "praying God to confound his foes".

Sheriffe committed them to Ipswich Gaol, where they continued for some time. Meanwhile he engaged in the "un-magisterial" practice of informing them by private letters of all that was intended against them, and suggesting they should produce certificates of good behaviour from prominent townsmen of Diss and Fersfield to help in their release.

They did this and as a result the three were liberated—all surviving to witness the Restoration of Charles II in 1660 ; and Womack to enjoy his living until 1685. (When the informers were individually examined by Thomas Sheriffe they confessed their story was a "malicious" one, from which they hoped to gain "some advantage)".

Nearby, at Dickleburgh, events had taken a very different turn. Christopher Barnard, Rector since 1622, was also a staunch Royalist but a man of impeccable character, to whom strife and political conflict were an abomination. When, in 1643 he had to choose between King and Parliament, he maintained his support for the King by refusing "to preserve the Reformed Religion" or to embrace the "Solemn League and Covenent", as prescribed by the Long Parliament.

In the eyes of the Parliamentary Party he was now a marked man, though in fact he had committed none of the offences—ecclesiastical, moral or political—for which 80 others of Norfolk's 500 clergy were dispossessed of their livings.

He suffered for the "unpardonable sin of loyalty"—with this consequence. Late one April evening in 1643 a Troop of Rebel Horse descended on the Rectory at Dickleburgh, "with pistols cocked and swords drawn", brutally dragged the Rector from his family circle, abused him with scoffs and jeers, showing no reverence for his calling, plundered his house of plate and linen, and made off along the turnpike across the moor, intending to plant him in Norwich gaol.

But Barnard and his family were deeply loved by his parishioners, who felt that to be deprived of him at such a time was the worst fate that could befall the parish, and an attempt to rescue him was quickly planned.

Events moved with amazing rapidity. Three parties were organised—one to pursue the plunderers along the turnpike—one to travel via Gunn's Bridge, Moor Road, and Sheckford Lane to reach the turnpike through Ram Lane in Tivetshall—the third, to skirt the moor on the eastern side, cross Semer Green, and reach the turnpike by Semer Lane.

All went well—near the "Ram" the raiders found themselves harassed from behind, and ahead, ambushed by the outflanking parties. A violent hand-to-hand scuffle ensued in the failing light—the Rector was rescued, and the disorganized and battered troopers escaped northwards.

Barnard was, however, officially dispossessed of his "cure" but, with his wife and ten children, remained in his Rectory, subsisting on the "fifth" of the value of the living granted by Act of Parliament to "sequestred clergy".

He spent 19 years in this state of enforced poverty but survived through the goodwill and generosity of his parishioners. His duties were entrusted to Elias Crabtree, a Puritan minister who lived with "Thomas Buxton, his beloved frined."

Barnard lived at peace with all but was of "firm perswasion of H.M.'s Restauration". He was restored to his living amid great rejoicings on September 22nd, 1662 at the same time as his son Edward became Rector of Diss, on the ejection of Richard Moore.

Richard Anguish, Rector of Starston, was also a Royalist and, like Barnard, was "dispossessed". But was not the same peace-loving, saintly man, "so much recommended to his parishioners by his excellent life and doctrine". Rather, Anguish was for those times a too-outspoken Royalist who taunted the Parliamentarians (in E. Anglia they formed the great majority of all sections of society) by preaching obedience to H.M., and disobedience to Parliament.

He denounced the payment of Parliamentary dues as a "sin"; he introduced "innovations" contrary to the dictates of the Reformed Religion ; he preached but once a day, maintaining that "He that preacheth twice, prateth once"; he condemned the removal of monuments from churches as "damnable sin";—his violent outbursts bringing him into conflict with the County Committee surveying the activities of the Clergy.

Ten witnesses spoke against him—his living was sequestrated —his private estate sold, and he was forced to live on the "fifth portion" granted by Parliament. He too was re-instated with the Restoration of Charles II, recovered his estate—then petitioned to settle in Montserrat, West Indies, where he died in 1668.

The Eye Anti-Felon Society
(PUBLISHED JUNE 1963)

IN reply to a Parliamentary Question on May 23rd, the Home Secretary stated that 62 persons were convicted of larceny of horses, cattle and sheep in 1961, that many cases went undetected, and that in the Dales and parts of Leicestershire the situation was rather out of hand.

Serious as this was in 1961, and a sorry reflection on our society, the problem was much more acute in the 18th and early 19th Centuries, when dire poverty drove many to steal, in desperation.

Widespread enclosure had deprived many a countryman of his "common rights" and curtailed his chances of eking out a precarious living. Rural poverty increased, and, as a noted historian on the 18th century has written—"Hungry men will snare and poach". In lean years despair among the poor became unendurable, resulting in widespread food riots, burning, looting and mob violence.

As a direct result of such tendencies to law-breaking, "Associations for prosecuting felons" became a feature of East Anglian life in the 18th and early 19th centuries. No regular police force existed then. The unpaid Parish Constables, often serving their year's duty very reluctantly, with much expenditure of time, and only a meagre allowance for expenses, failed lamentably to arrest the tide of crime, or to bring offenders to book.

Though savage sentences were passed on those who were caught, they failed to deter others spurred on to theft by dire need. The penalty for stealing a horse was public execution—for stealing a spade, a public whipping—for buying or receiving stolen yarn, transportation for 14 years. These were actual local examples of 18th century sentences, yet the wave of crime continued.

"Associations" sprang up in every 'Hundred'—in almost every Market Town, and even in individual villages. Thus "Guiltcross and Depwade" combined to form an Association—Diss had its own (1776)—so did Harleston, Bressingham and Roydon.

A late comer into this field was the Eye Association whose

first meeting was held at the "White Lion" on July 10th, 1810. Through the kindness of Mr. John Gaze I have been able to consult the records of this Assn. from its inception. Attended by over 50 persons from 16 parishes around Eye, the meeting approved the formation of "An Association for prosecuting offenders found guilty of Horse-Stealing, Burglary, or other Felony or Misdemeanours, committed against the property of any subscriber thereto".

A comprehensive list of 13 Articles of Government was adopted —covering election of officers, subscription, method of raising funds, times and frequency of routine meetings, calling special meetings to enlist the Association's help against offenders, forfeits for non-attendance, eligibility for membership, etc. But a long 14th article was added, detailing rewards offered to "Informers" who might help in bringing offenders to justice.

Here are some—"on the conviction of a Housebreaker, the reward for information to be 5£—of a person stealing a horse, mare, gelding, or any person receiving the same knowing it to be stolen, reward 10£—of a person stealing any cow, sheep, hog or cattle of any description, reward 5£—of every highwayman, murderer, or footpad, reward 5£—of a person stealing turnips, beans, pease, carrotts or other vegetables, fruit or wood, or damaging any hedge or other fence, or trespassing, or stealing any gate, plow or other Irons, or committing any other depredation or theft whatsoever, reward 10s." More reward clauses were added later as occasion arose.

Within two months the Association was asked for assistance when the barn of a subscriber was "robbed of 2 coombs of red wheat, the sacks containing it, and a waggon rope almost new". The Association printed and distributed notices of the offence, and offered a reward for information leading to conviction.

Crime followed crime. In December 1810 "a fowl house was robbed of 6 young Turkeys", in November 1811 "a chestnut mare was stolen"—the year following "a fowlhouse was robbed of 6 geese". (The Occold Constable received 25s. for carrying the offender to gaol in this case). In spite of the Association's activities, the period 1816-1820 inclusive saw a great upsurge in offences, some 24 cases being dealt with. They included—"Leg of an in-calf Heifer in the Barnyard, broken"—"yard robbed of a quantity of firewood"—"number of Pales and Rails pulled down, stolen and carried away from fence in Back Lane (Eye)"—"Two pigs killed and taken away from bullockyard at Abbey Farm, entrails left in yard"—"Hoggett sheep killed, stolen, and carried away from Brome Park, head skin and entrails left in adjoining hedge-ditch (N.B. remarkably well flayed and supposed to be done by a butcher)"—"barn broke open at Thrandeston"—"House burglariously broken open, piece of yellow stripe duffel Carpet stolen thereout"—"setting fire to bean stacks"—etc., etc.

1820 was followed for some years by decreased activity, though the Association was called upon to deal with sudden but short waves of offences in 1825 and 1838. In spite of their efforts and their "rewards" many offences remained unsolved, while only a few of the actual convictions were noted in the records.

Such entries as—"Reward 5s. for a letter from an Informer" —search warrant for loss of hog, 7s."—"Mr. G's servant, 5£ reward"—"S—— & L—— given 5£ for their exertion in discovering several persons guilty of sheep stealing"—"men watching for F—— £4—16—0 ; beer for them 17s " 2d " — "Expences sending men in search of horses £9—6—6"—"Reward for apprehending 2£—shed considerable light on methods adopted, and some successes achieved.

No expense was spared in pressing home a prosecution. In 1819 six men were apprehended for breaking open a barn several times, and "feloniously stealing divers quantities of wheat therefrom". Rewards paid amounted to £7, and prosecution expenses at Ipswich and Bury were £156 2s. 5d.

Two cases stand out prominently—one in 1818 when the Assn. pressed for Transportation of a persistent offender Thomas K——, but with what success is not stated. The other was in 1833 when William J—— "set on fire and burnt down a barn with several head of livestock therein". He was found guilty and the record states "he suffered death".

The Assn's. history presents a distressing picture of East Anglia in the early 19th century before the institution of a regular Police Force. In 1840, shortly after H—— had been convicted of "stealing a gig apron", and John B—— had been apprehended for "pickpocketing at Eye Races", the East Suffolk Rural Police Force came into being. The continual presence and vigilance of a full time force reduced the Assn's. activities. From 1840-1910 it took action in only 10 cases—of a somewhat minor character. It offered rewards for information in cases of "stealing beans"—"lost ducks"—"Game Trespass"—"Keeping dog without licence"—"laying poison to danger of dogs, birds, etc.". In fact though it remained in being with a membership averaging about 30—it became just a "Dining Club"—holding an annual dinner at "The Lion", and electing new members to maintain strength.

Nine new members joined on May 14th, 1914—the very last occasion the Association met. That evening they decided to hold all future annual dinners "before Lent"—but the Association has never met since. Many well known figures were among those who dined in 1913 and 1914—Dr. Edgar Barnes, Harold Warnes, Dr. Henry Barnes, C. A. West, Frank and Clement Gaze, H. M. Spiers, A. H. Jeffery, F. W. Hammond, F. W. Gill, Walter Betts, C. P. Hunt, A. C. Clarke and C. E. Rash. The last three are alive today, so though no meeting has been held since 1914, the Society is still in being, having never disbanded.

It would be interesting to keep it in being—but purely as an historical link with the England of George III.

Witnesses were paid 17s. 2d. for beer
(PUBLISHED NOVEMBER 1962)

WHEN the Eye Assoication for prosecuting felons held its annual meeting in May, 1914, elected five new members then dined sumptuously at the White Lion there was no hint of disbanding after its hundred years of history.

In fact, it was decided that in future the annual dinner should be held "before Lent." For some reason, the Association's activities were never resumed after peace in 1918, probably because its original functions had long since been carried out by the police.

The Association was one of a number of similar bodies existing in the 18th and 19th centuries. Its inaugural meeting took place on June 2nd, 1810, at the White Lion, Eye, where every subsequent business or social gathering was held. It was an age when poaching, petty-pilfering, arson and general lawlessness were rife. The original notice on behalf of the conveners, circulated by Thomas Wayth, of Eye, began, "Whereas from the frequent robberies committed within the town and neighbourhood, it is found expedient that an Association should be formed for prosecuting offenders who shall be found guilty of horse-stealing, burglary, etc." . . . then went on to invite "such gentlemen, clergy, farmers and others residing in Eye (and 15 named parishes within a radius of about four miles) as are desirous of becoming members thereof to pay 10s. each into the hands of the treasurer."

The next meeting was on July 10th, 1810—attended by 48 subscribers, including the Marquis of Cornwallis, It adopted a series of 13 articles of association and added a 14th of several clauses enumerating the rewards to be given to "informers" who helped in bringing offenders to book.

Thus—"for every housebreaker (if the offence be deemed a burglary), the sum of £5"; or "for every person stealing any horse mare or gelding, or receiving the same knowing it to be stolen, the sum of £10"—"for every highwayman, murderer or footpad, the sum of £5"—"for every person stealing turnips, beans, pease, carrotts or other vegetables, fruit, wood, etc., 10s."

Quarterly meetings were held at Eye on the Tuesdays preceding each Quarter Session at Ipswich—members not attending paying a forfeit. "Special meetings" could be called at any time by a subscriber seeking the benefit of the Association, when "a majority of not less than five subscribers who could conveniently attend" could take decisive action over publicity or prosecution.

In September, 1810, the first "special" was called by Samuel Gowing, "whose barn was robbed in the night of two coombs of red wheat, and a waggon rope almost new was carried out of the stackyard." The meeting agreed to print and circulate reward notices in the Association parishes, and to prosecute the offender if discovered.

The detailed records of the Association, I was able to see by courtesy of Mr. John Gaze, whose father, now deceased, was elected a member in 1902, and to whom the books were passed. Between 1810 and 1840, 47 special meetings were convened, and 24 of these were from 1816-1820, when the Association's services were in almost continuous demand to "prosecute" for a variety of offences. Among them were "fowl house broke open and robbed of six young turkeys"—"chestnut cart mare colt stolen from farmyard"—"leg of a with-calf heifer in the Barnyard, broke"—"yard robbed of a quantity of firewood"—"number of boards, poles, rails pulled down, stolen, and carried away from a fence"—"two pigs killed and taken away from farmyard at the Abbey farm—entrails left in yard"—"hoggett sheep taken, killed, stolen and carried away out of Brome Park, the head, skin and entrails left in hedge-ditch adjoining"—"quantity of oats mixed with carraway seed stolen from stable corn binn"—"windmill broke open and stone weight of wheat and sack marked 'John Cooke' stolen thereout."

In 1818 the Association endeavoured, by appeal at Sessions, to procure the "transportation or further imprisonment" of one persistently troublesome character—though the result is not recorded. They failed (1830) in a prosecution for firing a barn, but in 1833 the same offender, apprehended "for setting fire to the barn of Mr. Wayman, which was burnt down with loss of several head of livestock" was "found guilty and suffered death." This was the only case of capital punishment noted.

Other activities initiated by the Association are revealed in the accounts—"paid Bullock and Marsh for men-watching, £5 2s.; and for beer for the men, 17s. 2d."—"Expenses sending men in search of horses, £9 6s. 6d."—"allowed Mrs. Marsh's servant for discovering a person robbing the wood yard, 5s."

With the founding of the "Rural Police Force" in East Suffolk in 1840, much of the purpose for which the Association had been founded disappeared—prosecutions being undertaken by the police.

Between 1840-1914 only ten cases were followed up—for petty theft, corn stealing, keeping a dog without licence, etc. Its final offensive action was in 1899 when bills were posted offering a reward to any person "who shall discover the offender laying poison to the danger of dogs, birds and other animals."

From 1840 the annual meetings and dinner became a local "institution." Membership remained at about 30 throughout and never less than 20 supported the dinner. It was now really a "dining club." Nine new members were elected in 1913 when 24 dined, and of those who dined on May 14th, 1914, three survive—Mr. Alfred Clarke, of Mellis, Mr. Charles E. Rash, of Felmingham Hall, and Mr. C. Page Hunt, of Southwold.

Records rescued from the fire at Scole church

(PUBLISHED FEBRUARY 1963)

BY a great stroke of fortune all the Parish Registers were recovered after the fire which so tragically ruined Scole Church on January 7th. Sodden and charred, they were among the pile of books or in the iron safe which had been carried to safety in the vestry at the base of the tower.

The earliest register, dated 1561, had quite obviously been on fire, but the flames were extinguished at the critical moment. The 33 parchment leaves and limp skin cover were retrieved like a soaked mass of chamois leather. But they have dried out perfectly.

So good was the 16th and 17th century ink that almost every word remains legible.

The parish Registers are of course an invaluable source of many interesting details in the history of Scole. The earliest volume opens in this way :

"Osmondston als Skole Norff. This Booke or Register conteyneth all the names of such persons as wee baptized maried or buried in this parish of Osmondston als Skole in Norff. from the yeere of our Lord 1561 being the fourth yeere of the raigne of our most gracious Ladie Queene Elizabeth that now is. And so to proceed."

Family tragedy and a high infant mortality rate seem to stand out in the early books, from 1561. The following extracts, taken at random, illustrate these points.

    1564 : "John the sonne of Henry Chilver baptized the 17 day of April. The same John was buried the day following."

    1571 : "Anne and Cicely the twinlie Daughters of James and Cicely Johnson, baptized 6 of January which both were buried the 9 of January."

    1614 : "Willm the sonne, and Katherin the daughter of Robt. Blake, were bapt. the fourth daie of September.

Willm was buried the 5 daie of Sept. and Katherin was buried the 10 of Sept."

... Here is a real family tragedy, involving the death of a young mother and one of her twins : "Mathuselah Kemp, sonn of John Kemp and Eve his wife, was buried in the churchyard in Scole the 26 of Aug. 1620.

Eve Kemp was buried the 26 of August 1620.

Margaret Kemp, daughter of John and Eve, was privately bapt. in the house of John Kemp, situate in Scole."

Vagrants are frequently mentioned. They were, of course, all too numerous in the late 16th, 17th and into the 18th centuries. Their pitiful plight is reflected in those records. Many, in their wanderings, appear to have succumbed to hunger and privation, and to have died nameless.

1565 : "Ric. Saunders a poore vagrant buried the 20 of Januarie."

1574 : "Wllm the sonne of Gilbert Whitman and Anne his wife, a poore stranger, walking, was bapt. the 29 day of Jan. and buried the 30 day of same month."

1678 : "A travelin womman buried Aug. 14."

1681 : "Joseph and Mary, born of a stranger yt was brought to this town by a Passe and delivered as soon as she came hither, both bapt. Jan. 22."

1759 : "Nov. 3 a stranger woman was buried."

1760 : "Elizabeth, daughter of Eliz. Leney, born of a stranger at the sine of the Buck at Broom about the 18 of Januarie and was bapt. at Scole ye 15 of feburey following."

Some Parish Registers contain interesting additional details about the persons whose names appear in the list of births, marriages and burials. Those of Scole are certainly not deficient in this respect :

1602 : "Nicholas the base sonne of Wllm. Phillips and Triphena Ebitts his harlot, was baptized the 3 day of December."

1606 : "Roger Pyke servant of Mr. Hunnigs of Eye in Suff. being slaine in fyht the 5 of August was buried the 7 day of the same moneth."

1691 : "Joseph base child of ffrances Preston and as she saith of Joseph Benns, was bapt. July 15, aged then about 9 months."

1782 : "Aug. 21. George Norman was buried. He was killed on Diss Common by Mr. Simpsons broad wheel'd waggon on the 19 Instant."

1783 : "Buried Dec. 23 Wm Keely of Gislingham—a pauper—he died suddenly at the Grayhound."

1784 : "March 1st Benjemin Leftly buried. He hung himself at Frenze Parsonage."

The mention of "paupers" reminds me that the word "pauper" appears in the register no less than 77 times between 1783 and 1795. Thus "Ap. 5. 1785. Eliabeth Herrex, pauper, buried, aged 83 years." This might suggest that Scole was a village of paupers, but such was not the case—though there was great distress and poverty at this period.

In 1783, an Act of Parliament imposed a tax of 3d. on every entry of a christening, marriage or burial recorded in the register—except on those of "some poor persons, particularly circumstanced".

The tax was unpopular and "vexatious to people and Clergy alike". It was unproductive too, because many christenings were avoided altogether, and numbers of people were married or buried as "paupers", to avoid payment of tax.

The Scole book records : "Recd. the duty on five Burials 1s. 3d." and among other pauper entries is "1792 July 30. Buried Thomas Barker, Pauper, aged 24 years. He was killed in Mr. Mines Marl pit."

That Act was repealed in 1794.

We can imagine the whole village in mourning for "A boy called Stits, slaine with a cart" when he was buried in 1574, and also for "Mary Irelande a little girle or damsell buried 16 of Sept."

Then there were the dear old people who died in 1600—"Joane Deale, widow of great yeeres, and John Biggs widower of great age", and "Richard Biles, an ould Sexton, buried Aprill 14. 1678"—after years of faithful service.

When the Rector died in 1751, the devoted old Clerk entered this in the register—"Died the Revd. Abraham Cowper, Minister of the parish 56 years, buried 12 July in ye 81 year of his age. This memmoramdom by John Steward, Parish Clark to him from the year 1711 to the day of his death. Mementi Mory."

John lived for another 11 years; then, on August 18, 1762, died John Steward, "Clark of this parish 51 years, buried the 20 Instant in the 78 year of his age".

Judging from the marriages recorded, Scole was an East Anglian "Gretna Green". Marriage after marriage was between persons, neither of whom was resident in the parish. In 1605 "Owin Candler of St. Mary Tower parish in ypswich and Anne Penning of Eye were maried 28 of May". In 1610 "Wm. Borflit of Harwich and Eliz. Wile of Hoxen were maried in this Church ye 29 of May". In 1720 one couple were "John Butler of Stoke Ferry by Lynne and Alice Slapp of Rickinggale" and in 1741 "John Clark of Ipswich and Bridget Philips of Bungay".

The last of these irregular marriages, for such they were since neither party lived in the parish—was in 1743. The Hardwicke Marriage Act of 1755 required records of banns and marriage henceforth to be kept in "proper books of vellum, or good and durable paper". Clandestine marriages like those quoted, were stopped, and "Hardwicke Registers" came into general use.

In the early Scole registers the Christian names John, James, Thomas and William were the most common for boys, but Biblical names were very popular—Eleazor, Ezekiel, Jonathan, Nathaniel, Abraham, Samuel, Benjamin, Joseph, Isaac, Jeremiah and Zachoriah. So too was Methuselah (in a variety of spellings)—for the eldest son of each generation of the Kemp family bore the name "Mathuselah" for over 200 years, and many other families used the name too.

For girls—Mary, Elizabeth, and Anne, appear to have been most popular. These too, were frequently used—Merible, Prudence, Letitia, Appia, Theopila, Constant, Tryphena and Climenia. An interesting combination occurred in 1788—the Baptism of "Abraham the son of Isaac Barthorpp and Sarah his wife."

In 1643, during the conflict between King Charles and Parliament, Ministers of Religion were required by Parliament to adopt the practices of the "Reformed Church," as laid down in the "Solemn League and Covenant." Christopher Barnard, Rector of Dickleburgh, "generously refused to accept the implications of the Covenant" and was deprived of his living. But John Welles, Rector of Scole, accepted, and retained his office through the Commonwealth period.

Later, however, another Act (1653) deprived him of the right to solemnize marriages and of the care of the registers. An official known as the Register was appointed to keep the records and to be present at all marriages, which became civil ceremonies before a Justice of the Peace.

The Scole records include this : "We the inhabitants of Osmondstone, otherwise Scoale, whose names are hereunder written, doe make choice of Henry Theobald for our Register".

Those who testified were John Read, Thomas Jarman, William Brient, Thomas Sporle, Mathusala Kempe, Thomas Read, and on May 30, 1654, Henry Theobald was sworn "Parish Register", according to the Act, before John ffrere (a Justice).

The following March 26, a marriage took place and was entered thus : "Mathusala Kempe, of Skole, widower, and Ellen Sherwood, widow, weer joyned together in marriag by Thomas Sherif, of Dis, Esquier, their concent of marriag being published in the Parish Church of Skole three severall Lords Days before".

Henry Theobald made his last entry in 1659.

At the Restoration of Charles II in 1660, John Welles, the Rector, resumed charge of the registers, and was given the right to solemnize marriages.

In the year 1671 the register carries an item of unusual interest —mentioned also in Miss Mallows's *History of Scole:* "King Charles the Second passed through Scoale in his progress to Yarmouth and brake his fast at the 'White Hart' at the charge of the right honourable Lord Cornwallis upon the 27 of September in the 23 yeare of His reigne A.D. 1671".

A John Cornwallis was knighted by Henry VIII for bravery in Brittany and later he became Steward to Prince Edward's household.

His grandson supported Charles I against Parliament and accompanied the King's family into exile. At the Restoration he became Treasurer of King Charles II's household, and a peer of the realm in 1661. It was his privilege to entertain the King when he brake his fast at the 'White Hart'—no mean item considering the King was accompanied by the Dukes of York, Monmouth, and Buckingham, many other nobles and their numerous retinues.

Yarmouth—for which Charles II was bound—had proclaimed for Parliament against Charles I during the Civil War, and the corporation is said to have regarded the Royalists as "Sons of Belial" and "Children of Darkness". Those sentiments were now rescinded, and when Charles II entered Yarmouth at 5 p.m. on September 28, 1671, he was presented with "four golden herrings and a chain valued at £250".

In 1675 the Scole register records : "Scoale Bridge was fram'd by Samuel ffairchild, of Scoale, in the yeare of our Lord

1675, and finished 22 of Octob. In the same yeare the Towne of Scoale made a rate of fforty powndes for it. John Welles was minister ther then."

This would be a wooden bridge over the Waveney, superseded by the humped-back bridge of 1838, which in turn has been superseded by the modern structure of 1957 (Just as Denmark Bridge (1833) and the "Great Bridge" of Dickleburgh (1804) replaced former wooden bridges).

In 1694 mention is made of an Act "for granting His Matie certain Rates and Duties upon Marriages, Births and Burials and upon Batchelors and Widowers for the Term of five years for carrying on the Warr against France with vigour".

A minimum duty of 2s. per birth, 2s. 6d. per marriage, and 4s. per burial for all non-paupers was levied—with a sliding scale rising to £30 for the baptism of the eldest son of a duke, and £50 for a duke's marriage or burial.

The parson was to receive a fee of 6d. for each entry in the register.

Though 14 marriages, 23 burials and 27 baptisms took place in the five years, no record of any fees is given. Perhaps Scole was a law unto itself—certainly King William III reaped little from Scole in the vigorous prosecution of the war.

The 1561-1693 register carries on its back pages a detailed "Terrier of the Rectorie Dignitie or Parsonage of Osmondestone als Scole in 1634".

It refers to "sixe acres of lande abutting in part upon the Common pasture of Scole towards the South and upon the Perambulant waye towards the North". This would be the Old Rectory "with barne stalle and other houses of office as allso the Orchyard and Garden". (The present Rectory dates from 1863).

The last paragraph of the Terrier mentions the "Hempsacks" —glebe lands of 2½ acres on which hemp was then grown for making into coarse hempen cloth for smocks, sheets and bolsters; and even into fine linen, from the fibres.

The faithful old Clerk, John Steward, made a summary of Marriages, Baptisms and Burials from 1711 until he died in 1762, when another person continued it until 1804, when the second register closed. In the 92 years there were 341 marriages, 821 baptisms and 692 burials—yearly averages of about four, nine and eight respectively. In the last 23 of those years only 49 marriages occurred.

The 19th and 20th century registers are of a standard or regulation pattern and of particular interest because they record occupations of the fathers of children baptized (from 1813) and of brides, bridegrooms and their parents in the Marriage Registers (from 1837).

In the Scole Registers there is overwhelming evidence of the importance of the "town" as a coaching centre (in pre railway days) as a postal centre, for brickmaking, and for the flax factory at Waterloo.

Entries refer, of course, only to those baptized or married at Scole Church.

I counted no less than 22 different names of persons who were hostlers, post-lads, postillions, coachmen or horsekeepers—emphasising Scole's function as a crossways of north-south and east-west routes. There were, too, many wheelwrights, farriers, blacksmiths, harness-makers, and even a gig-maker and a coach-maker plying ancillary trades.

Postal officials—postmaster, postmen, mail-coachmen and mailcart drivers are numerous, too—and three generations of "Gipsons" appear after 1830 as brickmakers—this craft follows through till William Betts's sale in 1887.

But it is the flax-factory that seems to stand out so clearly, beginning with Andrew Wilson (flax-sorter) and James Corr (flax-dresser) in 1859. Twenty-six others connected with the factory are named, from C. F. Costerton (proprietor), David Boyd (manager) and William Murray (flax-sorter, 1861, and later overseer of spinners, spinning master, and foreman of works) to others described as scutchers or weavers.

Miss Mallows referred in her history to village fights in which Irish workers were involved—men from Ulster experienced in flax-growing and in processing it for spinning and weaving. Such names as William Murray, Hugh Mahaphy, Patric Corr, James Doran, George Mackinley, James Donley and William Crossin have an unmistakable Irish ring.

William Murray, I know, came from Belfast. Five of his children were baptized at Scole. A grand-son, Jim Murray, lives in Diss, and many of the Nunns and Kitchens are his descendants, to the fourth and fifth generations.

Other rural occupations, typical of the 19th century particularly, were those of thatcher, rat catcher, mole catcher, the osier merchant, the basket maker, and the drover.

Fred Thrower, of Mission Road, Diss, remembers his father driving cattle from Warren Hills to Norwich, leaving early on Friday morning, resting in Trowse Meadows for the night, before moving to the market on Saturday. The return journey with "stores" from Norwich began Saturday—the night again spent at Trowse—arriving at Warren Hills Sunday afternoon.

How fortunate that these registers, with their four centuries of Scole history, survived that tragic conflagration!

Dickleburgh's 18th century friendly society

(PUBLISHED JULY, 1963)

SUNDAY'S annual district parade and church service of the Manchester Unity of Oddfellows at St. Mary's, Diss, will mark the Order's 133rd anniversary, though it was stated in the souvenir brochure of 1960 that 1810 is regarded as the year in which the Order was established.

It had grown out of the Union Order, which resulted from the amalgamation of two earlier Orders, the "Ancient" and the "Patriotic". Both had been engaged in political, convivial and benevolent activities, but after the "merger", political affiliations disappeared and benevolence became the principal aim.

In medieval times the Guilds had performed the functions later assumed by friendly societies. The Guilds of St. Nicholas and of Corpus Christi in Diss, were founded to protect the interests of their members in many ways—to relieve them in sickness, in distress or when out of work, or too old to undertake it.

With the supression of Guilds and the confiscation of their funds and property during the upheavals of the 16th century, the sick, aged and infirm were left to the mercy of the Parish Overseers, who dispensed poor relief on a niggardly scale or offered a place in the poor-house with a pauper's burial at the end. Surviving Overseers' books paint a sorry picture of the poverty endured by many.

Against this distressing background, friendly societies began to arise in the 17th century. The earliest, in 1643, was known as the "General Sea Box", followed by "The Landman's Box" (1659) —the word "box" indicating the custom of keeping funds in large chests. Daniel Defoe (1660-1731) acclaimed the value of such societies and pleaded for their extension, but another century was to pass before friendly societies became a general feature of British social life.

Among the earliest locally was the "King's Head" club of

Dickleburgh, founded under an Act of 1793, the first general Act relating to friendly societies. Like its counterparts, it was a purely local club, but out of it grew the "Dickleburgh Union Society", from which in due course came the Dickleburgh Lodge of the Manchester Unity of Oddfellows.

Through the kindness of the Rector and wardens, I was able to examine the contents of the Dickleburgh Parish Chest recently, and there found a certificate dated April 23, 1795, admitting Matthew Dunn as a member of the "King's Head" club. It was signed and sealed by Joseph Buck and William Barker (Stewards, their "marks"—neither could write) in the presence of William Cattermole, Thomas Clarke, William Goff, James King, and John Reeve, all of whom signed.

To legalise the enrolment of Dunn, William Cattermole made oath before Thomas Maynard, Justice, of Hoxne, that "he did see the above-named Stewards make their marks".

So by April, 1795, Dickleburgh, to its great credit, already possessed a "club" with full range of officers. The certificate is, alas, the only evidence of that club. Its rules, aims and financial records have not survived.

However, Mr. Reg Woods kindly allowed me to inspect the various documents preserved by Messrs. William Smith & Sons and covering almost two centuries. In a vellum-bound book, I discovered the accounts of the "Dickleburgh Union Society" from their first meeting on April 19, 1804, until they ended abruptly in 1823.

The secretary of this society was the same William Cattermole who had "made oath" before Justice Maynard in 1795. The "King's Head" club had become the Union Society.

No rules or "articles" have survived, though the cost of printing them appears in the accounts, which alone remain to tell the story of this Union Society. It held regular monthly meetings. Each member contributed 1s. per meeting and was fined 6d. for non-attendance.

The first entry, for April 19, 1804, is : "Received into the Box at the first meeting, 18s." Four items on the debit side provide pointers to method of administration : "For 2 account books, 7s. 8d.; For making the Box, 16s.; For printing the Articles, £1 3s.; For a purse, 1s."

No calls for "benefit" were made in 1804. The first annual

feast, on January 12, 1805, paid for itself—so the second year began with : "Ballance in the Box, £5 18s. 4½d."

The feast however, was interesting. Members contributed £4 7s. towards it ; "the Brewers" gave 15s.; expenses were £4 3s. 5½d. (including meat £1 16s.; bread 7s. 4d.; 2 lb. raisons, 1s. 4d.; cheese butter, sauce, etc., 2s. 11d., old beer and porter, £1 13s. 4½d.; and "given to the maid", 2s. 6d.).

In 1805 there were again no calls for benefit—the Box now contained £15 19s. 8½d. For the annual feast on January 4, 1806, "4st. 5lbs. of Beef at 8s. 9d. per stone, 1st. 13½lbs. of mutton at 8s. 9d. per stone were provided, while beer, porter, etc., cost £2 7s. 6d. out of a total of £5 14s. 4d. This time the maid received 1s.

The first benefit was dispensed in 1806—"Wm. Harvey for one week in time of sickness, 7s. 6d." (a rate not much less than the agricultural wage of the time, 10s. per week). Jonathan Wood received six weeks' benefit, too—and a steward received a travelling allowance of 3d. per mile when visiting the sick.

In 1807 "William Cattermole, Clerk to the Society" received the first funeral benefit of £3 "in consequence of the death of his wife," but with no further calls the "Balance in the Box" rose to £30 16s. 11d.

But in 1808 there was a contretemps. At the meeting on July 2 Christopher Wingfield was called on to pay "2 weeks backmoney". He must have protested violently and abusively—for he was fined 3s. for swearing, at 6d. each time". Wingfield had already received seven weeks' sick pay, and another 10s. "during confinement in Bury Gaol". He was probably not typical of the society's members.

In 1809 Zachary Dixon died—his widow received £3 funeral benefit and £5 widow's grant—and his funeral was something of an occasion, for the members turned out in their new "hatbands and ties" (purchased for £7 4s. 7d. and 4s. 3d. respectively). These are the only regalia mentioned in the records.

The members' sorrow at losing Zachary Dixon was, however, somewhat mitigated by an expenditure of "10s. for beer at the funeral".

The years passed, with regular meetings, benefits and, of course, the annual feast with its emphasis on meat and beer.

The 1811 account for the feast reads : "Butcher's Bill at the feast, £3 16s.; shop things, 10s.; bread, etc., 9s. 2d.; 1 stone flower,

4s. 8d.; for egges and saws, 1s. 3d.; for the sarvant, 2s. 6d.; for beer, £3."

But 1813 was disastrous, though the monthly contributions reached their peak of £16 10s. 8d., including fines and forfeits. Four members received relief "in time of sickness", but a tragedy occurred—let the accounts tell the tale : "Lost out of the Box, £2 7s.; spent when Wm. Baker was taken into custardy on spision, 14s. 2d.; Box mended, 1s. 6d. : Journey to Diss for the Steward, 1s. 6d.; Clarke's fees, 1s.; Paid for assistance, 2s."

The balance fell by £5, but in spite of grants "in time of leameness, in time of sickness, and to William Coal on the Deth of his wife" the funds gradually increased.

By 1922 the "Ballance in the Box" was £128 16s. 10½d.

At this time consternation was caused by the passing of another Act for regulating friendly societies. It was widely (but wrongly) interpreted as a threat to tax the reserve funds.

But the Dickleburgh Society forestalled the operation of the Act by a grand share-out, £99 13s. 4d. being distributed among 25 members according to length of membership. Even William Baker, who had been "taken into Custardy on Spision" in 1813, received his share—there was no victimisation.

The society continued under difficulties, for in June, 1822, Edward Francis went sick—and continued to draw his 7s. 6d. per week until September, 1823.

When William Crisp and Thomas Shibley had received their travelling allowance for 23 visits, and when James Gillman, Robert Clarke, Jno. Etheridge and Thomas Ruddock also "went sick", the society faced bankruptcy. With reserves depleted, outgoings greater than receipts, and overseers refusing "poor relief" to the society's members—in September, 1823, it ceased abruptly.

The accounts were never balanced for that year.

However, the experience gained in conducting a friendly society proved invaluable. Before many years had passed a Lodge of the Manchester Unity of Oddfellows was founded in Dickleburgh, later to amalgamate with the Diss Lodge, after a long period of flourishing independence.

A highlight in the history of Dickleburgh

(PUBLISHED JULY, 1963)

ONE hundred and fifty years ago the London coaches still lumbered through Dickleburgh, and baggage waggons rumbled along the turnpike carrying merchandise to Norwich, returning with coal. The main street near the church was tightly packed with tenements, which continued north at intervals to the Great Bridge—recently built of brick and iron to replace the wooden structure. Half-a-mile along the Rushall Road stood the isolated parsonage, then moated on three sides. Noah Thrower's mill alone stood between parsonage and main street, while William Smith's windmill rose from the fields due west of the church.

High Common, on the Langmere road, was still an open common of some 80 acres, fringed with scattered homesteads. Summer Green, too, was unenclosed, extending to about 19 acres near the Pulham boundary. The dreary waste of The Moor, skirted by the turnpike, with its scattered cottages, was a wild, untamed, trackless swamp of some 60 acres, as yet undrained.

The Parish Workhouse was still functioning and the "Towne" had recently expended a considerable sum to repair it. Ageing woolcombers, linen weavers and glovers still plied their declining trades, but the young were not being apprenticed to these dying crafts.

Corn was still threshed by flails, though the first "thrashing mashien" was about to appear in Dickleburgh to "knock-out" 35 coombs of corn a day.

Life was hard for the many, for the Napoleonic wars dragged on, and parish rates helped to support militiamen's families and even to pay for a substitute, George Francis, who served in place of Robert Youngs, of Alburgh.

But in April, 1814, hostilities had ceased when Napoleon fled to Elba. The restrictions and privations of war-time were eased, and when the Diss Festival of June 21st was such a resounding success, a chain of similar events was sparked off in neighbouring villages.

But few achieved the magnitude, or were marked by such spontaneity of joy as the festivities in Dickleburgh. No event in the long history of Dickleburgh had evoked such outbursts of enthusiasm since the Rector, Christopher Barnard, was carried away by a posse of Parliamentarian troops in 1643, then daringly rescued by the swiftly-moving parishioners who ambushed the troops near Tivetshall Ram.

Towards the end of June, 1814, it was determined by the inhabitants of Dickleburgh that, "in commemoration of the Glorious Peace recently concluded with France, a Dinner should be given to the Poor belonging to, and residing therein".

Tuesday, July 12th, was fixed upon for the purpose and a subscription list was opened. It was generously supported, as the amounts against the 53 names show—the sum of £78 19s. being subscribed, representing an equivalent of over £1,200 at 1963 values.

A strong committee was formed, with the Rector, the Rev. Thomas Gilbank, and Mr. George Lee (a magistrate living a short distance up the Rushall road, on the left side) to superintend the general arrangements. With willing helpers they made preparations to feed 600 of the poor—a remarkably high proportion of the total population, then well under 800. Here are their detailed orders :

"36 stone of Beef at 10s. 6d. per stone, to be boned and baked by Jas. Saunders, and brought on Table, Hot." "120 Plum Puddings, weight of each $4\frac{1}{2}$ lbs., each composed of $1\frac{1}{2}$ lbs., flour, 1 lb. Raisins, $\frac{1}{2}$ lb. suet, 1 pt. of milk, 2 eggs and $\frac{1}{2}$ oz. of salt." "370 penny loaves (flour at 2s. 10d. per stone)." "6 Barrels of Beer at £3 10s. each, and sufficiency of salt."

July 12th proved to be a fine day. All details were planned with meticulous care, and at 12 noon all the inhabitants, "except those who from age or infirmity could not walk, assembled in the churchyard, and were formed into 11 companies," ready to move in procession to Rushall Road, where, under the rows of trees opposite Mr. Lee's house, 11 tables were garnished for the feast, each to seat 50 persons, a president and vice-president.

A mounted standard-bearer, carrying an enormous Union Jack, led the procession through the main street, where the houses were gaily decorated with garlands. A "band of music"—engaged at an expense of £5—came next, followed by the Rector and Mr. Lee, riding side by side on prancing steeds ; and behind them, marching four abreast, were the 11 companies, each preceded by a standard-bearer, a table president and vice-president.

The whole parade made a valiant effort to keep in step with the martial music and even the Norwich coach was brought to a halt as the procession turned the corner into Rushall Road.

Each company reached "its allotted table without the least confusion or disorder".

Amid silence, the Rector pronounced Grace—and then the feast began in earnest with an onslaught on 4½ cwts. of beef and 5 cwts. of plum pudding.

Even those confined to their homes were not forgotten, each receiving a plentiful supply of provisions and beer. Yet, when all appetites were satisfied and thirsts quenched "with all the strong beer the Dickleburians could decently carry," a considerable quantity of provisions and a barrel-and-a-half of beer remained.

The provisions were dispensed to the poor "as equally as possible" when they again assembled in the churchyard the next day, and the beer was wisely kept for distribution the following Saturday.

But there was a further treat, for the final accounts showed an "over-plus" of £5 which was spent on beer at a later date.

The feast concluded ; thanks were given ; and the King's health was drunk with great gusto. Then followed toasts to "Wellington and his Heroes", to "Peace and all its Blessings", "Our Military and Naval Sons", "Content to the Farmers", "Gratitude to Our Tradesmen" and "Comfort to the Poor."

Pipes, tobacco and snuff were then distributed and, after an appropriate interval for digestion—during which the band played popular airs—the company moved to the sports arena nearby. There carts and waggons formed grandstands for viewing "the various sports that were exhibited".

These continued till dusk, amid great mirth, then the day's events terminated with hilarious scenes, as an effigy of "The Tyrant" was committed to the flames on a bonfire, the like of which had not been seen in Dickleburgh since the days of the Armada.

"*Examinations for Settlement*"

(PUBLISHED JULY, 1963)

"AT a Petty Sessions for the hireing and retaining of servants held at Diss about three weeks before Michaelmas, 1754, I lett myself to Mr. James Gilman, of Shelfanger, Farmer, for one whole year at the yearly wages of two pounds and ten shillings for such my year's service. I went and served my said master the whole year at Shelfanger aforesaid and received the whole of my wages to my satisfaction."

This statement was made to a Justice of the Peace on October 21st, 1756, by Elizabeth Woodcraft, then living in Winfarthing, during her "Examination for Settlement". She had fallen on bad times and had been forced to apply to the Winfarthing Overseer for relief. This overseer, knowing something of her past history and being anxious not to saddle Winfarthing rates to support her, brought her before J. Mallom, Justice, to be examinated or interrogated, that he might decide where she had "gained a settlement", which would entitle her to "Relief".

By her year's service in Shelfanger with Mr. Gilman, she had qualified there, and to that parish she was removed forthwith for the churchwardens and overseers there to arrange for her support.

This examination, and the mention of a petty sessions at Diss, is one of a large batch recently discovered at Shelfanger Church, where they have been locked away for well over 50 years. They remind us again that September was, in former times, the great month for "Hiring Fairs", "Petty Sessions for Hiring and Retaining Servants", or "Statutes" as they were called.

The 18th century Norfolk newspapers contained dozens of advertisements at this time of the year, such as this : "Sept. 10, 1763. A Petty Sessions for the Hundred of Depwade will be held at the usual place, Forncett St. Peter, on Thursday 15th of this inst. September for Hiring and Retaining of servants. (Signed) Edwd. Copping, John Cole, Chief Constables."

To Forncett on that particular day, shepherds, ploughmen, labourers in husbandry, and maidservants would flock—seeking employment for the next 12 months—from Michaelmas to Michaelmas, their engagements being registered by the Chief Constables' officials.

Why for 12 months ? Simply because, by fulfilling a year's service satisfactorily in a parish, a single person "gained a settlement" in that parish, and thereby the right to poor relief in case of illness, accident, or unemployment. This was the legal position after the great Settlement Act of 1662, and subsequent modifications in the years before 1700.

Previous to 1662 ordinary workers had found great difficulty in moving from one parish to another, unless able to buy property outright. Few could do this, and if a person wished to move to obtain work in another place, it was necessary to find a guarantor who would "sign a bond" to provide support in case of distress, thus relieving the parish of any burden.

Since Elizabethan times every parish had been legally obliged to levy a poor rate to support its own poor.

Here is the case of Martha Ayton, of New Buckenham, who, in 1637, went to reside with friends in Gissing. The Overseer of Gissing was soon inquiring who would support Martha if she became ill. He reported to the Overseer of New Buckenham that "the inhabitants of Gissing were unwilling shee shoold inhabit there least in future time she may becom chargeable to them".

The Parish Officers of New Buckenham then sent a letter "to certifye that if at any time hereafter Martha Ayton shall becom chargeable unto the parish of Gissing by sickness lameness or owld age, then the inhabitants of New Buckenham doe promise to receyve her at any time when shee shalbe sent unto them".

This letter was signed by the "High Baliff" and other parishioners of New Buckenham and placed in the Gissing chest, where it has remained for over 300 years. Martha was allowed to stay.

A few years later, Robert Anger wished to settle in Diss, in 1645. His guarantor was "William Alpe, of Luddam" (known to the Diss officials) who "bound and firmly obliged himself to Stephen Burrell and Richard Shuckforth, Churchwardens of Diss, in 20 pounds of good and lawful money, to save, defend, and keep harmlesse, all and every the Inhabitants of Disse, should Robt. Anger his wyfe and children, as well borne as to be borne, become chargeable to the sd. Town of Disse".

The wardens accepted the "bond" and allowed Anger to settle, locking away the document in the chest, where it still reamins.

But not everyone could find a guarantor, nor would every parish do what New Buckenham did for Martha Ayton. Many who would have liked to move to seek work elsewhere were tied down by this system, and progress was stultified.

But the 1662 Settlement Act and the subsequent provisions by additional Acts, allowed a person to settle in another parish on production of a "parish certificate" signed by the churchwardens and overseers of that person's parish, in the presence of two Justices, guaranteeing to take him or her back in the event of illness or other incapacity.

Thousands of these are tucked away among parish records.

Here is one dated February 17th, 1699. "Wee the Churchwarden and Overseer of the Poor of the Parrish of Norwich Carlton in Norfolk, att the instance and Request of Joseph Rushbrook of our Parrish, pursuant to a late Act of Parlimt. doe hereby Certifie the Churchwardens and Overseers of ye Poor of ye parrish of Shelfanger or any other Towne in ye county, that the sd. Joseph Rushbrook and Elizabeth his wife are inhabitants legally settled in our sd. parrish of Norwich Carlton, and wee doe also promise yt if they shall become chargeable to them, wee will receive them when ever it shall be required. In wittness hereof wee have hereunto sett our hands and seals ye day and year first above written."

This was signed and sealed by Richard Wattson, Churchwarden (his mark), and Francis Osborne, Overseer (his mark), and allowed by two Justices, Robert Pepper and J. Harvey.

Once a newcomer came to another parish it was possible to gain a settlement in that parish (a) by a "hiring" for a complete year (b) by serving a parish office such as constable, overseer, surveyor or parish clerk (c) by occupying premises of more than £10 rent per annum (d) by paying parish rates or (e) by serving an apprenticeship for a full term, under indenture.

So, returning to Elizabeth Woodcraft, who had applied to Winfarthing for relief, she was adjudged by the Justice to have gained a settlement in Shelfanger by her "hiring" there for a year —to Shelfanger she was returned, under an official "Removal Order" signed by the Justice.

"Petty Sessions for Hiring" therefore became extremely important, as an officially registered and fulfilled "service for a year" gave the security of a right to poor relief, scant as it might be.

A further example : Thomas Baldry, of Shelfanger, labourer applying for poor relief in that parish, stated, in his "examination": "I was born in Roydon, where my parents were legally settled. Before Michaelmas 1823 I lett myself to Jeremiah Sparrow, of Fersfield, farmer, whose service I entered on Old Mich. Day and continued in the sd. service for the space of Two years and received my full wages. At Diss Petty Sessions before Mich. 1825 I lett myself to Lilystone Anness of Shelfanger, farmer, to receive the weekly wages of 9s. and my lodging, but no board. I continued in the sd. service for one whole year and received my wages to my satisfaction".

His service at Fersfield would have entitled him to "relief" there, but his subsequent service at Shelfanger also gave him a "settlement" in that parish and the "last" service always counted.

Occasionally the Justices were confronted with a difficult and complicated case and their decision might lead to litigation between parishes—since any parish had the right to challenge a Justices' order by appealing to Quarter Sessions if they felt they were having a family wrongly foisted upon them.

Here is an example of such a case ; Frances Hearne, a single woman, of Diss, was examined on April 1st, 1805, before two Justices. She said : "At Old Mich. 1801 I entered the service of John Rayson of Aslacton, farmer, in pursuance of an hiring for one whole year at wages of 3£. I continued in that service one whole year and received my wages, then continued in the same service at Aslacton one other whole year then ensuing with the sd. John Rayson at the same wages. I then left the sd. service. My master's house was situate in two parishes, that is to say part thereof in the Parish of Aslacton and part in Moulton. While I lived with John Rayson, one of the parishes 'went the Boundes' of their parish, but which it was I cannot tell, but they went through the kitchen and out of the Backhouse Door. I lodged in the chamber over the kitchen all the time I lived with the sd. John Rayson, and which part of the house I verily believe lies in the Parish of Moulton".

Frances made her mark, the Justices signed, and decided that Frances belonged to Moulton, the decision being determined by "where she lodged". The examination is endorsed "Removed from Diss to Moulton same day"—and there was no appeal.

Though hiring fairs gradually died out, "settlements" were

still gained, and "Examinations" continued to be held into the 1860s with families suffering the distress and inconvenience of arbitrary "removals" simply because they had fallen on bad times, and the old laws still operated.

An old Norwich friend remembered "bonny lasses coming in to the City by carriers' carts on Hiring Day, to offer themselves as servants—taking up their places near the Free Library"—even as late as 1880.

Diss maintained its "Sessions Fair" up to the First World War though hirings ceased in 1830. Today one never hears mention of Hiring Fairs or Settlements—the provisions of the Welfare State have removed the necessity and indignity of them.

Hard times in Brockdish

(PUBLISHED NOVEMBER, 1963)

FEW parishes possess a finer set of Overseers' Accounts than Brockdish, where the records for the period 1772-1854 constitute a parish social history in themselves. They contain infinite detail, the purpose of every item of expenditure being made abundantly clear. For 25 of those years (1798-1823) Joseph Chilver was Overseer. There was no school in Brockdish then, but he was described as a "schoolmaster" who combined the teaching of a few children in his own cottage for a few pence per week, with the more onerous duties of parish Overseer at a salary of £3 3s. 0d. p.ann. plus meagre expenses.

Chilver must have taken great pride in keeping his "Towne Booke". He wrote in a fine clear hand which never varied. His accounts were so neat and lucid that I am convinced he must have sensed that one day they would be studied for their historical and social content. He became Overseer at a critical time—a time of great privation and general shortages—of distress and highly fluctuating prices—of poor harvests and the cumulative effects of the long struggle with Napoleon.

Page after page of his accounts are disbursements to persons 'at need". For the year Easter 1800 to Easter 1801 he filled 22 long pages with well over 800 entries, revealing the dire conditions then prevailing. These are typical—"Abra. H— at need being lame 5s."—"Wid. H—, son not having work 4s."—"Jas. B— not having work 1s."—"Scipio G's— son towards a pr. of Highlows 2s."—Martha W— expences for the small pox £2—3—9"—"Chas. R's sons 2 slops, 3s."—"A pr. of stays for Girl W— 1s." 6d."

Chilver had the unenviable task of putting into effect the Justices' order "to provide sundry substitutes in lieu of wheat". His accounts show "loss by selling Barley Flour and Pea Meal to the Poor as substitute for wheat to diminish the consumption thereof".

A workhouse for the parish "paupers" was built in 1815, for those on parish relief unable to take care of themselves in their own homes. A recurring expenditure was "for the paupers' board"—(regularly recorded by Chilver's successor as "pd. for the porpers baude"). Chilver too had some difficult cases to cope with. He noted "Journey to Stratton with Maria C— to obtain mittimus for her to be committed to Bridgewell for obtaining money of the Overseer under the false pretence of being pregnant, it being proved on oath by Dr. Aldis that the whole was an artifice". Then there was "Wm. L— pretending to be ill" and relieved by Chilver with 2s. (in case the illness was genuine), and "a journey to Mr. Oldershaw with John M— for warrant of commitment to Wymndoham Bridewell for leaving his family chargeable to the parish 3s."— "B's wife at need 12s., he having absconded". B— was afterwards committed. Joseph Chilver died after 25 years of faithful service to the parish.

The population of Brockdish rose from 385 in 1821 to 482 in 1831. The parish then had 94 families in 69 houses. There were 227 males, 113 of them above 20 years of age. Alas ! there was not employment for all the men, let alone for the youths and boys, so the Overseer's record for 1831-32 is a very distressing one. His statutory task was to relieve the sick and aged, and "to set the able bodied poor to work". No fewer than 604 payments for relief occurred that year. Such reasons as 'illness'—'in need'—'loss of time'—'unwell'—'no work'—'for nurse'—'towards apparel'—'Relief for woman on the road'—follow in dreary succession. In addition there were 30 parishioners on "collection" (i.e. regular weekly relief)—and 39 others received relief for periods of varying length.

As in other parishes—for Brockdish was far from unique in its difficulties—the 'officers' did all in their power to relieve poverty and alleviate unemployment. Some men were given money "to go in search of work"—a few were persuaded to become soldiers (Robt. A— received 8s. "to go for a solger"). Others were set to work on the roads or to gather stones in the fields and carry them to the roads. This gathering of stones and road work were extensively and universally used as a means of providing work, improving the deplorable state of the highways in return for parish support through the poor rate.

But what work ! "Jno. W— 6 days digging Gravel in the pit 5s."—"R. L—4¼ days banking and scraping roads at 10 d. ; 3s."6½d." —"J— L— carting 82 donkey loads of stones and mould into Ingram's Lane at 1½d., 10s." 3d."—"L— carting stones into Great

Road, Duckspuddle and Tumbling Lanes 12s " 9d ". A normal load of stones was 72 bushels, for collecting which the prevailing wage was 7d. To earn 1s. 2d. a day 144 bushels had to be collected and carried to a cart or dumped beside the road.

It is hardly surprising that some became demented. We read that 8s. was paid to "Abra. S— and wife for setting up with H's wife 3 days and nights, she being deranged", and the Overseer received 7s. "for journey of self and wife with H's wife to Norwich Bethel". The same official paid 2s. 8d. "for stuff for a strait jackett". He also made a journey to Starston with L— to see Mr. Oldershaw (Justice). Making the "strait jackett" cost 10d. But that was not sufficient to control L—, it required "Lock and cheane to confine L— with, 2s. " 4d.".

Others were prepared to emigrate from Brockdish to the New World, but the Overseer provided little detail. On June 17th, 1832, the sum of £2 10s. was expended on "Journey to Yarmouth with Emigrants", while £1 10s. was the cost of sending Jas. Cole Walne (then the principal ratepayer) to Yarmouth to see the Emigrants sail and wish them bon voyage. Mrs. Wilby, wife of the Workhouse Governor, also received 12s. 0½d. for "making clothes for the Emigrants".

In March, 1833, Mr. Thos. C. Brettingham (of Brockdish Place) was paid £12 10s. "being first instalment to liquidate the sum of 50£ borrowed for purposes of sending Paupers to America, together with interest £2—10—0". The names of Emigrants are withheld — all we know is that Jas. Leaper "left £1—4—3 towards the expence of his American Expedition" — which appears as a credit in the accounts.

But emigration failed to solve the unemployment dilemma. The 'Towne Booke' provides details of an agreement entered into by the parishioners on April 2nd, 1835, to meet an acute situation. It was in all essentials like the Stradbroke Plan to provide maximum employment. It provided that "all occupiers of land in the parish shall and will take a good able bodied man to every 25 acres of land, and boys in proportion, reckoning the wages of a man at 8s. per week. Then if any men are out of work and not employed on the Roads, such men to be called Roundsmen and sent to occupiers, according to their occupations, free of expence, that is they are to be paid out of the poor rate. But only those occupiers that do keep their full complement of men are to be benefited by these

Roundsmen". A further part of the agreement stated "the quantity of stone to be carted by the occupiers into the roads, at their own expence". Thus Jas. C. Walne, with 254 acres agreed to employ 10 men and produce 85 loads of stones "to qualify for the services of Roundsmen at parish expence." The Overseer's accounts contained many items like this—"pd. Wm. Smith 2 days as Roundsman at J. Burgess 2s " 4d "—in addition to relief for "loss of time" —"in need"—and for work on the roads.

Thus Brockdish managed to tide over these distressing years, until the operation of the 1834 Poor Law Amendment Act relieved the Parish to some extent—especially when the Union House at Pulham was built 1836-7. Then in May, 1850, a parish meeting at the "Greyhound" decided it was "desirable to help George Randall to Emigrate". This led in due course to the levy of a 9d. rate "to cover the expences attending the Emigration of George Randall, Shadrach Elsey, and Joseph Walne". Brockdish thus produced a second batch of pioneers for the New World.

How interesting it would be to hear how these, and their counterparts from other parishes, fared in their new surroundings!

A Palgrave house with a history

(PUBLISHED JANUARY, 1964)

PALGRAVE had many associations with education long before the National School was erected on the Green in 1853. As far back as 1585, three years before the Spanish Armada threatened our shores, Simon Mure, headmaster of Sir Nicholas Bacon's Free Grammar School in Botesdale, moved to Palgrave to become Rector, and also "Headmaster of Palgrave School." The Palgrave Register notes that "Maria Moore, filia Simonis Moore" was buried on April 2nd, 1594, and that "Simon Moore Rector of Palgrave" was buried on Jan. 24th, 1600.

I have seen an original salary receipt signed by "Simon Mure", dated July 8th, 1581. It reads—"Rec. of Sir Nicholas Bacon of Redgrave in the Co. of Suff., Knight, by me Symon Mure scolemaister of the fre Scole in Botesdale for my quarters wages due at the feast of the nativitye of St. John Baptist, the some of five pounds of Lawfull Englishe money."

Though Palgrave School possessed no endowments like the Botesdale School (endowed by Sir Nicholas with £30 per annum for ever) it had an equally good academic standard. The records of Gonville and Caius College, Cambridge, show that in September, 1586, one "John Jewell of Carleton Rode, at Palgrave School under Mr. Mure"—entered the college as a scholar at the age of 18. The school was held in a large house on the west side of Palgrave Green, opposite the site of the National School and quite close to the scene of the recent disastrous fire. It was a "two storey double roofed house, with large central entrance, looking over a tongue of greensward towards the Village Church". There were 13 windows in the 70-foot long front. At the western end was a spacious schoolroom, at the eastern end of the edge of the Green was the 'Pound', where in former times the Parish Constable impounded stray cattle. A large scale map of Palgrave, dated 1823, shows the house and the pound—and a vacant space where the National School was later erected.

Palgrave School—once successful—appears to have dwindled

away in the 17th century, as did many similar small schools without endowment. The house then became a private dwelling. Here in 1723 Thomas Martin and his wife Sarah came to live. Martin was then 26. He lived until 1771, and visitors entering Palgrave Church by the south porch cannot fail to notice the tablet on the west wall to the memory of this "able and indefatigable antiquary".

Thomas Martin was a native of Thetford—the son of William Martin, Rector of Livermere and of St. Mary's, Thetford. He was educated at Thetford School, but "through lack of means, and to his lasting regret", he did not go up to Cambridge. Instead he became a clerk in his brother's Attorney's Office, and qualified as an attorney. But, disliking the office routine, he settled in Palgrave and stayed there for the rest of his life—"a zealous student of topography and antiquities". It was he who inserted the arms of Archbishop Sancroft in the upper central window of the house, where they remained until its demolition just over a century ago.

"Honest Tom Martin"—for he lived in hope that he would merit such a soubriquet—played an important part in the Church life of Palgrave. His elaborate signature with its many flourishes appears on the Wardens' Accounts and on many parish papers and contemporary documents. His great friend Francis Blomefield described him as "as good a drawer as any in England", and always referred to him as "Honest Tom".

The Palgrave Register makes sad reading in the years following Martin's arrival there. He lost a son and a daughter in infancy, and his wife Sarah died in 1731 ten days after giving birth to twins—"leaving him who was domestically helpless, surrounded by a family of six children". But the antiquary soon repaired the loss by marrying Frances, widow of Peter Le Neve, Norroy King at Arms. She was then living at Great Witchingham.

A "Suffolk Garland" records this interesting anecdote concerning the curious affair of the courtship. Tom Martin was executor to the late Le Neve, and one morning after poring over the manuscripts of his deceased friend, he was summoned by the widow to dinner. "He raised himself suddenly, threw himself back in his chair, stretched out his arms, and as it were yawned out 'O yes, O yes, who'll have me and my six children?'"

"That will I, Mr. Martin," said the widow, "if I like those which I have not seen, as well as those which I have seen". They were married shortly after, and the Palgrave Register records—

"Bapt. July 8th, 1733, Frances daughter of Thomas and Frances Martin." — to be followed by Robert (1734), James (1736), William (1737) and Matthew (1740). All alas ! died young.

Tom Martin died on March 7th, 1771, and was buried on March 12th. The memorial was erected by his great friend, Sir John Fenn, who in 1787 edited a selection of the famous Paston Letters from manuscripts formerly in Martin's possession. The Paston muniments had descended to William, second Earl of Yarmouth, on whose death in 1732 Martin had acquired them.

Tom Martin's "History of Thetford" was a lasting memorial to his work, and he also furnished Blomefield with much material for his "History of Norfolk". He was a member of the "Gentlemen's Society" and his "hoary hairs were said to be the crown of glory at the annual gathering of the Society of Antiquaries".

A friend who stayed at Palgrave and also met Martin at Caius College (whose master, Sir James Burroughs, was Martin's cousin) described him as "a blunt rough honest downright man of no behaviour or guile—often drunk in the morning with strong beer. His thirst after antiquities was as great as his thirst after liquors".

The next occupants of this house restored it to its former use as a school for small boys. Here in 1774 came the Revd. Rochemont Barbauld and his bride Anna Laetitia, formerly Miss Aikin, daughter of John Aikin, D.D., Professor of Theology at the Dissenting Academy in Warrington.

Mr. Barbauld was of French Protestant extraction. His grandfather, when a boy, was literally smuggled on board a ship, "enclosed in a cask and conveyed to England", when the family fled from the Protestant persecutions of Louis XIV of France. His father was a minister of the Established Church, and Rochemont was sent to the Warrington Academy. There he met Anna Laetitia. They both flourished intellectually in the intensely stimulating atmosphere among famous scholars such as Dr. Priestley (the discoverer of oxygen), T. R. Malthus (a great economist and theorist of population control) and John Wedgwood (father of Josiah).

Mr. Barbauld became a Presbyterian, and in 1774 was invited "to take charge of a small Dissenting Congregation at Palgrave, near Diss, combined with the management of a boarding school for boys". The Dissenters met on the Suffolk side of 'The Lows', using as their meeting house a barn then standing on the site of the present Unitarian burial ground, and erected in 1697. Mr. Barbauld was ordained here on September 13th, 1775.

The school blossomed under the inspiration of the Barbaulds, and the house was henceforth known as "Barbauld House".

The School at Barbauld House, Palgrave attracted a succession of brilliant young scholars, many of whom were to become famous in later years. Here were instructed in their early years Sir William Gell—"explorer of the plains of Troy and the ruins of Pompeii" —many sons of the nobility, and that most eminent lawyer, Lord Chief Justice Denman.

To their great disappointment the Barbaulds had no children of their own. In 1776 Mrs. Barbauld wrote to her brother, Dr. Aikin, saying "We have a request to make which may seem rather singular—but is actually seriously in earnest. You enjoy a blessing of Providence hitherto denied to us—the blessing of children. You have already several, and seem likely to have a numerous family. Our request then is this: that you will permit us to adopt one of your children. Now my dear brother and sister, if you consent, give us which of your boys you please."

The upshot was that Charles Rochemont Aikin was adopted at the age of two, and Mrs. Barbauld made his upbringing and education her special care and study. For his use she devised "Early Lessons for Children" which also filled an important need in the schools of the day, and became one of the earliest standard primers for the young. It was translated into French and met with success equal to the same author's "Hymns in Prose for Children".

But however enjoyable and successful school life might be, it was undoubtedly exhausting, in spite of visits to literary friends in London and Norwich, during vacations. Mrs. Barbauld's father had died, and early in 1784 her mother died at Palgrave, where she had lived since Dr. Aitkin's death. The Palgrave Register records—"Buried Feb. 3rd, 1784. Mrs. Aikin."

In September, 1785, the Barbaulds sailed for France—where they travelled extensively, returning in 1786 to settle in Hampstead. Here Mrs. Barbauld continued her literary activities, writing and publishing essays supporting good causes—those struggling for civil and religious liberty.

Mrs. Barbauld is represented in the latest Oxford Dictionary of Quotations by five excerpts from her works—one of them "The world has little to bestow, when two fond hearts in equal love are joined" — and another "Society than solitude is worse, and man to man is still the greatest curse." The latter gives much food for thought in the troublous times we live in nearly two centuries later.

One of her poems also appears as a hymn in the Revised A. & M. Book. It seems to depict the seasonal changes in the peaceful Palgrave countryside of the 18th century.

>"For the Blessings of the field,
>For the stores the gardens yield,
>Flocks that whiten all the plain,
>Yellow sheaves of ripened grain,
>All that Spring with bounteous hand
>Scatters o'er the smiling land;
>All that liberal Autumn pours
>From her rich o'erflowing Stores.—
>These to Thee, my God, we owe;
>Source whence all our blessings flow."

Among the assistants in the Palgrave School from 1775-1781 was Simon Westby. From Mrs. Barbauld he derived inspiration and enthusiasm for teaching and an insight into her gift of arousing interest and a sense of purpose in her pupils. After his studies at Cambridge he devoted his energies to teaching the youth of Diss — for he was the successful headmaster of the Guildhall Grammar School from 1791-1820. (He was also for a time Curate of Shelfanger, and Rector of Kenninghall 1803-1820).

Barbauld House School next came under the control of the Rev. Nathaniel Phillipps. His advertisement, which I have frequently seen in Norfolk weeklies of the time, gives an inkling of the kind of establishment he ran. "PALGRAVE SCHOOL—30 young Gentlemen are educated in various branches of Literature upon the following terms — Entrance 2 guineas: Tuition and Board 25 gns. per ann: Under Tuition will be comprehended The Latin, Greek and French Languages, English Grammar and Composition, Writing, Arithmetic, Book-Keeping. Geography and the use of the globes will be charged separately, as also a Course of Lectures in Experimental Philosophy which will be delivered if required to such pupils as are of proper age. N.B. a quarter's notice of removal will be expected."

The school was patronized widely by the sons of country squires, clergy and landowners. Parson Woodforde mentions in his diary for July 21, 1788, "Hambleton and George go to school tomorrow to Mr. Phillipps of Palgrave", and on December 20 of the same year "Mrs. Custance with her two sons Hambleton and George, who are just returned from school at Palgrave, made us a long morning visit. They both look well." (They were the sons of Squire Custance, Hambleton being then 9 years old).

Mr. Phillipps was succeeded by the Rev. John Tremlett, who in turn handed over his combined scholastic and pastoral duties to Dr. Charles Lloyd, a man of remarkable forcefulness. Lloyd had been a master at Swansea Grammar School, but was urged, by no less a person than Dr. Joseph Priestley, to be ordained. He subsequently studied at the Presbyterian Academy in Swansea, and received his LL.D. from Glasgow University. He came to Palgrave in 1803 on the same terms as Mr. Barbauld came in 1774. He was a brilliant teacher, who "grounded his pupils well in the classics". His vivid portrayals of the lives and personalities of classical authors were said to be most stimulating. His biographer says "he was sensitive, and suspicious of affront", and that he had a "warm temper". Perhaps it was a combination of these qualities which led him to "correct his pupils passionately".

Dr. Lloyd was known by his pupils as the "Quantity Doctor", but whether from the amount of punishment he meted out, or from the amount of work he demanded from them — is not clear. Among his pupils was Edgar Taylor (b. 1793), son of Samuel Taylor of New Buckenham, who became articled to his uncle, Meadows Taylor of Diss, in 1809. The last minister to officiate at Palgrave was the Rev. John Fullagar, who declined school in 1818. The old meeting house on the Lows went out of use at this time, and the chapel in Park Fields was erected in its stead, and came into use in 1822.

The boys' school faded out — and Barbauld House became the home of Mrs. Tilbrook's "Establishment for young Ladies", which was later taken over by Mrs. Hart, who made it the leading local girls' school. Mrs. Hart, like Mr. Phillipps, was a great believer in advertising. Her announcements proclaimed that "Parlour Boarders" were taken at an additional fee of 5 gns. per ann., presumably to share the good food and elegant conversation at Mrs. Hart's own table.

In 1859 this house of historic and honourable associations was purchased by the owner of the adjoining property, and in the words of Wilton Rix, a 19th century antiquarian, who left personal impressions of the place, "it was swept away". He had seen "the names and scribblings of generations of aspiring or idle pupils, on the long casemented window of the schoolroom", and had talked with elderly Palgravians who remembered "the Great School" and its famous pupils who had performed their plays for the delight of the villagers.

Those days of fame were gone — and in 1859 the old house went too. Mrs. Hart removed to "The Laurels", Mount Street, Diss, and crowded her young ladies into the house still standing back beside "The Cedars".

Tragedy in Gawdy Wood

(PUBLISHED FEBRUARY, 1964)

A GLANCE through the Norfolk Chronicle of 1826 shows that in spite of the vigilance and the deterrent influence of the many "Associations for prosecuting felons," crime was rampant, and punishments were severe. Sentence of death was passed at Thetford Assizes on three prisoners convicted of sheepstealing.

Another prisoner was sentenced to "7 years transportation," (for stealing a watch), while a female prisoner was "Transported for life" for stealing 45s.

"Unlawfully entering a plantation and having in possession pheasants" — "poaching" — "armed in the night-time with intent to take and kill game contrary to Statute" — these were typical of a seemingly interminable succession of offences, while theft of corn, wood, meat and poultry were commonplace.

The "Harleston Association" included representatives of 18 villages around the town, stretching from Hoxne to Hardwick, and from Dickleburgh to Flixton, including Starston. Its members, numbering about 100, were pledged to report every infringement of the law, and to use the Association's resources to track down offenders and bring them to trial.

Even this had not deterred many of the more cunning and hardened marauders, as for some years the nightly depredations against private property in Starston had been so numerous that the leading inhabitant organized a regular watch and patrol to frustrate potential offenders. This "Vigilance Committee's" efforts had been so successful that by 1826 it was felt expedient to dispense with the watch, but this led to a renewed outburst of poaching and pilfering.

By some means it came to the notice of the Committee that certain notorious characters would be out in the woods near Starston on the night of November 27th, 1826, and that if they failed to take game, they would resort to poultry stealing — many poultry having already been stolen from the parish. The committee decided to go out in force that night, in two parties, moving in pairs at intervals along different routes to an agreed rendezvous in Gawdy Wood. Four men were armed — the Rector (the Rev. William Whitear), Charles Etheredge, Daniel Denny and Thomas Pallant — while the remainder carried heavy sticks.

The night was very dark — certainly the tenseness of the occasion and the blackness of the night were such as to test even the hardest nerves. Recognition under such conditions would certainly be difficult, and the tragedy that followed was due to loss of nerve and the failure to distinguish friend from foe.

Charles Etheredge had 'paired' with the Rector, and a letter of his has survived describing the sequence of events. After patrolling their allotted beats — "Five of the party arrived at the place appointed and agreed to keep about 100 yards apart till the others should come up. A few minutes from this time two men made their appearance and jumped over the hedge into the road within a few yards of where Charles Etheredge stood. He immediately called out that all was right, supposing them to belong to the watch. One of them appeared much alarmed, and in an instant at 4 yards distance snapped his gun at Etheredge, which providentially missed fire. He then turned and made off in the direction of where the Revd. Whitear stood. Etheredge repeatedly called out that they were of the same party. Then Mr. Whitear met the man and opened his dark Lanthorn to discover who it was, when the person immediately shot Mr. Whitear in the right side, at a distance of about 4 yards. Etheredge was at this time about 10 yards from him, and seeing Mr. Whitear fall on his back, immediately shot at the man, who then fled and escaped into the darkness, though not before Mr. Whitear had raised himself and fired."

In this dramatic way the night's activities ceased. The severely wounded Rector was assisted home. Two days later, on the 29th, it was stated that though he was severely wounded, no unfavourable symptoms had developed, and his medical attendants entertained great hopes of recovery. Pallant had sustained the loss of a thumb and first finger, and on arrival home maintained he had been wounded by a poacher — little realizing that it was either the Rector or Etheredge who had wounded him.

Up to December 9th Mr. Whitear made excellent progress towards recovery. He constantly enquired after Pallant's condition, and expressed the conviction that he himself had been shot by misadventure. On Sunday, December 10th, his condition changed suddenly — and he collapsed and died, to the great sorrow of all his parishioners.

The Coroner, Mr. Daniel Calver, held an inquest lasting six hours on Tuesday, December 12th, when a verdict of "manslaughter" was returned against Thomas Pallant, a "steady, harmless young man of 24" — brother-in-law of Daniel Denny.

Pallant appeared before Mr. Justice Gaselee at the Thetford Lent Assizes in 1827. On being arraigned he appeared deeply affected and cried bitterly. Having heard the evidence the Judge acquitted him as at the relevant time "he was in such a state of trepidation as not to know what he was about". He was taken home in an insensible state.

The evidence at the Assizes was much as Etheredge had stated in his letter, but John Nunn who 'paired' with Pallant said they thought they were surrounded by poachers, and that on the approach of what was in fact the Rector's party, he himself had exclaimed "Lord have mercy! — there they come, four or five of them!" This precipitated Pallant's loss of all self-possession, and led to the final tragedy.

The Judge concluded by reproving those who had carried arms on this occasion. Although they were out, quite commendably in his view, for the apprehension of poachers, that did not entitle them to carry and use fire arms.

The victim of this tragedy — the Rev. Mr Whitear, was the son of a Rector of Hastings, and had himself bee· Rector of Starston for 23 years, after being a 'Wrangler' at Cambridge, and spending two years as a Fellow of St. John's.

The tablet to his memory in Starston Church makes no direct reference to his untimely end, but mentions "his varied fund of Theological, Scientific and Practical knowledge, his piety and benevolence, which prompted him to apply it to the best purposes in zealously promoting the spiritual and Temporal improvement of his Parish."

But his interests extended far beyond the confines of the Parish, for he was very active in furthering the progress of popular education, through the Norfolk and Norwich Society, of which he was a founder. For many years he was a magistrate, and a Deputy Lieutenant of Norfolk (which incidentally makes it seem strange that he should be carrying fire-arms). An obituary notice refers to "his happy temperament, directed by clear and sound understanding" — and to "the excellent constitution, which enabled him to employ his powers of mind and body in obeying calls of duty, friendship and humanity, with cheerful and unceasing assiduity".

In the course of recording hundreds of parish papers I have repeatedly met Mr. Whitear's signature among those of scores of justices who signed warrants, removals, parish certificates and the like. I have often wondered what manner of man was Justice ——? So it was with William Whitear. An agreement he made with Elizabeth Love, of Pulham, widow, to become his housekeeper, just sparkles with sincerity and generosity.

Another document concerned a dispute between Dickleburgh and Rushall (of which Whitear was also Rector) over their respective contributions in 1825 "to build an additional gaol House of Correction and Shirehouse for the County". Whitear's letter showed a conciliatory, purposeful, and common sense approach to the dispute in order to bring the matter to "an amicable adjustment".

I felt I could share in the sentiments expressed on the memorial in Starston Church which states that "he died deeply lamented by a circle of afflicted relations and affectionate friends, fervently attached to him by his estimable and amiable qualities".

Old customs : Chalk-back day

(PUBLISHED SEPTEMBER 1960)

THE third Thursday in September was "Chalk-Back Day" to our forbears in Diss — a name that survived until the beginning of the present century. In the course of time it had also assumed another name—"The Sessions"—and the two names, though distinct in origin, were used as alternatives.

The origin of "Chalk-Back Day" is obscure, but the custom of chalking crosses on people's backs is thought to have derived from Holy Cross Day, September 14th, the day of the "Exaltation of the Cross."

The celebration of that ancient church festival was suppressed at the Reformation, and the marking of chalk crosses on the backs of others, and even on their doors and window-shutters, was a mute and defiant reminder that their religious belief and practices could not so easily be put aside.

"The Sessions" developed from "The Hiring Sessions," usually held after harvest in late September, when workers of all ages and both sexes congregated at the Hiring Fairs to strike bargains and seal contracts with employers for the succeeding year.

"Chalk-Back Day" and "The Sessions" were thus close together in time, and in Diss the third Thursday in September became the appointed day for both.

Hiring Sessions arose after the "Black Death" of 1348, which swept away between one-third and a half of the entire population. After it had spent its force and taken its cruel toll of human lives, there was a great scarcity of workers and, of course, food prices soared.

To prevent the wealthy landowners from attracting an undue share of the available labour force by offering wages above the average, the Act known as the "Statute of Labourers" was passed in 1351, pegging both wages and food prices.

Although this was not universally observed—there were black markets in those days, too—it did prevent flagrant abuses. The yet authorised Statute Hiring Fairs or Sessions—regarded by the workers as indispensable at that time.

Different places selected their own days for "Hirings," but all fell round about Michaelmas time. At Harling it was Tuesday after Michaelmas, at Botesdale the Thursday before, and at Wymondham the second day after Old Michaelmas, and so on.

In Diss, on the appointed Thursday, men and maids seeking work resorted to the churchyard with their friends, ranging themselves in rows on the path leading from the south porch to the Market Place—men on one side, facing women on the other. Some wore badges or tufts in their hats to indicate their particular line of work—the carter a tuft of whip-cord, the cowherd one of the cow's hair.

The employers arrived, sauntered through the ranks in search of a likely horseman or a buxom housemaid. Discussions and bargainings ensued, for there were more things than just wages to consider—housing, hours of work, rights of gleaning, turfage, sticking and rabbiting.

Amid a babel of voices contracts were sealed by word of mouth and by the giving of a "fasten-penny" (in Diss it was a shilling). So the various folk obtained their new work—trusting and hoping that their mutual judgments would turn out well.

Meanwhile, mischievous boys were unable to resist having their fun. While adults were pre-occupied with their haggling over terms, hirer and hired were liberally chalked with crosses as if to give a special seal to their contracts. Many were pinned or tied together—a practice that led to many embarrassing situations.

As the 19th century progressed the whole idea of Hiring Sessions was increasingly regarded as degrading and reminiscent of the slave markets of Southern U.S.A. Reforms were being enacted, education becoming more widespread, and the spectacle of human beings being "exposed for sale" was repugnant.

"Happily such ideas are becoming extinct, and the orginal intention of making a public exhibition of one's self for the sake of being hired is fast dying out. While not in favour of sweeping away all old customs, for many have elevating tendencies, those relating in any way to serfdom should not be tolerated in England."

So wrote a contemporary in 1860. Referring to Diss, he continued: "Within the last quarter century hundreds, nay thousands, have been herded like so many beasts at a fair, in the churchyard at Diss, there awaiting, possibly with anxiety, their future masters."

So, with reforms afoot, opportunities for emigration to the lands of opportunity and the expansion of industry in the "shires," the Hiring Sessions gradually faded out. In one place we are told that by 1844 "they were of trifling consequence"—in others they were already dead. In Diss they petered out about a century ago.

The parents of the older among us talked of seeing a few people congregating in the churchyard for the last of the Sessions.

"Chalk-Back Day," however, survived longer—though its earlier significance was lost. It was an occasion for high spirits, but, like many such occasions, it was abused and degenerated into an orgy of chalking on walls, shops and shutters as well as on others' backs.

The Press referred to it as a "senseless and absurd custom." In 1869 bills were distributed in the town threatening prosecution for juveniles guilty of such practices, but this did not prevent "chalking backs to a slight degree."

Eventually, the custom discontinued. One of today's septuagenarians, at school in 1900, remembers the very last of it. Surreptitious markings in school, when the teacher's attention was otherwise engaged, were the last known. Stern parents find deep-seated chalk markings difficult to remove and put a finishing touch and dealt a final blow to "Chalk-Back Day."

Camp Ball

(PUBLISHED DECEMBER 1961)

DISS almshouses have gone, a hatchery has risen in their place where once was an expanse of common. Soon the chirp of day-old chicks will be heard where years ago the full-throated roar of the Camp Ball partisans rent the air.

For it was on Diss Common, now "enclosed," and traversed by the railway and dotted with factories, maltings, garages and other premises, that the most famous "Camping Match" of all time took place, just over 200 years ago—a county struggle between the men of Norfolk and Suffolk.

The name "Camp Ball" comes from an Anglo-Saxon word "cempan," to fight. It was a primitive form of football, with rules, if any, suited to local conditions. Many East Anglian Camping Closes or Pightles have existed since the 15th century.

An Elizabethan writer described the game as "a friendly kind of fight, a bloody and murdering practice with everyone lying in wait for his adversary to pick him on the nose and dash him against the heart with his elbows."

A century later "the husbandmen killed the fat swine on approach of winter, and blew the bladder great and thin, to try at football with their shins." King James I forbade the game at Court" as meeter for lameing his subjects than making them able." He preferred them to engage in archery.

Numerous accounts exist as to how the game was played in its many varieties. The two sides consisted of 10 to 20 players, referred to as "combatants," from the nature of the game. They invariably stripped to the waist and wore colours in their belts, though some "camps" were fought out in brightly coloured flannel jackets.

The Camping ground was slightly larger than a modern soccer pitch. It might be a flat "piece of plough," roped off for the occasion to restrain supporters from entering the lists, or it might be the village Common with its natural hazards of bush, hillocks and rabbit holes.

Occasionally, a plain shiny turf was used, or even the village street in some places for this "free for all." The goals were marked by crude stakes for special occasions, though heaps of discarded clothes provided improvised posts for the ordinary village camps.

The rules varied, for there were "civil camps" (in which boxing was forbidden) as well as "Savage Camps," "Fighting Camps," and "Rough-Play," which never ended "without black eyes, bloody noses, broken heads or shins, or other serious mischiefs." Under one set of rules the ball might be kicked, carried or thrown through the goal, under another set "carrying" only was allowed.

It was common to play "Nine notches up" in the early days, when scorers cut a notch in a hazel stick for each goal scored.

This proved a most exhausting game, often lasting for hours, so later the result was decided on goals scored after an hour's play.

Men of the Hundreds of Taverham and Blofield were to have engaged in "Camping" on Crostwick Common in July, 1806—the prizes offered being "Hats"—presumably as we award "Caps" today. Three thousand spectators assembled to enjoy the fray, but alas! the Blofield men defaulted and the men of Taverham "walked over the ground—and then walked off with the Hats"!

Norfolk and Suffolk met in a 10-a-side encounter at Kirby Cane in 1818 for a prize of £10, this being the first "thorough boxing camping match that had taken place there for 35 years."

Few of the 20 had ever before engaged in such a pugilistic contest, yet a spirit of gallantry animated both parties, the reporters said. Several thousands witnessed the "Camp," including many of rank and fortune.

The "Camp" between Happing and Blofield Hundreds at Ranworth in 1822, for £14, must have had a Wembley atmosphere about it. To see this, 15 wherry loads of spectators crossed Ranworth Broad, and the roads to the ground were thronged with carriages, carts and pedestrians—no less than 7000 assembling to enjoy the struggle.

The 10 members of each side marched hand-in-hand to the centre stake, shook hands with their adversaries, gave three lusty cheers, then retired in line for a few yards. An "indifferent" spectator threw the ball high between them, made his escape, and so started "the great rush to catch the falling ball, in this most desperate trial of skill and strength."

An hour-long struggle failed to produce even one goal, so the prize money was shared. The last 10 minutes of this severely contested match ended in "fighting most furious."

The mammoth game between Norfolk and Suffolk took place on Diss Common nearly a century before. It was truly a "savage camp." Tradition says there were 300 a side, and that the game lasted 14 hours.

The Norfolk Campers entered the combat with tremendous confidence, tauntingly asking their rivals at the line out: "Have you brought your coffins?" Suffolk, however, were not easily intimidated, and had the "punch" and endurance to vanquish their northern rivals.

No quarter was given in this rough, fighting camp, and nine of the combatants died of their injuries within a fortnight.

A few years later two deaths occurred at Easton, in Suffolk, following a "savage camp" there. The game then fell into disuse, particularly in Suffolk between the Orwell and the Alde, where it had been most popular.

It survived longer in Norfolk, the last recorded Camp being in 1831 when "neither the camping nor the subsequent wrestling were well contested."

Now, in 1961, the game is perpetuated by such names as the "Camping Close" at Eye, the "Camping Pightle" at Hawstead, the "Camping Land" at Stowmarket, with others at Swaffham, East Bilney and elsewhere.

Beating the bounds in Rogationtide

(PUBLISHED MAY 1962)

THE ancient custom of "perambulation," or "beating the bounds," was revived, many years ago, by the late Canon Nock, of Bressingham, and continued annually until his death in 1960.

In the cool of a Rogationtide evening, just before Ascension Day, the Rector, his wardens, Anglican supporters, Free Church people and Salvationists, assembled near the village memorial. After a welcome, and prayers, the procession moved along High Street, to the melodious accompaniment of the Diss Salvation Army Band, halting to sing hymns at the cottages of the aged who could not perambulate.

Blessings were invoked for a bountiful harvest by representatives of the various groups, and so they continued through the village for a final rally about a half-mile "up the Common" (all traces of the former Common have gone, though many houses "stand back" on its former boundary).

In keeping with tradition, the participants resorted to the Village Hall for refreshments—the hall being an ancient barn, restored and adapted for community use.

Bressingham is rich in its parish records. The ceremony of perambulation can be traced through nearly four centuries. Even in the reign of Queen Elizabeth I, "Goeing the Boundes" was a convivial occasion, for the church-wardens recorded paying "for bere at the perambolation," and later "for beere and cakes when we went procession."

In the 17th century, other luxuries were added, for "bread, cakes, chese, bere, tobaco and pipes" appeared in the accounts. So, too, did the expense of providing "wooden crosses," which were erected at strategic points in the parish boundary, or nailed to prominent trees.

Beating the bounds was no casual country ramble, for ploughed fields, hedges, ditches, ponds and streams all had to be negotiated in this exacting 12-mile test of endurance. Small wonder that they halted at vantage points to rest, offer prayers, consume those provisions and smoke their churchwarden pipes !

A detailed description of the "Bounds of Fersfield as perambulated by Francis Blomefield, the wardens, overseers, constables, surveyors and other inhabitants, on 17 May in Rogation Week 1735," remains to this day, in the historian's own handwriting. The text is punctuated with decorative tree-like "crosses," at points where they were actually affixed to particular trees.

It is fascinating to trace Blomefield's itinerary on a modern map. It can be done extremely well, in spite of the changes in field boundaries and the masking of many details by subsequent enclosures.

Fersfield adjoins Kenninghall, whose "place" was a Royal residence in Tudor times. Blomefield wrote: "We enter Queen Elizabeth's Lane, now called Besses Lane, till we come to Fersfield Lodge. We enter the Backhouse Door and make our cross (+) on the doormand, and going out by the same door we enter'd, go to the pond over which we cast a stick unto the Common, levell with the ditch that bounds the said Common."

The difficulty of buildings, ponds and streams straddling parish boundaries often caused complications in many places. Boys were frequently recorded as receiving half a crown for wading through, or swimming across, a stretch of water, to demarcate the boundary.

The Diss perambulation of 1794 is described, with meticulous detail, on four stained foolscap sheets in the Parish Chest. After placing crosses at many points, the foot-weary company reached the northernmost point of their 17-mile trek, where, "In the Boot Lane or Tibenham Long Row they made a cross, bumped the boys and others asses against trees, ate cakes, drank half a barrell of beer, and made a cross dividing Tibenham from Diss."

Bumping the boys was a common practice, to remind them of the salient points on the boundary, in readiness for future occasions. In the last recorded Diss perambulation, in 1825, the Rev. William Manning and 39 others went the bounds, accompanied by "music." The wardens' accounts show that each one to complete the course received "a shilling for dinner, a shilling to drink, the 'music' being allowed expenses for dinner and drink, and 30s. besides."

Tythe and ordnance maps in the 19th century defined boundaries clearly and officially, so the custom of perambulation gradually ceased. Some of the later ones in Norwich, too, appear to have degenerated into occasions of "wanton levity and vulgar mirth," for the Vicar of St. Peter Mancroft and his followers, in 1827, were "assailed by fellows with pails of water, and on Hay Hill the Vicar was drenched from head to foot."

The 20th century revival of the Rogationtide procession has restored some of its earlier religious significance and form—whether at Dereham, where the Vicar keeps a portable harmonium for accompanying the hymns; at Redenhall, where a violinist provides the music; or at Bressingham, where the full strength of the S.A. band has been mustered.

All signify our dependence on a Bounteous Creator, and help to promote Church unity.

On Rogation Sunday, May 27th, 1962, the Bishop of Norwich, accompanied by the Rector and parishioners of Itteringham, went in procession through the village, halting at several points to bless fields, gardens, a stream, a farmyard, and the village centre. On the same day, members of various Lowestoft churches, led by the Salvation Army Band, joined in a Rogation Day procession—stopping here and there to offer supplications and to sing hymns of praise. At Walberswick, the previous day, the old custom of "Beating the Bounds" had been revived, some of those taking part actually traversing the entire parish boundary of several miles.

In many other places, too, the ancient practice of perambulating the parish in solemn religious procession, chanting litanies and prayers, begging God's blessing on the fruits of the earth, and entreating that the rights and properties of the parish might be preserved, was carried out, though in a somewhat abbreviated form.

Perambulations are mentioned in Court Rolls of the 13th century. Originally they consisted of "walking round a territory, forest, manor or parish for the purpose of asserting and recording its boundaries, in order to preserve rights of possession"—simply, "beating the bounds.".

Later, the ceremony assumed a religious significance—the boundaries were perambulated at Rogationtide and the opportunity was used to invoke God's blessing on the crops, and on the industry of man.

A typical setting is described thus in the *History of Hawstead, Suffolk* (**1784**): "Upon the parish bounds grew a majestic tree—the

Gospel Oak. It stood on an eminence, commanding an extensive prospect. Under its shade the Clergyman and his parishioners used to stop in their Perambulations, and, surveying a considerable extent of fruitful and well-cultivated country, repeated prayers proper to the occasion."

It was Henry VIII who passed an Act (1540) ordering "12 Discrete persons of each parish to make perambulations and to appoynt wher the boundes shal extend". *Machyn's Diary* picturesquely describes an early Rogationtide procession of 1554: "The iii day of March at the Cowrt of San James, the quens grace whent a prossessyon with harold and serjants of armes and iii bysshopes mytred and all iii Rogation dayes they whent abowt the feldes."

At this time (circa 1550) many of our local Parish Churchwardens accounts began, so giving us details of expenses incurred and providing an insight into the happenings of perambulations.

In 1588 the Bressingham Towne Book had this entry: "Payd for Bere at the Perambulation, iiiid." Later, greater stress was laid on festivity: "Layd out for bread and beare and a side of chese when we went perambulacon, 4s. 6d."

By Charles II reign (1666) a new element, tobacco, had crept in—with the provision of long churchwarden clay pipes: "Pd. for bread, beere, chese, cakes, tobacco and pipes at our perambulation, 11s."

There is also reference to wooden crosses, which were fixed at special points on the boundary, sometimes driven into the ground or nailed to prominent trees. In 1629, the Bressingham Carpenter, Andrew Barker, received 9d. "for mackinge the crosses"; and in 1632 William Keene received "VId. for parringe the crosses"—presumably, 'repairing' them.

The first reference to a Diss perambulation occurs in 1691, when Churchwarden Camell's accounts included: "At ye longe Perambulation by 13 men, besides boys, for meat drinke and cakes, 6d. for a Guide, and 1s. spent at Tibenham Long Row, in all 16s."

A very detailed description of the perambulation of 1725 has survived. It runs: "Disse: From Tottington (the Checquer or Cockstreet Green) thro Mr. Burton's meadow to Mrs. Sherriffe's pasture close called three corner pightle, to the willow Close of hers, downe Brumble lane to Shelfanger Lane, thence to Crucknells Hempland gate. There a cross is made: thence almost thro the strait lane to Westbrooke Green" . . .

Try to follow this Diss-Roydon boundary. Mr. Burton's meadow is now the Long Meadow, and Mr. Scoggin's house is in the three corner pightle, then called "Farthing Cross".

The journey continued Northward touching Bressingham, Shelfanger and Winfarthing until "comeing to Mr. Boon's Pightle, turn on the right-hand and make a Crosse dividing Winfarthing and Disse on any Oak or Tree, thro that into Boot Lane or Long row.

"There under a coppice of trees we make a Cross, Bump the Boys arses against Trees and eat cakes and drink halfe a Barrell of ale, make a Cross dividing Tibenham and Disse. From thence cross the Green - - - " and so down the eastern boundary touching Gissing and Burston—"till we come unto Disse Common or Moore and there the County river bounds Diss against Sturston and Palgrave".

Bumping the boys was common practice, forcibly to impress on their memories the salient points of the boundary for future reference.

Diss regularly "went the bounds" through the 18th century. The last occasion was on May 9th, 1825, when the Rev. William Manning (then 54) and 39 other parishioners perambulated, "the expence thereof amounting to £23 - 14 - 2".

The regulations were that 20 men that went the bounds should each be allowed 1s for dinner and 1s to drink—the music to be allowed expence for dinner and drink, and 30s besides".

To complete that course of 17 miles through meadows, lanes and spinneys, over swamps, ditches and streams, was no mean achievement, especially for the fiddlers, flute and clarinet players. Weary in wind and limb, they must have felt relieved to reach the county river.

These perambulations of parish boundaries were of great importance until the early 19th century. Each parish was then responsible for the support of its own poor through a parish poor rate—for maintaining its roads by a surveyor's rate—and for sending a number of men to the militia. Thus, it was essential to know in what parish every family lived. Disputes and delicate situations often arose, especially where houses were built astride the actual boundary.

An interesting case occurred between Wortham and Burgate because the "Dolphin" then straddled the boundary of the two parishes. In a "settlement" case at Ipswich Sessions, the question arose as to which parish one Thomas Woods belonged and the Court was asked to decide. Woods had been employed at the "Dolphin" and had slept in the middle bedroom of three. His bedstead was close against the wall, the head of the bed being immediately over a beam in the kitchen, the beam marking the parish boundary.

A witness, Simon Frost, who had "perambulated" with the Burgate parishioners stated that they "entered the 'Dolphin' at the front door, went straight through the kitchen into the wash-house, put a stick through the sinkhole at the right hand corner, returned to the kitchen, went out at the back door and round the wash-house, then took a circle round some fields and returned through the 'Dolphin'. On one occasion they pointed at the beam."

It was argued that by taking the beam as a boundary line, only 11 inches of the bed in the room above would be in Wortham, and that four or five inches at the most of Wood's head could have slept in that parish. The rest of his person must have slept in Burgate.

As a result of this complicated argument with its legal niceties, Counsel maintained that "Woods belonged to neither parish, as he had slept in both at the same time."

He was returned to Eye, whose parish officers had obtained an order for his removal to the "Dolphin"—but Wortham and Burgate had contested it.

In the early 19th century a variety of maps came into general use—Enclosure maps, Tythe maps, Estate maps and Official Ordnance Survey maps—all delineating parish boundaries with great accuracy.

"Beating the Bounds" thus became irrelevant, but Rogation-tide processions through streets and fields continued in many parishes, intermittently. Recently the practice has increased, partly as means of Christian witness, also to help in promoting unity among the denominations, and by no means least, to demonstrate man's dependence on a Bountiful Creator.

A system savouring of slavery

(PUBLISHED OCTOBER 1962)

IN former times autumn was traditionally the season for hiring farm and domestic workers for one year from Old Michaelmas. Early newspapers advertised many hiring sessions, and this announcement of about 200 years ago is typical:

"Hundred of Earsham. A Petty Sessions for hiring and retaining servants will be held at Harleston, September 18, when, upon application to the Chief Constable at the 'Crown', all agreements between Masters and Servants will be registered gratis.—John Tuthill, Chief Constable."

This was the prelude to one of the many Hiring Sessions or "Statutes" which reached their peak between 1750 and 1800, then gradually faded away in the nineteenth century. How widespread they were may be gauged from the fact that no less than 25 of them were advertised in Norfolk alone—from Downham to Acle, from Holt to Harleston; and these were a mere fraction of the national total.

"Hirings" originated from the Black Death of 1348-9, that scourge which decimated a third of our population. Surviving workers demanded very high wages, until the Statute of Labourers (1351) fixed rates of pay and allowed any workers in excess of the needs of their own parish "to carry the implements of their husbandry openly to market towns, there to apply for hire in a public place".

So began the hirings, and the practice of displaying emblems.

The Poor Law of the fifteenth to seventeenth centuries definitely restricted the free movement of workers. As every parish was, by law, responsible for its own poor, newcomers who might be a potential burden on the parish rates were far from welcome.

But an Act of 1697 encouraged movement from place to place "for the better conveniency of living", provided the home parish granted a certificate promising "poor relief" if such should be necessary.

Mobility thus increased, and hiring sessions became both

popular and numerous in the eighteenth century. In the reign of George II (1727-1760), authority to hold them was delegated to the Chief Constables of the Hundreds. Harling held a sessions for "Guiltcross"; Harleston for "Earsham"; while a large village like Kenninghall held its own. Even larger places, like Wymondham and Bungay, held two sessions.

By September, the harvest gathered in, men and maids sought new masters and mistresses—perhaps at better wages. The old custom of bringing the tools of the trade was replaced by the wearing of "tokens"—the horsemen, a whiplash round his hat; the shepherd in his hempen smock, a knot of sheep's wool; the dairy maid, strands of cowhair in her bosom; the cook, red ribbons; the housemaid, blue streamers.

On the spacious approach from the Market Place to the porch of Diss Parish Church a vast array of men, young women and boys assembled to be hired on the third Thursday in September.

The grandparents of our older residents used to mention the table in the porch where the Constable sat—they recalled the haggling for wages and the babel of voices, the "earnest money" given to seal a bargain, and the exasperating practice of Diss urchins who pinned together hirer and hired during the heat of bargaining, to the embarrassment of some and the amusement of many.

The profusion of "Examinations for Settlement" in our parish records provides abundant evidence of the sessions.

Susanna Page, of Diss, "hired herself at Diss Petty Sessions, Mich. 1759, to Mrs. Jacob, of Eye, upon liking for a month, which time she served, and continued until Old Mich. 1760, at the rate of 6 guineas a year, a month's wages, or a month's warning".

Henry Sillett, gardener, entered the service of Sarah Smith, widow, of Diss, "in pursuance of an hiring at Diss Petty Sessions, 1760, for one whole year, at 5 guineas yearly, and 2s. 6d. hiring money".

Conditions of hire varied widely. William Bunn, farm servant, "let himself at Harleston Sessions, Mich. 1801, for one year, to Mr. Paul, of Starston, received a shilling hiring money, and was to have 10s. 6d. per week for his service, and milk for breakfast every morning".

But Robert Salter "let himself at Wymondham Second Statutes at Old Mich. 1816, as Hostler at the 'Maid's Head' at Newton

Flotman, with board and lodging, no wages, but was to take to himself the advantages of his situation as Hostler".

Judging from hundreds of "Examinations" perused, and these but a fraction of total hirings (since they referred only to persons seeking poor relief)—hiring sessions reached their greatest popularity between 1750 and 1800.

The earliest actually noted in Diss was 1747, the latest 1814. Advertisements for them in Norfolk decreased from 25 in 1762 to three in 1822 and only one in 1824.

According to "White's Norfolk", Harleston alone survived in 1883.

Though these occasions brought new masters and servants together, and afforded workers a chance of discussing rates of pay, they grew unpopular on both sides. Absence from work to attend sessions aggravatingly interrupted farm routine and more enlightened people thought it repulsive to see human beings offering themselves for hire.

The Editor of the *Diss Express*, a persistent campaigner against the system, wrote in 1868: "Happily such practices are becoming extinct—this custom, savouring of slavery is now almost obsolete".

Two friends remember hirings in the north even into the twentieth century.

Florrie Cutting, now 90, has told me she heard vivid accounts of the later sessions in the churchyard (c. 1830) from her employer, Rosetta Welham, who witnessed them and who died in 1907 at the age of 85.

The "Sessions Fair"—held from "time out of memory" on the day following the hirings, was banned from the Market Place by The Fairs Act of 1872, but many remember it continued on "Hewitts Meadow" until the First World War.

Then it was suspended—never to be revived and with it passed the last connection with the "Diss Hiring Sessions".

Help in distress—South Norfolk briefs

(PUBLISHED FEBRUARY 1963)

ON the very last page of the oldest Scole register is written: "Breifs: January 16, 1680, collected for Tadcaster in ye west riding, York, 2s." and "April 3, 1681 collected for Duxford in Cambs. 2s. 1½d."

The places mentioned had suffered some disaster from fire, flood, storm or pestilence, and these sums "collected on briefs" in Scole Church were to help them to rebuild.

It may be that in future months the Rector, wardens and treasurer of Scole Church will issue a national appeal for a fund to rebuild the burnt-out St. Andrew's, with the approval and under the patronage of the Bishop. In former times such an appeal would be known as a "brief".

Many of us can remember parish briefs—when someone in the parish suffered a grievous loss and went to the Rector to draw up a brief for him, a subscription list to help him overcome his setback.

In "Requests at the House" I came across this one: "Francis Ready have had ye misfortune to loose a poney as such Beg a Littel assistance Toward ye Loss". The churchwardens granted him £1 and doubtless others contributed too, to re-establish him in his carrier's business.

The earliest briefs were authorised by the Pope as head of the Church; then, at the Reformation, the prerogative passed to the Crown, and briefs were issued as letters patent under the Great Seal, with the instruction that they must be read in church during divine service.

I have a copy of one issued by Queen Elizabeth in 1560 "for the poore people that be strykene by the hande of God from there wyttes, kepte and mayntayned in the hospital of our Lady of Beddelem untyle God caule them to his marcy or to ther wyttes agayne".

It went on to authorise certain persons to traverse the country asking alms for this institution.

Briefs, then, were Royal Warrants to collect for some charitable object. In early Stuart times a petition for a brief had to be accompanied by a commendation from Quarter Sessions, testifying the genuineness of the appeal. After the Restoration (1660) the Lord Chancellor issued briefs and the collection was farmed out to "undertakers".

These examples are from South Norfolk records to illustrate the varied objects for which collections were made:

An early one from Gissing was in aid of Chard, in Somerset, which had been devastated by fire—"a collection gathered in the Parishe Churche of gyssinge in northefolke the 2 day of Nov., 1578, for the erecting of the Town of Chard". (The sum collected was "XXIId" of which Mr. Kemp gave "VId", and 23 others the remainder).

In 1644, when a Sessions certificate verified the extent of the damage and Parliament issued the authority, we find the churchwardens of Bressingham paying 2s. 6d. to "a man authorised under ye hands and seales of ye Parlamt. men for a losse of fyer done at Brinton in Warwickshire by Prince Rupert with ye losse of 10 men with other cruelties".

Loss by fire was the basis of most briefs. At Southwold on April 25th, 1659, "a fire whose destructive fury was heightened by a violent wind", consumed in the space of four hours the town hall, market house, market place, prison, granaries, shops, warehouses and 238 dwelling houses, with movable goods, nets and tackle for fish . . . and a variety of merchandise. The damage was estimated at £40,000 and 300 families were ruined.

Parliament granted a brief. Among the parishes which subscribed was Roydon, where "the sume of eighteene shillings and sixpence was collected June 24, 1659, towards the releife of the inhabitants of Southwold".

A similar calamity befell Holt on May Day, 1708, when "a great part of the town was destroyed by an accidental fire which burnt with such fury that the butchers could not save the meat on their stalls".

In the Billingford Register of Briefs appears: "1709, for Holt fire Norff. loss 11,258£, given 5s. 3d."

Redenhall papers include a contribution for another disastrous fire: "1641 gathered at the Church for Relief of Stratford upon Avon a towne in Warwickshire wch was burnt (pt. of it) with losse of 20,000£, gathered I say XXIs IIIId. Recd. this money Aprill 7.

1642. Chr. Smithe Collector of Briefs".

Archbishop Laud secured a brief for rebuilding St. Paul's in 1634—it was then in a state of decay and much abused. Redenhall responded with 68 subscriptions "as a free benevolence to his Maties' Justis at there meeting at Harleston by the inhabitants of Harlston and Redenhall for the Reedifyinge and bewtiffyinge of Paules Church in London"; while Bressingham contributed £3 15s. 4d. for the same object—there were 44 subscriptions, 1 at 4s., 3 at 2s. 6d., 2 at 2s. and the rest from 1d. to 6d.

Losses due to storm damage and personal losses of all descriptions were the subjects of briefs. Billingford records payments in 1660 of "1s. 8d. for Capt. Harrison", of "1s. 3d. for Edward Chastian" and "1s. for Robt. Endsdell" without disclosing what the losses were due to.

In the 17th century when there was much dissension in England, there were many hostile raids on our coasts. A notorious one occurred in July, 1691, when a French squadron "played the cannon of their galleys upon the Town of Teignmouth, Devon, and shot near 200 great shot thereunto. They then landed about 1700 men, who ransackt and plundered the town, burning and destroying 116 houses, 11 ships and barks in the Harbour, entered two churches in a most unchristian manner, tore the Bibles and Prayer Books in pieces . . . etc."

In all they did £11,000 worth of damage. A brief was granted and Bressingham records giving "the sum of 2 shillings and two pence upon the Brief for the relief of the Inhabitants of Tingmouth".

Any form of persecution of Protestants seemed to touch the hearts of Englishmen and to evoke a more generous response to a brief than usual. Billingford gave £1 in 1699 for "Persecuted French Protestants" and 10s. 6d. in 1680 for "Irish Protestants".

Redenhall was most generous in 1641, as it records: "Gathered by warrant dated 19 March, a particular of all the persons yt gave their benevolence for ye relefe for the distressed protestants of Ireland, £40-0-9". There were 372 donations.

Yet another cause which prompted ready response was the ransoming of captives taken and held by the Barbary pirates— either from audacious raids on our coasts or by preying on our shipping in the Mediterranean. It became the custom to free these captives by payment of heavy ransoms, though this did not abate the scourge. The Gissing Booke contains "a purticular of wt money was collected in ye towne of Gissinge uppon Sunday 29 of Dec. 1669 to a breife granted by His Matie to levie 30,000£ for ye redemption of Captives in ye hands of ye Turkes". There were 47 donations, in all £2 4s. 5d., of which John Gibbs, Rector, gave £1. In 1680 Billingford gave 12s. "for Christian slaves taken by ye Turks".

But briefs were unpopular, simply because they were abused. Many were so vague as to seem almost a "racket", and one is hardly surprised to note that Billingford contributed only 2d. towards "Jo. Wakelin's fire loss" in 1707 and Scole gave only 1s. 3d. in 1682 "for a town in ye West riding, Yorks".

Even Pepys condemned the traffic in briefs. On June 30th, 1661, he wrote: "To church, where we observe the trade in briefs is come now up to so constant a course every Sunday that we resolve to give no more to them". John Bryars, the forthright Rector of Diss and Billingford (1714-1728) entered this note in his Billingford Register, "I have always protested against these Briefs which I look upon as one of the Grievances of the Nation".

In the 19th century the response to an almost continuous flow of briefs became less and less—largely because the "Undertakers" swallowed up as much as two thirds of the proceeds in expenses—e.g. 1823. Brief for Fylingdales Church—(damaged £561 18s)—Collected by Brief £339 18s. 8d.—Expense of Patent £76 6s. 10d. —Collector's salary £158 5s. 8d.—Net result £105 6s. 2d. (less than one-third of the amount given).

Diss records 140 briefs between 1813-1827. The maximum given to any one was 9s. 6d., four produced nothing, and 119 just a shilling each. The total for the 140 was £8 9s. 2d.

These figures are significant of the attitude to briefs. For years there was controversy about them—well-known writers exposed their abuses. Having outlived their usefulness and acquired such an unsavoury reputation, they ceased under an "Act to abolish Church Briefs", 1828.

"Burial in Woollen"

(PUBLISHED FEBRUARY 1963)

AMONG the parish papers of Billingford I came across a scrap of paper containing these words:—*"Norff: Aug.* 30, 1729. Elizabeth Maston, of Thorpe Parva, made oath yt ye Body of Thomas Green, of Thorpe Parva, lately deceased, was buried in woollen only, according to an Act of Parliament made for that purpose. Sworn before me Abra: Cowper, Rector of Scole in ye presence of Eliz. Cowper, Isaac Cowper."

This was an "affidavit" required under a law which came into force on August 1st, 1678, and which stated: "No corpse of any person shall be buried in any shirt, shift, sheet or shroud or anything whatsoever made or mingled with flax, hemp, silk, hair, gold or silver, or in any stuff or thing made of any other material but sheep's wool only, upon pain of the forfeiture of £5".

The law further required ministers to keep "a register of all and every person or persons buried in their respective parishes", and that "some one, or more, of the relations of the deceased shall, within 8 days next after the interment, bring to the Minister an Affidavit in writing under the hands and seals of two or more creditable witnesses, stating that the deceased was not put in, wrapt or wound up on any shirt, shift, etc. . . . or in any coffin lined or faced with any cloth, stuff, or any other thing mingled with flax hemp . . . etc.".

The woollen industry of this country was then at a low ebb, and the purpose of this unusual Act was "to lessen the import of linen from beyond the seas, and to encourage the woollen and paper manufacturers of this Kingdom".

The law was observed strictly at first, and I have been able to examine the many ways in which a number of South Norfolk parishes recorded their "burials in woollen".

At Burston and at Wymondham a special register was kept, described as "A Register of Buryals in the parish of B (or W) in the County of Norfolke since the 1st day of August 1678 in pursuance of an Act Intituled 'An Act for Burying in woollen', made the 30th yeare of the Reign of Charles the Second 1678"

The Wymondham register was quite comprehensive, with names of deceased, the witnesses swearing the affidavit, and the Justice or Minister before whom the oath was made. There were some 2,500 entries between 1678 and 1735 when the record stopped —and probably observance of this tiresome Act ceased too. Witnesses might have to trudge miles to find a justice, so the Act was unpopular and irksome and ignored wherever possible.

The following extracts illustrate the varied ways in which Registers record the observance of the Act:

At Needham, the first mention was in 1698, when "Hannah Brad an Infant was buried according to a late Act of parliamt. Affid. Nov. 9". In 1712 "Roger Green was buried in woollen ffebruary 25, as appears by Affidavit made before Mr. Munns, Curate of Redenhall ffeb 28". In 1722 "Henry Flack was buryed March 17. affid: made in due time". No reference appears after 1728.

At Roydon—"Mr. John Dawney Rector of this parish died March 22 and was buried 24th. Certificate of his burial in woollen was made March 30. 1705 by Mr. Tilney Rector of Bressingham". In 1705 "Mary ye daughter of Samuel Roper died June 3rd, was buried ye 4th, certified ye 9th". Eight in all were "certied"—then there was no further reference to the Act.

At Wreningham—"Oct 4. 1721 Edmond Herrison was buryed". Oct. 6. 1721 "Mary Stagg made oth that ye bodye of Edmond Herrison was wrapt in and buryed In woollen only according to the Act of parliamnt sworn before me R. Branthward by Elize Jay and Mary Blogg". At Wreningham I found this gem (for spelling) —"Samial browen jun. made oth that the body of Samuel browen sen. was wreapted in wolen only according to the act of parliment, before Elezebth Jay, Mary blogg, before me R. Brant ye 15 day of october 1721". Starston continued to observe the law until 1798, but records appear in the Overseers' Accounts. "Old John Prime" had been on the parish relief for several years. In 1780 he died, and the expenses of burial appear thus:

"Laying John Prime forth 2s 6d; cleaning and washing for do. 2s 0d; Chas Tuthill for diging the grave 3s: for a coffin for do. 9s: for ye Bearers for do. 3s: for the Affidavit 6d". At Diss, Affidavits are recorded between 1685 (from which year accounts survive) and 1771—usually in the overseers' accounts. In 1688 "layd out for a coffin for Len Atkins 5s: layd out for 1 yd ½ White Baise to wind him in 3s: being with him and laying him forth 2s 6d: for Beere 12d: for an affidavit 6d". Another in 1693—"for woollen to winde wid Titshall 1s 4d; for winding her and making Affidavit 1s". The last reference to the Act, in 1771, was almost a casual one, "To Chas Ayton for making the grave, and Affidavit for wido Algers child, 1s 6d".

At Scole the law was observed immediately it came into force, but the Clerk who made entries in the register found considerable difficulty in spelling "affidavit". The first "Buriall in woollen" was recorded thus—"Sepult. John Baxtur and sunne of Omphery Baxtur and Mary his wife was buried September 4. 1678. and alphidavit of the same".

This was the last—"Sepult. Elizabeth Nicholes Buried Aug. 2. 1679. Alfedave of the same."

The most complete affidavit survives at Fersfield—"Norff. These are to certifie whome it may concern that Thomas Mallows and Mary Thrower made Affidavitt before me this day that Margrett Mallows being interred in the churchyard of ffarsefeild within eight days last past was not putt in, wrapt, wound upp or buried in any Shirt Shift Sheet or shroud made or mingled wth fflax Hemp Silk Hair Gold or Sillver or other then wt is made of sheep's wooll only Nor in any Coffinn lined or faced with Cloath Stuff or any other thing wtsoever made or mingled with fflax Hemp, Silk Hair Gold or Sillver or any other materiall but sheeps wooll only. Dated this 28th day of September 1679. Thomas Mallows (x his mark) Mary Thrower (x her mark) before me F. Bickley (Curate)".

Wymondham Register notes a case where the law was defied or ignored. In 1680 "Will Jubbs, Gent. Stephen Burrell, Gent. and Mary Low were buryed, of whose Interment no affidavit being brought according to the Act, for default the persons concerned were certifid and payed as the Act enjoynes".

In 1700 Thomas Deye, Sr., was buried at Eye in a linen shroud thus contravening the Act. A fine of £5 was exacted, and duly recorded in the parish register of the borough.

A few parishes observed this strange "protectionist" law until it was repealed in 1814—but in most places it had been, at the best, only partially obeyed.

Alexander Pope, in Epistle I of his "Moral Essays" (1733), ridiculed the provisions of the Act thus:

"Odious ! in woollen ! 'twould a Saint provoke !
(Were the last words that poor Narcissa spoke).
No, let a charming Chintz, and Brussels lace
Wrap my cold limbs, and shade my lifeless face:
One would not, sure, be frightful when one's dead —
And—Betty—give this Cheek a little Red."

The rustic sports of a century ago

(PUBLISHED AUGUST 1963)

RUSTIC sports were an essential part of all the great festivities of early 19th century, whether festivals of peace or Coronation or jubilee celebrations. They invariably followed the gargantuan dinners provided on such occasions for the poor, who, having regaled themselves lavishly, relaxed to enjoy themselves. Those were the days before spiked shoes, starting blocks and track suits or the 4-minute mile, and the emphasis was on entertainment and fun—the more comic the spectacle, the more popular it was.

Rustic sports of 1814 were described in different places in various ways—"Races on the Common, with other rural enjoyments"; "lots of fun"; gambols and other rustic amusements"; "rural and laughable sports"; and "sports and merry dancing".

These tags give an idea of the light-hearted atmosphere that prevailed, for these sports were intended as a feast for the eyes, a sort of dessert following lashings of beef, huge slices of plum pudding and copious draughts of strong beer—hardly the basis for serious athletic contests.

Fortunately the actual programmes of rustic sports at the Festival of Peace celebrations of 1814 in many East Anglian parishes have been preserved to provide a comprehensive picture of such proceedings.

The only events approaching anything in the way of atheltics were races for lads under 16 (usually for a pair of shoes as a prize), races for men (for hats or pairs of gloves); and flat races of a furlong run in bare feet, trousers and shirt.

Prizes offered seem rather strange to us today. For girls there was a "chemise race"—a universal favourite, so called because the prize was a chemise. At Framlingham "a chemise elegantly decorated with true blue ribands" was the first prize, while the second was "a pair stockings and garters with the Trafalgar motto —'England expects every man to do his duty' ".

And to add colour and gaiety to the occasion, each entrant received "two yards of riband to decorate the hair".

A reporter at Halesworth was carried away by the fleetness of foot of the competing Suffolk lasses, for he wrote "The airy competitors for the chemise flew like arrows to the goal".

At Hingham girls ran foot races "for gown pieces and shoes". Nor were the more portly matrons overlooked—for women over 30 ran for tea kettles—the winner at Framlingham receiving a copper tea kettle valued at 12s 6d, the second prize being a "tin tea kettle, value 5s".

For general popularity nothing gave greater pleasure than the sack race—an event which lingers on into our more athletic age of the 1960s.

It was, as it is now, for less athletic types, the lean and the portly, the swift of foot and the slow coach. All types had equal chance when "jumping in sacks", which favoured cunning rather than athletic prowess.

Donkey races, or "Jerusalem pony races" as they were often termed, were universal favourites, because of the unpredictability of the donkey's response. Sometimes they could be coaxed into activity but at others they would stubbornly refuse to budge, and quite often would throw their riders. Competitors invariably provided their own mounts, and the popularity of the races could be gauged by the valuable prizes offered (for those days)—£1 for the winners at Framlingham; a "new pad and bridle" at Hingham.

While the pig remains passive in the modern bowling-for-the-pig event, in the early 19th century it was the most active participant in the "pig hunt" or "Royal pig hunt". It was customary to turn the animal loose in the arena with a number of lusty men and the prize went to the first competitor to hold the pig up by its tail.

At the Bungay Festival the task proved impossible for there, according to reports, "A pig with his tail smoothly shaved and glibly soaped was let loose among 20 contenders for the prize. He who could fairly hold him up by the tail, was entitled to the grunter, but no one succeeded in catching the elusive animal".

At Halesworth "One pig worrior, with astonishing dexterity, caught and supported the grunter by its tail in about the time a man of energy could take up a stone".

Framlingham's programme included a diversion not noted elsewhere—a "smoking match" in which "one pound of tobacco was smoked for by six men". each competitor being provided with a churchwarden pipe and a quantity of tobacco, the first to reduce his quota to ashes receiving the coveted pound of tobacco.

Jingling matches were part of every programme. Jingling was a diversion in which all ten players were blindfolded except one, who kept ringing a bell in each hand while the others tried to catch him. The jingler himself was a nimble elusive customer, capable of frustrating the clumsy gropings, snatchings and stumblings of the contenders.

Less and less physical effort was called for as the sports progressed—the emphasis being on the ridiculous. "Grinning matches" or "Grimacing" appeared in every programme—in which, according to a Lynn writer, "pre-eminence was sought by distortion of the physiognomy".

The head was thrust through and framed by a horse collar, the prize going to the competitor making the greatest facial distortions, and Coltishall boasted one performer "so perfect an adept in the art that the contending parties speedily resigned the prize to him".

Events thus far had engendered much mirth and provided lots of fun, but the concluding events must have caused sides to ache.

At Coltishall they were billed as "Diving into Bowls of Flour". The competitors, with their hands tied behind their backs, were expected to plunge their faces into large bowls of flour to retrieve hidden apples in various stages of decay.

Such antics caused tremendous hilarity, as did the variation at Wiveton, said to be "a new species of musement", in which six men with their hands tied behind them dived into a large tub of water for oranges.

Only at one place, Ranworth, was a "camping match" part of the 1814 celebrations in Norfolk. That ancient and crude forerunner of football was contested (or fought?) between teams of ten men a-side representing Ranworth and neighbouring villages.

The game produced "some good set to's" and "a few bloddy noses", but Ranworth, long a centre of this rugged game, triumphed, "shook hands with their opponents, drank their ale, smoked their pipes and cracked their jokes with greatest good humour". Several thousands watched this battle, the prizes being ten hats for the winners, and ten pairs of gloves for the losers. Such were the rustic sports of the early 19th century—successors to the more vicious and barbarous "sports" of earlier days, such as bear-baiting, cockfighting, and bull-baiting, though these were still carried on surreptitiously for some years into the century.

Old trades

(PUBLISHED AUGUST 1962)

SOUTH NORFOLK is particularly fortunate in its wealth of 18th century parish documents, containing details of apprenticeships, warrants, removal orders, affiliations and poor relief, invariably signed by Justices of the Peace.

A careful study of some hundreds of such papers from several parishes has provided a picture of the variety of work carried on by a good cross section of the people, since trades or occupations were usually recorded at the examination before the J.P.s.

No less than 77 distinct occupations were noted, and this, of course, was in no way an exhaustive list. Many of these are still carried on, others have completely gone. Some, like the blacksmith, the wheelwright and the thatcher have almost disappeared. The trades named below were used by specific individuals when describing themselves at an interrogation by a Justice or Overseer.

By far the largest groups were connected with the land—the yeomen or "freemen" who owned land, the husbandmen or farmers who rented land, and the servants in husbandry (labourers) who hired themselves by the year at the annual hiring fairs at Diss, Harling and Kenninghall.

There were, too, the goose drovers who specialised in steering flocks of hundreds of geese along the quiet country roads and lanes to the Michaelmas and Christmas Goosey Fairs, not so today, with the whirl of traffic! Men described themselves as colt-breakers and jobbers in cattle—the former taming the fiery spirits of young horses and accustoming them to bit, bridle and harness, ready for cart, chaise or waggon—the latter, the jobbers, were just dealers.

The products of the land provided a livelihood for the miller, the butcher, the baker, the maltster and the beer brewer—the latter supplying the alehouse keeper (just a seller of beer) and the innholder (who sold beer but provided food and accommodation, too). An interesting group derived their living from hides and skins. The fellmonger bought up the raw skins from the slaughterer, to sell them to the tanner, who used local oak bark in his tanning pits at Diss and Buckenham to convert hides and skins to several kinds of leather. The curriers dressed and prepared the rough leather for the glovers, the cordwainers and the leather staymakers. The glover cut and hand-stitched his gloves on different types to meet the needs of fine ladies and beaus, as well as rough hedgers.

The cordwainers were shoemakers, a very numerous group then, for all footwear of leather was stitched by hand. The name cordwainer came from a French word cordouannier or cordonnier, a worker in leather from Cordova, in Spain. The name is perpetuated by a City Livery Company of London.

The waste wet hair from the currier was sold for mixing in with plaster—the churchwardens of Shimpling paid 1s. 6d. for carrying of ten bushels of wet hair from Diss for the steeple.

An 18th century description of Diss states, "An important craft in Diss affording employment to many, is that of leather staymaker." The humbler classes wore stays of stout leather, while ladies wore stays of canvas and jean, stiffened by whalebone.

"Both types are equally pistol proof and rigid." Happily both types have long been obselete, though staymaking survived in Diss till the 20th century. Saddlers and harness makers plied their trade in every village, but their craft has declined to small proportions today, as tractors have replaced horses.

Among the craftsmen in wood were the clogmaker, the wheelman (wheelwright), the cooper, and the chairmaker. The last named bodged or turned the legs of his crude chairs under a canvas awning in the open air—using a primitive treadle lathe. Basket makers were numerous, and there was an occasional lath-river, who rived or split his lengths of wood, to prepare irregular and twisted laths for the rough lath and plaster work of many cottages and barns. At a later date (19th century) I noted an advertisement for a cricket-bat-river.

The skilled tradesmen were the plumber, the brickmaker, the bricklayer, blacksmith, whitesmith (or tinman), glazier and thatcher. One man described himself as a brickstriker—and he had gone from Diss to Swardeston for his apprenticeship—his job, to strike off or level the clay in the wooden brick mould, just as today we would strike off a piled up peck of grain. Other skilled workers were the watchmaker, the watch chain maker, the bucklemaker and even one corkscrewmaker. The last three stated they had served their time as apprentices in Birmingham, before coming to S. Norfolk—but it took seven years to become an expert corkscrewmaker or bucklemaker.

South Norfolk crafts

(PUBLISHED AUGUST 1963)

JUST over 300 years ago—in 1636—a Diss Manorial Court confirmed that "the tenants of Diss Mannor have been accustomed time out of mind to make Hemp pitts upon Diss Moore and Cockstreet Green for the Retting of Hemp." Some years earlier, in Queen Elizabeth's reign, following a dispute between Parson Coxe and his Rectory Manor tenants, it had been agreed that "time out of memory of man the tenth shofe of Hemp had been brought to the Church Porch ready retted," in payment of tithe.

Retting was the first stage in the extraction of the valuable fibres of locally-grown hemp. From seed sown in April and May, the plant was ready for pulling in August, when it was tied up in small sheaves or "baits". Hemp stems were hollow, with a "thin bark of fibres" encasing the tender brittle woody part. When retted, or steeped in water, the softened fibrous bark was loosened from the "cambuck", or woody part, ready for the next stage —"breaking".

It was the practice in some places, notably at Hinderclay and Thelnetham, to "grass" the freshly-pulled hemp or lay it out on a meadow for "dew-retting". This process occupied about five weeks, and necessitated "turning" two or three times a week according to the weather conditions, whereas "water-retting" in ponds was completed in four to five days, depending on weather and temperature of the water. The expert retter could detect the completion of the process, by "feel".

Breaking came next. The "baits" were bundled together and removed to farm barn or cottage shed, where the stems were beaten with a wooden "swingle" to break the wood and detach the fibres, though with larger producers this was performed by passing the stems through a mangle-like machine with fluted rollers.

Scutching followed. It was really the completion of the breaking process, ending in the separation of cambuck from fibre. The former—known as "hemp-offal" was a useful fuel and even a saleable product. The word "scutch" was derived from a Scottish dialect word, meaning to beat or drub.

The raw, tangled fibre was next passed to the heckler, who heckled or combed it into various grades from fine to "tow". The word heckled—according to an old dictionary of 1842 presented to me by Mr. Ernest Hose, and an invaluable help with these curious words—appeared in several variations: Hickler, higlar, higler, hackler or hatcheler.

The German word was hechel, Dutch hekel, Danish hegle, Swedish hackle, Slavonic hakel—all meaning a "rake". Thus a hatchel, hackle, or heckle was "an instrument formed with long iron teeth, set in a board, for cleansing hemp from tow (the hards or coarse parts) i.e. it was a large species of comb. Some hackles had fine short teeth, others long coarse teeth."

The tangled fibres from the scutcher having been graded by the heckler, were then made up into 14lb. bundles of fine, coarse, or tow, ready for the market or for the spinner—for hemp was sold "by the stone". A good crop of hemp would produce 40st. of fibre per acre.

Chief markets were at Diss, Harleston, Bungay, Halesworth and East Harling. In Diss business was transacted near the parish pump on Market Hill (just below the present Barclay's Bank), since the official Town Scales for weighing hemp were kept on the premises now occupied by Mr. Brame.

The various grades of fibre were next passed to the "spinners" —usually women or children who carried on the work in their homes. It is said that hemp was easier to spin than wool, and that children of five or six years could easily acquire the art—and in fact were taught to spin. Payment for spinning was proportional to the fineness of the yarn produced.

Finally—though most hemp yarn was "woven brown", its natural colour, some was grassed for whitening or bleaching in the sun. While laid out on a meadow, it had to be kept moist.

Thus the stages in processing hemp for weaving were: Pulling, retting, breaking and scutching, heckling, spinning, and grassing.

A detailed study of the parish papers of border villages leaves no doubt whatever as to the importance of hemp growing, and of the trades or crafts to which it gave rise, along the Waveney Valley, from Elizabethan times to the mid 19th century.

Every farm and every cottage with suitable soil grew its patch of hemp, which provided fibres for making so many articles used in everyday life. In fact, next to yeomen, farmers, husbandmen and labourers in husbandry, naturally the most numerous groups in South Norfolk and North Suffolk, workers in "processing hemp" came a very close second.

The parish papers I have examined include apprenticeships, parish certificates, examinations for settlement, removal orders, bonds of indemnity, orders in bastardy, constables' warrants, inventories, and many other deeds and documents (where they have survived). They cover some 300 years—but only refer to those persons who for some reason or other "clashed with" or sought help from parish officers—a mere fraction of the total population.

Thus we find that Frances Peartridge, or Starston, applied to the overseer for the maintenance of her illegitimate child. She was asked the date of its birth and could only recall that it was "born in August in the hemp-pulling season" (1747), she having missed the chance of earning a few extra shillings at hemp pulling because of the arrival of the baby.

In 1764 the Churchwardens of Diss "placed John Catchpole, a poore child, apprentice to Nicholas Syder of East Harling, Higlar (i.e. Heckler) until the full age of 24 years, to be taught and instructed in ye art of yo Higlar".

Most parishes had hecklers—Robert Burcham (aged 29 in 1762) stated he had been a heckler at Bressingham with his uncle Samuel (also a heckler) since he was nine years of age. Peter Pearse, in a maintenance order of 1786, was a hickler, while Joseph ffisher (1762) and Robert Orford (1764), both of Bressingham, described themselves as "hemp dressers".

At Needham several men described themselves (18th century) as hatchelers, so, too, did Jonas Keeble, of North Lopham, as late as 1823 when describing his occupation for the registration of his child.

Starston has many references. In 1768 Jonathan Day "made agreement with James Walne, of Starston, to learn the trade of hickler, to serve one year and a quarter, to board and lodge himself, and to have for the same service 10s. in wages."

Thomas Bowen, of Starston, was apprenticed in 1752 to William Matthews, of Needham, as hickler, for five years, and was plying his trade in 1770. The Starston overseer, in his accounts for 1787, included 2s. 6d. "for a journey after fetching Davises Hickles from Hoxne".

Then there was the Barker charity school at Bressingham, founded in 1731 by Elizabeth Barker, widow of the Rector of Fersfield. Mrs. Barker was buried in a massive altar tomb on the south side of Fersfield Church. The inscription records that she "settled a tenement and land lying in Bressingham, upon the Rector and Wardens, the clear profits therefrom to be applied to teaching as many poore children of the parish above 8 years and under 10, as the profits would pay for, to read, write, spin and learn the Catechism".

The tenement remains to this day—and the schoolroom too, where children were taught to spin hemp over 200 years ago.

In 1774 John Barrett received 1s. 5d. for mending the children's wheels.

Hemp growing and processing survived well into the 19th century, for Alfred Fisk described himself as a hemp dresser in 1860 when he witnessed his son's marriage. Overseers' accounts teem with references to "tow wheels", issued to the poor by the parish to enable them to supplement their meagre earnings by spinning hemp tow into coarse yarn. Both Diss and Harleston boasted a "Tow-wheel maker" in the early 19th century.

Such names as "Heckfield Green" at Hoxne, mentioned in John Sherwood's will of 1572, leaving an "aniutye to the poore Inhabitinge in Brockdish"; "Spinners' Bridge" a quarter mile east of the Green; "Bleach Green Farm" at Wingfield; "Pit Lane" at Hoxne, the "Rettery" at Eye on the Hoxne Road; and the other "Rettery" at Eye where the Reading Room stands—all remind us of those earlier days when hemp growing and processing were a principal feature of Waveney Valley life.

Spinning was in school curriculum

(PUBLISHED AUGUST 1962)

HEMP was widely grown in South Norfolk villages in the 18th century. Processing it afforded a livelihood to more people than any other industry except husbandry. Small enclosures, rarely more than two acres, known as hemplands, dotted the lower parts of the countryside, usually near the cottages.

Hemp, much like a giant nettle, up to 12 feet high, was cut and spread out on the meadows for some weeks to rot. The heckler (or hickler) then beat the stems with a swingle (a wooden implement two feet long, like a large knife) to break the woody parts from the fibres. Then with a hatchel, or crude comb made from nails driven through a length of wood, the scrutcher combed out the fibres.

The hemp dresser cleaned them, the grasser or whitester laid them out on the grass to bleach in the sun, sprinkling frequently with water to prevent them shrivelling up. Women and children spun the yarn for the linen weavers to make into hempen-cloth for smocks, sheets and towels, working their simple looms in lean-to sheds beside their homes.

This weaving industry survived until 100 years ago—with Diss as the chief market. The Lophams had 47 hemplands as recently as 1833, and the Lopham churchwardens' books noted the purchase of hemp for the workhouse inmates "for spinning 92 clews of yarn £1 17s. 6d."

A Bressingham boy was bound apprentice to Gabriel Mallows to learn the art of "lening" weaving, while another Bressingham boy went to John Haylett of Buckenham, a twine spinner.

Two hundred years ago many commons had not been enclosed. Sheep were far more numerous than today. Woolstaplers, woolcombers, worsted weavers and hosiers carried on their trades here in considerable numbers. The staplers sorted the wools according to quality and length of fibre. The combers combed the finer yarns for spinning into yarn for the dyers, who in turn provided the worsted weavers with their raw material. Coarser wools were used by the hosiers, as stocking making was widespread.

Thomas Leech, of Diss, who died in 1845, was one of the last of the woolcombers. He is said to have led a great procession of his craftsmen in Diss in 1783, while his son, also Thomas, was described as "the last of the woolstaplers for which Diss was noted." when he died in 1872, aged 71.

Spinning of both hemp and wool was done mainly by women and children, the latter being taught the art from an early age. The rules of the Charity Schools at Banham, Bressingham and Diss expressly stated this, and spinning and weaving were regular occupations for the inmates of workhouses.

A traveller passing through Scole 300 years ago noted that the women "went spinning up and down the way, with rock and distaff in their hands." A spinster then was one who spun—an unmarried woman always being termed a singlewoman.

Wigs were on their way out in the early 19th century, but one man professed to be a barber and perukemaker, presumably to meet the demands of the dandies who came to the Diss Market and clubs. One singlewoman was a mantua maker—or mantle-maker Breeches makers were numerous, and a local tailor would advertise for breeches-hands or trouser hands.

Among a miscellaneous group were an ostler, who worked just for his keep and what he could pick up extra, several higlers, really hagglers who tramped the countryside buying and selling trivial goods, and haggling for the last penny; a riding officer of Customs; a razor grinder, who learned his trade in Birmingham; a chandler and soap-boiler; and a chimney sweep and fire defender.

The last was a Diss boy, apprenticed in Shoreditch for seven years to learn the art and mystery of a chimney sweep and fire defender. His memoirs — after squeezing through the dark and grimy chimney systems of old houses—would make interesting reading to the modern electrically-aided chimney sweep.

Finally, an unusual trade, a bottom-fyer. He spent his time wading in the Waveney, cutting down the weeds and crooming out the mud. He was the 18th century river dredger, and for his thankless and exacting task would receive 6d. per rod of $5\frac{1}{2}$ yards, and be lucky to earn 1s. per day.

Grow hemp or be fined

(PUBLISHED AUGUST 1963)

HEMP frequently achieves an unfortunate notoriety through its association with the drug traffic—less than a month ago coconuts containing hemp were sent by post from Jamaica to drug traffickers in this country. Two years ago a pianist was imprisoned on a hemp charge, having been tempted to smoke an Indian hemp cigarette—after which, he said, he could "improvise and concentrate better" when playing. And, more recently, detectives investigated the growing of hemp among winter cabbages in a Kent field because it was thought to be destined for drug traffickers.

A little over 100 years ago South Norfolk, and the Waveney Valley in particular, were noted for hemp growing—not for drugs, but as a source of fibres for making hempen-cloth, a coarse material then widely used for smocks, sheets and bolsters, and for "picklin", or bed tick.

The "Hempsheaf" Inn at Stradbroke and "The Hemplands" of North Lopham are a reminder of the days when small fields or patches of hemp were a common feature of our countryside, for hemp was grown on the same land year after year—hence the word "Hempland" to denote such land.

True hemp (*cannabis sativa*) is a temperate crop, a bushy plant up to about 10ft. high with nettle-like leaves. Its stems contain the valuable fibres which the Russians (now by far the principal growers) market in seven different grades, from very fine to coarse.

Nearly 4,000 years ago the Chinese grew hemp to produce fibres for making a range of products from fine fabrics to coarse ropes. In due course hemp was introduced into England via Brittany, where it was grown until recent years.

The dead were buried in shrouds of hempen cloth or linen in Saxon times, a practice that continued in England until Charles II enforced "Burial in Woollen". A local overseer's account of **1630** reads: "Paid to Mare Dausonne to bye her hempe for the laying forthe of ould Eyve and the sowing of him when he died . . .iis. viiid."

Table and bed linen, ropes, nets and sails were made from hemp fibre, so too were tents and hammocks made from canvas—a corruption of "cannabis".

By about 1200 A.D. hemp became so important that it was listed as a "tithe-able" crop. Later, Edward III's Queen, Phillippa of Hainault, encouraged weavers from her native Flanders to settle in England and introduce the making of finer linen goods—particularly in East Anglia.

Henry VIII (1533) and Elizabeth (1563) both encouraged the growing of hemp "for the better provision of nettes for help and furtherance, of fishing; and for eschewing idleness, in such counties or parts of counties where it shall be commodious and profitable".

Henry ordered one rood of hemp to be grown on every farm of over 60 acres. Elizabeth increased this to one acre "on pain of a fine of £5 instead of 3s. 4d." for not complying with the law.

The gathering of fines was farmed out under Royal Letters Patent. In East Anglia "Kirke and Garter" were granted a 7-year monopoly for collecting fines for non-observance of the Statute. Many farmers protested that their land was totally unsuitable for hemp and refused to grow it, but were forced to pay their fines.

So many complaints about "extortions" by the taxgatherers were received by the justices that an inquiry was instituted, and the indignant yeoman of Eastern England forced the repeal of the Act in 1593.

However—the soils and the climate of the Waveney Valley, especially "old meadows and low bottoms near rivers", were so ideal for hemp that it became a regular crop on thousands of holdings and cottage gardens, South Norfolk alone producing one eighth of the country's output of hemp.

One cannot peruse the records of any border parish without finding references to hemp. In Queen Elizabeth's reign (1594) a dispute arose between Richard Cox, Rector of Diss, and a number of his manorial tenants, over payment of tithe.

At the Court of Inquiry six elderly Dysseans—one aged "fower skore and ten yeares"—were interrogated concerning the "anncyent custom within the said parish between parsons and parishioners for the tyethes of woolle, hempe, honye and hoppes". With their long experiences of "fifity yeares and upwards" they all declared in turn that "tythe hempe was brought and left for the parson in the Church porch, every tenthe sheffe ready retted in the dry shofe".

The Scole Register of 1604 referred to the "mightie greate and fearefulle haille which did great hurt in corne, hemp and fruit", while the Scole Terrier for 1634 mentioned "two acres-and-a-half of Glebe land called by the name of Hempsacks".

The Palgrave Terrier (or inventory of lands and goods) of the same period noted: "There are no tythe customs, except 4d. for every milch cow yearly in lieu of tythe milk, and for every peck of hemp-seed sown, 8d. and no more".

Denton, Starston and Diss are rich in tithe records of the 17th century.

Entries like this are common in the Rector's book: "John Smythe of tythe Hemp, 1 peck sown 1s. 1d." (a peck would sow roughly one tenth of an acre); and "John Bidbanke, his ffarme ffor 2 pecks hempe sown 2s." (1678).

In 1700 the then Rector of Starston, Mr. Wiat, recorded in his little book: "I received likewise of Simon Wainforth 3s. for tythe Hempe." With some tenants tithe had already been commuted to a fixed annual payment. One tenant paid £5 15s. per annum for seven years "ffor all tithes", but he also agreed to provide, in due season, "a fat goose, a fat turkey and 2 dozen and halfe pigions" each year.

Moving to the 18th century we have abundant evidence of hemp growing. Kirby, in his *Suffolk Traveller* (1732-4), wrote: "The district in which Hemp is chiefly found extends from Eye to Beccles, spreading to the breadth of about 10 miles, which oblong of country may be considered its Headquarters. It is in the hands of farmers and cottagers. With Cottages it is the practice to sow on the same land each year. Manuring of 16 loads of dung per acre receives great attention. Sowing is from mid to end of April, but it will bear till May. No weeding is given, for Hemp destroys every other plant."

Hemp reached its maximum production in England about 1780, and when Arthur Young, a noted Suffolk writer on agriculture, visited Norfolk and Suffolk between 1804-13, he found "the Culture of Hemp much declined, scaroely one tenth of what it was some years past, chiefly due to the high price of wheat".

Still, he listed the border parishes and their acreages of hemp, the Lophams leading with 30 acres (divided among a host of patches varying from one tenth of an acre to four acres), Banham and Buckenham (20 acres each), Winfarthing (12), Bressingham,

Fersfield, Diss (ten each), Needham, Brockdish, Garboldisham (eight each); then Kenninghall, Roydon, Shelfanger, Burston, Gissing, Dickleburgh, Denton and Starston with smaller amounts.

Although "in decline", hemp continued in production as late as 1870, though in very small quantities. Mr. Reg. Woods, of Dickleburgh, has farm accounts for Bridge Farm, complete in every detail from 1808 to 1823. These show that in 1817 "£5-0-9 was paid for 26 Pecks of Hemp Seed at 3s. 10½d. per peck"—sufficient for 2¼ acres. Details of the costs of harvesting the hemp, processing it and making the fibre into hempen cloth are also given.

An item of news in an early number of the *Diss Express* (1865) carried the heading "Gigantic Hemp"—it went on to describe a stem of hemp in Mr. Martin Howe's garden at Brockdish "12ft. 9ins. high, measuring round the branches 19ft., girth above the ground 8½ins." Mr. Howe had several other plants ranging from 8ft. to 12ft. in height.

It is only about three generations ago that hemp disappeared from our countryside. Mrs. Roger Baker, of North Lopham, who died in 1962 at the age of 89, told me that her mother spun hemp; and Mr. Arthur Pearce, of Bressingham, has said that his grandfather was also a hemp spinner.

Finally—to confirm hemp growing a century ago, a note in *East Anglian Miscellany*, from a Suffolk man of 70, read: "When I was a boy (c. 1860) hemp was much grown, and I well remember seeing it at Worlingworth and Kenton."

Now it is a forgotten crop . . .

Woolcombers and worsted weavers

(PUBLISHED MARCH 1963)

DESCRIBING his impressions of East Anglia in his "Tour through Great Britain" in 1722, Daniel Defoe wrote "When we come to Norfolk we see the face of diligence spread over the whole Country. The vast manufactures carried on by the Norwich weavers employ all the country around in spinning the yarn for them." And some 40 years earlier Thomas Baskerville, touring with his friend Baker in 1681, came to the Scole Inn where he found "good wine and beer," but particularly noted that the women of the district "went spinning up and down the way, with rock and distaff in their hands."

Though Diss, just off the great turnpikes of those days, never achieved the same eminence in the woollen industry as its more illustrious neighbours, Norwich and Bury St. Edmunds, there is however abundant evidence that it was a centre of very considerable importance for woolcombing, spinning, worsted-weaving and hosiery making.

The earlier indications of this are perhaps fragmentary, yet quite definite. They occur before 1200 A.D. when a company of foreign weavers settled in the town. Among them were "Walter and Leurie sons of Dering", named in a document of 1195. The Diss manor had been granted by Henry I to Sir Richard Lucy, whose daughter married a Fitz-Robert, to whom the manor passed. In 1298 a descendant—Robt. Fitz-Walter—granted "William Partekyn, a Dier, the liberty of washing his wool and cloths in Diss Meer" on condition that "the gross die should be first washed off and that he should not suffer the drain of his dying office to run into the Meer".

One of the oldest surviving "deeds" I have seen, relating to Diss, records the purchase of property adjoining the Mere, by Wm. Cristernesse a "litster" (or dyer)—dyeing being an ancillary industry to the woollen industry. (Five centuries later, that property passed to the Aldrich family, and on the site today is Larter and Ford's).

Much more open common land existed in those days and sheep rearing was both widespread and profitable, particularly on the light Brecklands to the west of Diss. Thus Garboldisham became an important woolcombing centre—with two churches in close proximity. The Earl of Oxford, Patron of the livings, designed to allow one Church, "All Saints", to fall into decay because "it was difficult to procure a Clerk". The parishioners would not countenance this, and under the dynamic leadership of a "tailor" and a "woolcomber" raised funds to restore the church. The symbol of the tailor—a "pair of shears"—is carved in stone on the west face of the now ruined tower, and is still visible today, 10ft. from the ground. Ten feet further up is a "woolcomb" (now obscured by ivy)—the symbol of the woolcomber under whose leadership the tower was completed.

Peter of Disse—a "worstead weaver", is mentioned in Henry VIIIs reign—Michaell Goddard, another weaver, gave evidence in a tithe dispute in 1594, while Joseph Tainton plied the weaver's trade in "spacious sheds" in the Burston Road—(where Trenance is now). Several Diss families became opulent through engaging in the woolcombing business—among them the Camell family (Charles Camell, woolcomber, 1690) and the Wisemans (Edward Wiseman, Hosier 1734). John Gooding (1680) and John Hunt (1704) were specifically mentioned in the Burial Register as "Combers".

Many Indentures of Apprenticeship of "poore boys" to woolstaplers, combers, weavers and hosiers are preserved in the parish chests of Diss and nearby villages. Thus "Henry Andrews apprenticed to Edward Ruddleditch of Dickleburgh, 'wosted weaver', 1693"— "Robert. Baxter to Edwd. Archer of Diss, wollcomber, 1723"—"Wm. Smith to Thomas Driver of Diss, hosier, 1740" —"Rich. Lord to Robt. Smith of Old Buckenham, Worstead Weaver, 1772"—"Francis Riches to John Tight of Carleton Rd., Worstead Weaver, 1767"—"Joseph Cunstable of Dickleburgh to Samuel Browne of Frenze, woolcombers, 1796." Similar indentures have survived at Gissing, Pulham, Starston, Needham, Denton and Bressingham.

These—with the evidence from hundreds of "Examinations for Settlement" and "Removal Orders" which record occupations—indicate the widespread nature of the domestic woollen crafts in the 16th-18th Centuries. Wm. Brown of Needham (1761) describes himself as a woolcomber, so did Francis Aldis and Stephen Gissing, of Dickleburgh (1788 and 1776), George Raven, of Starston (1766), Wm. Barker, of Bressingham(1772), Moses Bingham (1734) and the Howard Brothers of Gissing (1772). Wm. Jex of Denton was a worsted weaver 1765, while Isaac Fitch (1793), Robert Rudd (1753), Henry Legate (1790), Edward Barrett (1804), Robt. Wright (1802) were all woolcombers in Diss.

The names quoted were only of those who for some reason or other had dealings with the Parish Officers—doubtless there were many many more whose names and occupations were never recorded.

The work of a woolcomber or stapler in the early days before machinery was invented for carding and combing wool, was an unhealthy occupation. Crude hand combs, like rakes with several rows of teeth, were used to disentangle the knotted and matted wool. One comb was fixed to a post—the tangled wool placed upon it, and another comb was then drawn across it to separate the "noil" (short and broken fibres later spun into yarn for hosiery) from the "tops" (long smooth fibres spun into worsted yarn). To maintain flexibility in the wool, the combs were heated over charcoal stoves or "combpots" which gave off noxious fumes unpleasant and often injurious to the "comber". It was this that caused many an apprentice to dislike combing and obtain a Justice's release from his indenture.

From the early 18th Century, when the Diss Charity School was founded, we get more than a hint of the importance of the domestic woollen industries in and around Diss. The School opened in 1714, on the ground floor of the old Guildhall, where "30 boys were taught reading, writeing, and their Church Catechism", while 12 or 15 of them were said to be "capable to spin if a stocke could be provided". An appeal (extant) was launched "to raise a sum to purchase a Stocke to putt such of the ladds as are fitt and capable, to the spining in the woolling manufacture, and make the schoole to flouresh".

Numerous inventories of household goods are also preserved —among them many references to "wool wheeles". Anthony Balls of Diss was in the Castle Gaol in 1710. Among his effects sold to raise money "to buy him out" of gaol were "ffoure wooll wheeles for his wife and children to spinn att". Overseer's accounts too provided much evidence of distribution of wheels to the poor—"to set them to work"—"a wool wheel for Rose Guch and one for Dame

Tuttle" (Gissing)—"wido Bird a wheel" (Diss) and "Spinning Wheel for G. Self 1805". The workhouse records of Diss mention no less than 66 wool wheels among "Requests at the House" (1810-1820).

But what happened to the combers' "noils" and "tops"? As already mentioned, they were given to the spinners after being stretched out into a series of strips called "slubbings". Smooth yarn for worsted weaving came from "tops"—fluffy fuzzy yarn for wool garments and hosiery spun from the noils. Most of it went to Norwich to be woven—in the "city of vast manufactures".

The opulent Camells and Wisemans died out—but one family lived for over 200 years and through six generations, on Market Hill. It was the Leech family, who first appeared in the middle 17th Century—David Leech was the first—and five generations followed (all named Thomas). They were variously described as woolcombers, woolstaplers, hosiers. The fifth and last Thomas Leech died in 1872, aged 71, and was stated to be "the last engaged in this manufacture for which Diss was once famous". Thomas's father had died in 1842 (aged 85) and in the first half of the 19th Century the Leeches were employing Robt. Hall, James Buttle, John Bishop, Chas. Williams, Edwd. Barrett, Robt. Wright and others as expert combers. They were old hands—but no apprentices enrolled then, as the industry was in decline here, as it expanded in Yorkshire and other parts.

When the workhouse was converted to almshouses in 1834, many wheels, looms, and a warping bar were found unused in the attics. Long before that there were indications of decline as the machine age slowly stifled domestic industry.

Even in 1781 Sam Thurlo, of Dickleburgh, "forsook combing" to take charge of the parish workhouse—Henry Woolsey (1796), of Diss, changed from a comber to a sawyer—Robt. Buxton "left the trade"—and even Thomas Leech became a tax collector as his woolcombing business dwindled. His combing sheds, 35 x 11 yards and 26 x 10 yards, were only demolished a few years ago. They were behind the U.D.C. offices overlooking the Mere.

In 1877 the official town weights were sold to Joseph Fisher, of Barnham Broom, for £24 12s. 6d. Each unit was marked 'Diss'. That marked the real end of the woollen industry in Diss. The only existing reminder of a once flourishing industry and its manifold activities on Market Hill where raw wool and finished yarn were bought and sold—is the wooden block and wheel in Mr. Brame's premises, from which the town scales were suspended. And I often wonder if the profusion of teazles in a field at the Heywood are descendants of those grown in the heyday of the woollen trade, for 'teasing' the surface of finished woollen products.

Saint Blaize—Patron of the Woolcombers

(PUBLISHED MARCH 1963)

NO account of the Woolcombers would be complete without mention of their patron Saint, St. Blaize, for it was on or near St. Blaize's Day, February 3rd, that they staged their great pageants and celebrations, reminiscent of the Guild processions of pre-Reformation days.

St. Blaize was Bishop of Sebaste in Cappadocia, a part of Asia Minor, in the 3rd century. Beloved and saintly, he used to retire from the throb and bustle of town life when his official duties were completed, to spend hours in private meditation on an eminence overlooking the town.

To his retreat—a cave in the hillside—came animals and birds, with which he made great friends and which are said to have nourished him in times of necessity.

It was during his term as bishop that one of the periodic persecutions of the Christians took place, in the reign of the Roman Emperor Diocletian. Driven from his home, St. Blaize sought refuge in his hillside cell, where he was sustained by his animal friends until apprehended by the Roman soldiers who arraigned him before the Provincial Governor.

He maintained and stoutly defended his faith and beliefs as a Christian, and even under cruel physical torture he refused to deny his Master, even when his flesh was lacerated with crude iron combs such as those used by woolcombers. His spirit remained undaunted and when finally he was beheaded in 289 A.D., on his way to execution he extracted a fishbone from the throat of an ailing child. Thereafter, his blessing was always invoked for ailments of the throat.

St. Blaize is said to have visited England and to have lived in Cornwall, giving his name to the village of St. Blazey, not far from Fowey and St. Austell. The former custom observed there, of lighting bonfires on his feast day is reputed to be derived from a pun on his name: "Making a blaze."

His figure appears in stained glass windows and on inn signs—in districts where, at some time, the wool industry flourished, though many inns have changed their names as circumstances have changed. An inn in Kendal, Westmoreland—once a centre for combers and weavers—has a fine modern sign showing St. Blaize.

He is usually depicted in his bishop's robes, bearing in one hand a comb (because to him was attributed the invention of the woolcomber's art), and in the other a lighted taper, symbolising him as a "burning shining light" among Christians. At his feet rests a swine's head to mark his conquest over worldly desires, and surrounding him are beasts and birds—his friends and companions in his seclusion from the world.

Because combs were used to torture him, and because of his alleged invention of the woolcomber's art, he became the patron saint of all woolcombers. In districts where the art was widely practised, it was the custom to mark his feast day with pageants and processions.

Norwich, Bury, Bradford and Colchester were among the towns where the custom persisted into the 19th century, and Diss, in a smaller way, staged similar events until past 1800. One publication, *A Picture of Diss* records that "Masters and men (staplers and combers) were wont to celebrate St. Blaize's Day with a grand pageant, last observed in Diss in 1801".

It was in this pageant that Thomas Leech represented Bishop Blaize—the last-but-one "Thomas", who died in 1842 aged 85. The occasion followed a traditional pattern: A long, picturesque and impressive parade through the streets, with halts for "orations" at various points, to eulogise the bishop and to offer up petitions for peace and prosperity for the craft.

Central figure was St. Blaize himself, though Jason and the Argonauts who went in search of the Golden Fleece to Colchis, played conspicuous parts.

The procession on St. Blaize's Day in Diss in 1801 was led by trumpeters, immediately followed by "the Marshal-man". Then came "Peace", represented by a damsel on horseback, "richly robed and caparisoned" and bearing a dove and olive branch on her head. Elegantly dressed children bearing wooden bowls, replete with fruit and nature's gifts, or bearing sheaves of corn, escorted "Plenty"—another beautiful girl, also on horseback, followed by a group representing the Argonauts accompanying the athletic figure of Hercules.

A richly-draped palanquin, borne aloft by four sturdy men, was next in the procession. On it rested the "Golden Fleece" —Jason, in a phaeton drawn by four horses, flanked by Castor and Pollux and attended by more Argonauts. The Militia Band then heralded the approach of the venerable Bishop Blaize (in the person of Thomas Leech) in another phaeton, drawn by six horses, and attended by his chaplain, pages, and vergers. He was richly robed, and bore a curious mitre of wool upon his head.

Bringing up the rear were some four score workers "ingeniously and fancifully dressed and embellished" to represent the many individual trades connected with wool production and processing —shepherds and shepherdesses in immaculate smocks, bearing their crooks—sheep shearers with their "croppers"—combers with crude iron combs—spinners with rock and distaff—"twisterers" —dyers—weavers—pressers and packers

The procession assembled on Diss Common, near the old workhouse. It moved to "Pound Corner"—where the Church Hall now is—where "Peace" eulogised St. Blaize to the crowd assembled in "Pound Piece", on the south side of Back Lane, thus:

"With boundless gratitude illustrious Blaize
Again we celebrate and speak thy Praise.
Britons do still revere, and Fame proclaim
To wondering nations, thy auspicious name.
Thousands to thee, the Founder of our Art
With thy Great Sire, their equal warmth impart.
With breasts inflamed we now our Homage pay,
And sound thy worth, on this thy Festal Day."

Then followed tributes to Jason and to the art of the wool-comber, and an appeal to St. Blaize to continue his blessing on the craft, and on the country's struggle against Napoleon.

"While you assist, Commerce can never fail
Nor other Powers o'er Britain's sons prevail."

The cavalcade moved on to the Market Place, where "Peace" made a further oration from a special dais. After lamenting the disastrous effect of "all-consuming war", which caused industry "to droop her head", she concluded with an exhortation to "let wasteful war retire, and Trade, on soaring wings to fame aspire".

Passing up Market Hill—still the centre, but once the thriving hub of the woollen industry of Diss—the procession wended its way, via Cock Street, to The Green, where "Plenty" invoked the Goddess of Peace to "smooth the brow of care" and to dissipate "pining want and grim despair". The final appeal and charge, uttered with considerable feeling, was —

>"Come Goddess ever dear —
>Let Music's all delighting powers
>Awake and charm the soul —
>And let the mirth elated hours
>In gay progression roll."

So ended the organized and official celebrations—but, alas, many interpreted the last two lines rather too literally, by patronizing the taverns and drinking houses all too freely, and with sad results.

St. Blaizes' Day had gradually become associated with "Bacchanalian revelry"—hence the expression "drunk as blazes".

These celebrations of 1801 were the last ever held in Diss to mark St. Blaize's Day, but similar events were held in Bradford in 1825 and on a magnificent scale in Norwich (1836) at the opening of a new yarn factory.

Diss weavers

(PUBLISHED AUGUST 1963)

SIDE by side with the growing and processing of hemp in South Norfolk went the weaving of hempen-cloth, a strong coarse material used for sheets and shirts, slops, smocks, frocks and picklin (tick), and many household linen articles.

Francis Blomefield, beginning his *History of Norfolk* with a description of Diss (1736), wrote: "The Market is kept weekly on Friday, the chief of which consists in the linen-cloth manufacture for which the Market is famous, great quantities being sold here."

This was obviously no new feature of the market, but one of very long standing. Blomefield attended school in Diss for a while and as he wandered through the market he would have seen the bundles of hemp and rolls of hempen cloth offered for sale. Much of both was produced in Diss itself, and large quantities came in from the neighbouring villages from cottage spinners and weavers.

Of few local industries can there be a greater wealth of historical and documentary evidence, than of the Diss linen industry.

In *Betts of Wortham* mention is made of a handmade linen tablecloth, with the head of Queen Elizabeth on it, "woven by the weavers of Diss long famous for their skill". That was over 400 years ago.

One linen weaver who at the age of "three score and seaven yeares" gave evidence in the 1594 inquiry into the Customs of the Manor, must have been an apprentice at the time Queen Elizabeth was born, and was a journeyman weaver some years before Henry VIII died.

The deeds of the house now called "Trenance", at the junction of Mount Street and Walcot Road, show that Samuel Bolter, a master linen weaver, occupied the premises "with spacious outhouses and weaving sheds" in 1628. Not long after, it was burnt down, but on the same spot another house and buildings were erected. Later they become the home of generations of Eatons, who were noted linen weavers until the early 19th century. The house was known as "Eaton Lodge".

Evidence of the large number of weavers in Diss has been gleaned from the hundreds of parish papers surviving. These papers became much more numerous after 1696-7, when William III passed Acts of Parliament enabling persons "for their better convenience of liveing to remove into towns or parishes where the increase of manufactures would imploy more hands".

Right through the 18th century a succession of apprenticeships, bonds of indemnity, and so on, provides a picture of a very considerable hempen-linen weaving industry, mainly domestic, but with a few larger employers like the Eatons, George Wharton, and George Womack, who employed several journeymen and apprentices.

Eaton's premises have been mentioned; Wharton's were behind what is now Lloyds Bank, and Womack's adjoined the "Saracen's Head" yard and bowling green. Scores of individual weavers worked in their own homes—like James Quantrill, near the "Cock" Inn—all training their apprentices.

Here are a few instances from the numerous papers in which Diss weavers were named:

In 1653, "laid out to Sam Wiseman with Popey to be bound the trade of a lininge weaver, 2£—from the churchwardens' accounts when 'Popey' was bound apprentice

In 1764—"Wm. Dixon, a poore child, apprenticed to John Dixon until the full age of 24 years to be taught and instructed in the art of linnen weaver".

In 1738 Thomas Margerom, a linen weaver, was charged before a magistrate with being the father of Elizabeth Dunk's illegitimate child. He signed a "bond of indemnity" in the sum of £40, agreeing to support the child until it should reach 14 years.

In 1785 John Hubbard's wife applied to the overseers for relief. Her husband, a linen weaver, had "run away and left his wife and family chargeable to the parish of Diss". From the Justice, John Frere a warrant was obtained to apprehend Hubbard, and bring him, before a Justice for appropriate treatment. (He spent some time in 'reflection' in Wymondham Bridewell).

In 1786, Henry Knowles, a linen weaver, obtained work in Diss, and according to custom, presented his parish certificate from Metfield, showing that that parish, his place of settlement, would take him back if circumstances compelled him to apply for relief. Henry found work in Diss congenial and regular, for in 1787 his brother Sam, another linen weaver, arrived from Bungay to work here, as did John ffarrant, from Palgrave. The parish certificates they produced have been preserved.

In 1789 Sir Thomas Maynard, of Hoxne, a Justice, signed a warrant to apprehend William Ashman, a linen weaver, suspected of being the father of a child or children expected by Mary Hines. He, like Thomas Margerom, signed a bond of indemnity to come into operation when the child (or children) arrived.

These examples, with a host of others, indicate the extent of the 18th century linen weaving industry in Diss. They refer, of course, only to those who came directly under the scrutiny of the parish officers, and it should be realised that the great majority of weavers carried on their work peaceably, and without leaving any written record.

Judging from all the evidence—a mass of it indeed—the industry reached a peak in the second half of the 18th century. Home production of hemp and cloth had been stimulated by the war between Russia and Sweden in 1741, when imports of hemp from the Baltic were curtailed. Rivalry on the high seas between Britain and France during the Seven Years War (1756-63), and later when France sided with the American Colonies in their bid for Independence, interrupted trade. Prices of home-grown hemp rose—and the growers, scutchers, hecklers, spinners and weavers were very busy.

But during this period of boom there was considerable crime in connection with hempen cloth—thefts of large quantities being frequently recorded in the weekly news-sheets.

Much cloth from Diss was sent by road for sale in Norwich —and events such as this have their counterparts even in 1963. On February 13th, 1770, William Norris, of Diss, was charged with stealing 26 yards of cloth from the stage waggon of John Bray, of Diss, on its way to Norwich. Norris was apprehended and, after detention in Norwich gaol, he was sentenced to "seven years' transportation" to a penal settlement overseas. The material —hempen cloth—would be worth 1s. per yard, and the value of 26s. for the piece would represent about one month's wages.

In 1776 John Bruce stole 27 yards of linen cloth from a carrier's waggon, but greater leniency was shown to him—he was merely "publickly whipt in the Market Place at Norwich".

Organised gangs, too, raided "bleaches"—meadows where the cloth was laid out for bleaching by the sun. A Palgrave man,

Edward Grimwood, was instrumental in discovering a "gang of 13" including men from Snetterton and Attleborough, involved in the theft of "20 score of fine hempen cloth"—from a local bleach in April, 1761. Transportation followed their arrest.

But decline set in. Arthur Young (1813) noted the decrease in hemp acreage in South Norfolk, and parish papers reveal that after about 1800 many young weavers turned to other work. Jacob White, weaver of Diss, applied for relief in December, 1815, "having had no work since Michaelmas". George Hey, another weaver, undertook the onerous task of "Governor of Diss Workhouse" —not a lucrative appointment by any means.

Fewer "tow-wheels" and looms were requested from the overseers, and they accumulated in the dust of the workhouse attics.

Fewer boys became apprentices. John Smith, whose father and grandfather were weavers, "took to weaving in 1803 at the age of 12". He first made a piece of hemp cloth, and in 12 months was "master of his business", progressing then to twills and huckaback, all linen fabrics, until 15 years of age. By 1819 he found work so irregular that he sought work in Norwich making "Bombazines".

Yet the industry lingered on, the old weavers sticking to their trade. In the 1830s the sorry plight of the handloom weavers generally led to an investigation of their state by a Government Commission. A report on "The State of the Handloom Weavers" was published in 1839.

The Commission visited Diss, where only one manufacturer, Henry Warne, was giving out work for making drabbett, huckabacks, sheeting and shirting from hemp fibre. He employed 63 persons—40 men, 20 boys and three women. His premises were those now occupied by International Stores, and the adjoining property to the north.

Warne told the Commission that competition from power loom products had not as yet affected his market, and he was anxious, in fact, to expand, but had failed to increase his staff of weavers.

One weaver, John Bradley, was interviewed. He had fought for five years under Wellington and was a Waterloo veteran. Now he was working 15-16 hours a day "which, deducting time for meals, left 13-14 hours actual work, for 16s. a week from weaving two chains of hempen cloth per week at 8s. per chain". His output was far above the average.

Samuel Crick, another weaver, made 1½ chains a week and earned 12s., "giving him 10s. clear after deducting 1s. for winding quills, 6d. for starch, 6d. for candles".

The report stated that weaving "was heavy for women". Only three engaged in it, earning 5s. to 6s. per week, a little above the average for female labour in East Anglia.

Some weavers worked in their own homes, earning wages above average, for "though they had less companionship than in the workshop, they were not so readily led away to spend their money on drink". The Diss weavers were commended by the Commission. Of Haverhill, where 100 looms were idle, the report stated: "From evidence obtained at Diss there is good reason to believe that the weavers of Haverhill might do much more work if they exerted themselves."

The old weavers retired, or died, and the industry finally came to a halt. Yet in the Parish Registers (1813-1861) no less than 31 linen weavers are named, with a smattering of 'hemp dressers', a 'cloth-bleacher', a 'linen hawker' and two dyers.

Times were changing indeed. More men became employed in the newer industries of mat weaving and brush making, while to replace hemp, now out of favour, flax growing was being encouraged and eventually the new factory at Waterloo, Scole, was to employ many.

The adventurous, too, were lured to join the great stream of migrants to the New World.

Shortly after the report was published, Henry Warne closed his Mere Street factory—but the ageing weavers stuck to their work to the end and were doing "home-work" for him until mid 19th century.

Today we have only the evidence of parish papers, guide book references and Drapers' Alley to remind us of a once thriving industry with its weavers' halls at both the "Saracen's Head" and "Greyhound" inns.

18th Century weavers of the Waveney Valley

(PUBLISHED AUGUST 1963)

SINCE writing of the Diss weavers I have seen an interesting notebook on Shelfanger and have had the opportunity to study the Shelfanger parish papers, locked away in a chest for many years. There are indentures of apprenticeship of Shelfanger boys to "hicklers" and to "linen weavers"—of whom there were many in the village in the 18th century. One 1755 indenture notes that Joseph Battelly had at the time of his apprenticeship as a hickler "wearing apparrell as follows, viz., one Duffile Coat, one Duffile waist coat, an old coat, two new shirts and two old ones, one pair good sheepskin breeches, one new pair of shoes and a tollerable pair of shoes more, two pairs of stockings and an indifferent Hatt."

This discovery of a hempen linen industry in Shelfanger is a reminder that though Diss was by far the principal centre for the weaving and marketing of hempen cloth, there were many other centres in neighbouring villages.

Mr. Harrison, the Rector of Shelfanger (1897-1912) who compiled the notebook on the village, referred to a document of 1681 in which a "Wm. Chapman, linnen weaver" was mentioned, and added that for several years after he came to Shelfanger (1897) an old man who was born in 1813 and died in 1906, aged 93, could remember "when weaving was largely carried on in the village and many cottages in Shelfanger had looms in them."

Shelfanger was but one centre and not by any means the most important. Recently, looking through the Roydon Register, an unusual series of entries confronted me, under "Burials". There were the names of no less than 11 linen weavers who died between 1726-1743, for instance: "1728. Wm. Algar, linnen weaver, buried March 30" and "1736. Thomas Holmes, linnen weaver, buried March 15".

It was not the normal practice in those days to record occupations in the register—hence the importance of these. We lose touch with the Roydon weavers after this—parish papers have not survived—until the new Baptismal Register of 1813, which, by law, required the trade or occupation of the father of a child to be stated. The first entry at Roydon, in 1813, was the baptism of "Charles, son of Samuel Woodrow, weaver", followed by "Sarah, daughter of Wm. Anness, heckler"

The word 'weaver' occurs 27 times until the last in 1842, and there are 13 hecklers, two hemp dressers, a hawker, a whitester and a bleacher.

The Roydon Marriage Register from 1837 also recorded many weavers, but it was the "Sempstresses" that caught the eye. Emma Downing, a bride in 1839, described herself as a "Sempstress". In the same year Wm. Thurlow, weaver, of the Fen, married Jane Baldry, sempstress, also of the Fen.

No less than 21 sempstresses are mentioned as brides between 1837-1859, without doubt working in their own homes on "piece work", stitching up smocks, sheets, pillows and bolsters for sale in the market and shops of Diss.

By the mid-19th century the hempen linen industry of Roydon had died out—and both men and girls trudged into Diss to work in the matting and brush making industries, as the Register shows.

Another concentration of linen weavers occurred at Palgrave. One would suspect this after reading the earliest "Terrier" mentioning the Guildhall—the old Tudor House near the "Swan" —with its "hempland" adjoining.

But it was a flimsy-thin Register of "Births, Marriages and Burialls, 1698-1706" that revealed such a wealth of information. Entries were made by the Parish Clerk in what was probably a rough book containing names for transfer to the "fair copy" in a more substantial Register later.

It included the occupations of all who died, and of the fathers of all children baptized—something exceptional for that period. Thus: "July 16th, 1699. Birth. Elizabeth, daughter of John More, linnen weaver, and Elizabeth his wife"; and "Burial. Anne, wife of Samuel Algar, linnen weaver. Jan. 18, 1699".

Among the many weavers named at Palgrave was Thomas Gooderham, father of another Thomas, baptized in 1705. The young Thomas also became a weaver, for the weekly paper of March 28th, 1770, showed that at Bury Assizes Benjamin Batterby was sentenced to seven years' transportation for stealing a quantity of hempen cloth from the workshop of Thomas Gooderham, of Palgrave.

A blank occurs in the Palgrave story in the 18th century but in the new style Registers of the 19th century we find 13 linen weavers named between 1813-1849, along with Rachel Aldridge, sempstress, so the industry appears to have succumbed here about 1850, as in other places.

Bressingham was another great hempen cloth weaving centre. In 1635 the churchwardens there paid 4s. 8d. "for Hempe for a Bell Rope and making thereof", and in 1701 they placed "Samuell Manneing apprentice to Thomas Okly of Bressingham, Lening weaver"

A steady stream of apprenticeships occurs there, which, with information from a fine set of parish papers and the 19th century Registers, gives a fair picture of a considerable and continuous industry in the parish until 1856—through generations of several families For instance: "1840 Jeremiah Brown (21), weaver, son of Wm Brown (weaver)"; and "1842 Benj. Francis (weaver), son of Robt Francis (weaver)" appear in the Marriage Register

No less than 58 weavers are named, with their accompanying hecklers, etc , before the industry dwindled away in the mid-19th century

Dickleburgh, too, was another scene of the hempen cloth industry, with many 18th century apprenticeships and other references. But probably the most interesting information comes from the early 19th century farm account book now in the hands of Mr. Reg. Woods.

In 1809, J. Rout was paid 1s 8d. "for Bunshing 1st. of Hemp at Michaelmas time" and Berry Leggett received 11s. 6d. "for 'waveing' 21½ yds. of cloth". Berry was still weaving in 1811, for he earned £4 11s. 8d. "for manufacturin 4st. of Hemp into Cloth".

Then, in 1817, Robt. Woods was paid £1 for "waveing" 30¾ yds. of cloth at 8d. per yard. "Waver Woods" was subsequently employed as a jobbing gardener when the hemp-cloth industry declined, for he received "1s. 6d. for 1½ days gardning".

There is a record, too, in Dickleburgh, as in other places, of some irregularity: "Reeling false and short yarn". This was an offence, and quite a widespread one. A woman spinner from

Dickleburgh was sentenced at the Norfolk Assizes July 1770, to detention in Wymondham Bridewell for committing such an offence.

Moving down the Waveney Valley we find great weaving activity at Brockdish, Needham, Starston, Harleston, Denton, Earsham and, of course, at Syleham, Hoxne, Bungay and Beccles on the Suffolk side.

At Needham the names of 23 linen weavers were recorded between 1719 and 1831—the Frewers, Reeves, and Matthews, families practising the craft through several generations.

All the processes from growing hemp to weaving and finishing product were carried on—it was here I first encountered "hatchelers", interspersed with apprentices, hicklers, hacklers, weavers and tow-combers.

In Denton and Starston—quite considerable centres for hempen cloth making—the industry had died out by about 1830, the last to be mentioned being James Keable, journeyman weaver at Denton (1826) and Daniel Smith, Whitester, at Starston (1830).

At Harleston the decline of a once large and prosperous industry must have been complete by 1810, for no references to any linen crafts appear in the parish registers—and the parish papers have not survived to provide any clues.

Harleston, in fact, came under the influence of Norwich, and by 1800 was engaged in making bombazines for the City merchants.

At Brockdish "Benjamin Harper, linnen weaver" appeared in a ffeoffment of 1696, and "Heckfield Green" was mentioned in 1572, so the village had a long tradition of "hempen-linen" making.

But while the industry died out in other places, it survived and expanded in Brockdish, though the actual work was carried out at Syleham Mill.

The names of a succession of weavers occur in the 19th century registers. From 1838 no less than 85 are named in the Marriage and Baptismal Registers. The old water-driven Corn Mill was converted in 1839 to the double purpose of grinding corn and driving looms, lightening the task so women could engage in weaving

Fifty-three of the 85 named were women—brides and mothers. In 1850, Wm. Atkins (weaver), son of Benj. Atkins (weaver), was married; in 1853, Henry Randall (weaver) married Eliza Green (weaver); and in 1854, Simon Finch (a deaf and dumb weaver) married Susanna Smith (weaver).

Then, in 1860, John Petts (weaver), son of Thomas Petts (weaver), married Eliza Crick (weaver), daughter of James Crick (weaver).

The making of drabbet, shirting, sheeting and huckaback was continued under Messrs. Chase, Edwards and Holmes, who assumed control of the factory when Mr. Charles Warne became insolvent. Later still, the Syleham Drabbett Co., linen and smock manufacturers, owned the mill and the making of "cloth" ceased towards the end of the 19th century.

Space prevents more than a passing mention of Hoxne—where hemp was grown and processed in considerable quantities and where looms were worked by a water mill—as at Syleham—but the industry ceased well before the middle of the 19th century.

A search through Bungay "papers" revealed that in the 15th century every house of importance in Bungay wove its own hempen linen, the last cloth being made in premises in St. Mary's Street, where six looms worked until 1855. Charles Chapman was the very last hempen linen weaver there—26 were named in the Registers from 1814 to 1838, with three hicklers and a sempstress.

A combination of circumstances led to the extinction of this once-important Waveney Valley industry. Hemp ripened just at harvest time, and was a labour consuming crop when labour was needed elsewhere.

Railways, too, had spread throughout the country and had made possible the wider and cheaper distribution of softer and more refined cotton fabrics.

The Syleham factory is really the only survival, though its raw materials are no longer locally produced, and weaving has ceased. Of course, the Lopham linen industry continued until 1925, but that was so specialised as to deserve special mention in a subsequent article.

The great days of Lopham linen

(PUBLISHED SEPTEMBER 1963)

THE Commissioners investigating the conditions of the handloom weavers in the 1830's must have been very depressed by the sorry plight of many skilled craftsmen in the declining weaving industry up and down the country. But when they came to the Lophams they found "the one green oasis in the vast desert of discontent in which their inquiries had been conducted."

Chris. Land, Michael Barman and George Shaw, all prominent weavers, met the Commissioners at the "Bell" on February 15th, 1839. When questioned, they disclosed that "trade in shirting, sheeting and table linen was 'pretty middling', that their net wages averaged 10s. a week for 12 hours work a day, after deducting two hours for meals, leaving ten on the loom. Occasionally, to execute a special order on time they worked perhaps 16 or 18 hours a day, but ten hours at the loom was all men in general could endure for a permanency".

Later the three were joined by Coleby Cobb and George Shaw sen., and together they went over the names of all the weavers in the parishes, which amounted to 50, while there were nine "masters" and one in London. The report emphasised that the material used was hemp, raised in the counties of Norfolk and Suffolk, some beautiful specimens of very fine thread being shown, spun by hand in the neighbourhood, mainly across the Waveney in Suffolk.

Here then was a well-established and highly organised hempen cloth business—flourishing in 1839 just as others were in decline. How and when did it arise? There is abundant evidence of the intensive growth of hemp in the belt from Harling, Kenninghall, Banham, Lopham and then along both sides of the Waveney Valley. "Linnen Weavers" were practising in Kenninghall in Queen Elizabeth's reign, for "John Barnarde a linnen weaver" was involved in a subversive plot in 1569: The craft may perchance have been introduced even earlier, for Flemish weavers came into East Anglia in the early 14th Century. At all events hemp was an important crop and when Arthur Young came in 1803 he gave the acreages for these villages, while the Tithe Commutation map of 1845 showed North Lopham with 20 hemplands varying in size from 1 rood 2 perches to 2ac. 0r. 39p. and totalling 14ac. 0r. 33p., and South Lopham with 43 hemplands varying from 1 rood to about 4 acres, totalling 55ac. 2r. 16p. Thus the Lophams had 60 acres of hemp—producing some 15 tons of fibre—and this "much decreased" from what it had formerly been.

By the early 19th century the Lophams were making far more cloth than required for parochial needs so they began peddling or hawking their wares further afield, eventually to London and throughout Great Britain. When similar industries declined in other centres the Lopham weavers displayed this great initiative of going out to seek markets—as instanced by entries in the Overseers' accounts: 1833 "pd Christmas Ludbrook towards buying a donkey 1£"—1844 "Thebbill towards donkey 1£". Several similar entries occurred. Rolls of cloth carried on donkeys were sold far afield. Still later when hemp cultivation died out, and railways made possible the wider distribution of competitive powerloom fabrics in other softer fibres, the Lopham weavers resorted to 'vans', bought flax from Ireland, and introduced Jacquard looms from Scotland, complete with an instructor James Strahan, to make the intricate damask linen goods as fine as those produced anywhere.

Through the kindness of the Rector, the Rev. C. E. Beevers, I have been able to spend many hours studying the Lopham registers, which with the Tithe Commutation Map, the Churchwardens' and Overseers' accounts, and three valuable books salvaged from the great sale in 1925 recording details of the day to day workings of the linen business at its peak, provide a picture of this amazing village industry—for amazing it was, in quantity, quality and variety of output.

One wonders how such an industry could become extinct. I quote from a letter I received in 1960 from Percy S. Beales, a descendant of both the prominent linen families, the Beales and the Buckenhams. "At the zenith of this remarkable industry, miles of roller towelling, sheeting, and household linen were despatched to Eton and Harrow and to many another humbler institution, while to many noble homes from the Queen's Palace downwards, were going regular supplies of the finest damask".

Here then is the evidence. The Registers described Jonas

Keeble (a prolific father) at various times as Hatcheler (1819), Hickler (1823)—Francis and Jonas his sons, as hemp combers or hemp dressers (1856-7). Robert Huggins was "hawking linen" in 1817, so too were John Pitcher, Wm. Bowell, Robert Nunn, Christmas Ludbrook, John Leeder, Chris Land and Walter his son, and others, in succeeding years. After donkeys, vans were used to carry more goods greater distances—and as the fame of Lopham linen spread the patronage of Royalty was achieved. Then on T. W. & J. Buckenham's van was emblazoned the Royal Crest surmounting "Linen Manufacturers by appointment to the Queen".

In one of her many cherished letters to me, Mrs. Mary Gooderham, that fountain of Lopham lore, who died on August 5th, 1963, at the great age of 97, wrote: "I remember John Shaw—a weaver and a great personality, who entered the employ of Mr. Buckenham as a boy and continued with him all his life, becoming the driver of the linen van and accompanying Mr. Buckenham on his journeys which often took them away for three months. John knew his way about London and the Home Counties and went to Buckingham Palace quite frequently—but stayed outside with the van, while Mr. B. 'went inside'." John Shaw lived until he was nearly 90, and died as recently as 1949. His daughter, Miss Nora Shaw, has shown me many of her treasures.

To give some idea of how the linen industry was integrated into the life of the Lophams I would quote these "statistics". In the North Lopham (Marriage) Register 1837-1897 the names of 98 weavers occur as "bridegrooms" or "fathers of bridegrooms". In 21 cases the groom and his father were both weavers. In South Lopham the names of 93 weavers occur as grooms or fathers of grooms, and in 19 cases both were weavers. These figures 21 and 19 bear out the Commissioners' point that the craft was passed from father to son to maintain the supply of weavers.

In the Baptismal Registers for North Lopham 1813-1882, 202 of the fathers were weavers. Of Baptisms in 1814, six out of 14 were weavers, and in 1815, 14 out of 41. For North Lopham 1813-1897, 316 fathers were weavers. The last dates when weavers registered baptisms were 1882 and 1897, for the young fathers were by then engaging in other work and the weavers still practising were ageing.

Typical marriages were: "Chas. Land (28) weaver, son of Seth Land (weaver) married Susan, daughter of Uriah Leeder" in

1839. "Chas. Land (27) weaver, son of Chas. Land (weaver) married Melvina Bowell (25) d. of Wm. Bowell (linen manufacturer)".

One of the books Percy Beales rescued in 1925 contains the day to day despatches of linen from Lopham. To show the varied and distinguished purchasers I quote at random from January, 1875. "To Mrs. Buckenham 65 Berners St. London" (the London store). "To O. Browning Esq. Eton College"—"To H.R.H. Princess Mary of Teck, Kensington Palace"—"To Mr. Kirby, Livery Office, St. James Palace"—"To Mrs. Packer, 19 Esplanade, Lowestoft"—"To His Grace the Duke of Norfolk"—"The Travellers' Club, Pall Mall", etc.

These travelled by van, passenger and goods trains. An analysis of total despatches from 1871-1893 shows a peak period from 1875 to 1886, after which decline became very marked. In 1893 despatches were only one-sixth of those in 1883, when some 100 weavers were busy in their simple lean-to sheds, or in the larger shops of the "master weavers".

A record of "giving out yarn" appears in another book. On the left side for July 7th, 1881, Thomas Shaw, weaver, received yarn for 120 yards "Spider web"—thus—"16 and 120, 200, 120, 74, equals 530" being details of yarn required to warp and weave 120 yards.

On September 20th he returned "12—10/4 at 8s." 9d. and was paid £5—5—0" also "6—10/14 at 12s. " 3d. and received £3—13—6".

Walter Huggins was one of the whitesters or bleachers—laying out unbleached cloth on grassland reserved as "bleaches". On December 3rd, 1877, he received 90 yards of 32, ¾ Huckaback and on December 17th he returned the bleached 90 yards of 32 ¾ and received £1—3—0.

After the peak—the decline. The Lophams pinned hopes on a projected railway from Harleston to Thetford through Wortham, Redgrave and Hopton. The Parish Magazine of 1898 refers to a "petition" for this railway (my own father was one who signed it for Redgrave)—which would improve the ways of getting Lopham products away and assist in checking the drift of population. The young people were leaving Lopham and no young weavers were coming on. The railway never materialised. From 1,536 (in 1836) to 1,563 (in 1854) the population dropped to 1,500 (in 1860), to 1,203 (in 1880), to 1,074 (in 1890) and to 1,049 (in 1908) for the combined parishes. The boys were leaving the villages—many to go to sea, like Wm. Long in 1851, for whom the Overseers paid £3 10s. 9d. for "binden him apprentice to sea sarvise for 4 years". In 1852 they paid £5 0s. 8d. "for binden J. Long prentis to sea to Mr. Turner of Blyth, ship Tomas, Captain Geo. Brown". (This was probably a coastal collier trading between Blyth and Lowestoft). Not a single one of the many apprenticeships was to a "linen weaver".

The masters refused to take apprentices "under 20£" (1839 Report) in addition to paying 50s. to the journeyman who taught an apprentice, for loss of time. This, they said, saved the trade from "overwhelming ruinous competition", but it also led to a drying up of the supply of young weavers.

Herbert Crook (born 1886), of Lopham "Bull"—who wound bobbins and carried linen to the Bleach at Roydon, and his wife, whose father, H. Goddard, kept the "Chequers" near Lopham Gate in the hempen era, attributed the decline to the lack of male successors in the Buckenham-Beales families, to direct the industry. They thought the railway might have helped to preserve it, and they agreed with the 1839 Report's hint at excessive drinking among the weavers, which turned the young against the trade. Percy Beales, too, in one of his letters referred to the weavers as a "hard drinking lot". But competition from power-loom products, the restrictions on making luxury linens during the 1914-18 war, soaring flax prices, the popularity of cheaper cotton damask cloths, and the fashion of having polished tables and mats—were all inimical to the Lopham industry.

Several factors, then, caused decline—the end came in 1925, though Albert Tyler continued making huckaback towelling for a few years more. The grand three day sale in November, 1925 was the finale, when 300 lots of "the celebrated damask linen table cloths, bleached and unbleached sheeting; buckaback, diaper and other towelling"—with many looms, were disposed of.

Thousands of these treasures are still in use or hoarded as souvenirs, with their exquisite designs of roses, thistles, acorns, oak leaves, or spider web, or Travellers' Club motifs. They will eventually wear out and pass away. Mrs. Roger Baker who died in March 1962, had marked sheets and towels in red cross-stich with the Royal monogram, while her mother had spun hemp and had also hand stitched or "made" the ends of towels and sheets cut from the long rolls of cloth. Mr. Yeates—now of Roydon watered bleaching linen laid out at the back of the "Limes". Others —ageing—who remember the last days of the industry will disappear from the scene one day. Museum looms too may survive for many years.

But certain enduring memorials will remain when tangible products, and human contacts with Lophams' linen industry, have passed away. The Bells of North Lopham church ring out to the memory of Stephen Beales, a leading linen manufacturer, while the east window there is a memorial to another noted family—the Buckenhams. Both families carried the fame of Lopham products far and wide.

It is, however, the stained glass window in the Lady Chapel of the ancient South Lopham church to the memory of Louisa Buckenham that is the most appropriate and symbolic memorial. Mrs. Buckenham was another member of the famous family, and a great public benefactor. The window depicts three scenes from the story of Dorcas (told in the Acts of the Apostles ch. 9 verses 36-42), Dorcas was a woman "full of good works" who made coats and garments for the poor—as shown in the left panel. In the centre, the sorrowing widows are showing St. Peter a linen garment made by Dorcas, "when she was with them". Dorcas raised from the dead appears in the right hand panel. Surely this lasting memorial will remind future generations of the families of the Lophams of one of their greatest wonders.

Costerton's flax factory at Scole

(PUBLISHED OCTOBER 1962)

A CENTURY ago the road from Diss to Scole would have presented a very different scene from that of today. Instead of stubbles and fields of roots on the north side were the broad acres of William Betts's closely-cropped market gardens with their own private railway. On the south side, with its great chimney towering above the landscape, was the extensive flax factory, of which the present red brick farmhouse is but a tiny relic.

No swiftly-moving cars sped along the road, but many leisurely horse-drawn farm wagons lumbered along loaded with sheaves of flax for the factory. As many as 20 to 30 wagons from farms within a radius of 20 miles were often seen lining the roads near the "White Hart"—their horses contentedly engaged with their nose-bags, while teamsters enjoyed a refreshing drink after the dusty work of unloading.

It was Charles Fisher Costerton, of Eye, who began that factory, partnered by his brother-in-law, Peter Nayler. Costerton had become, in the mid-1840s, clerk and later registrar and auditor to the Hartismere Union. This brought him into direct contact with the acute poverty of the rural districts at that time.

Conscious of the need for alternative employment to agriculture, he conceived the idea of persuading farmers to grow flax, and himself erected a factory for processing the fibres into twine, rope and sacking—all needed in agriculture and industry.

His flax factory at "Waterloo", Scole, beside the Waveney, was erected in 1854 and proved an immediate success.

Associated with it, and built at the same time, were a processing factory at Eye—controlled by the brothers Chase—on the site now occupied by the Reading Room in Lambseth Street, and the "Rettery" on the Hoxne road, half-a-mile beyond the Abbey Bridge.

These ventures were complementary and, when in full swing, gave employment to 100 people in Scole and 100 in Eye.

Supported by Sir Edward Kerrison, a keen farmer and flax

enthusiast, Costerton conducted a vigorous campaign among farmers and farmers' clubs to convince them of the value of flax cultivation, both for its fibres and for its oil-containing seed.

By lectures, demonstrations, advice on cultivation and seed selection, he succeeded in his efforts and the countryside around Diss in summer became dotted with the delicate blue of flowering flax.

The "Costerton and Naylor" Cup for the best three acres of flax was a coveted trophy, presented each year at an annual dinner at Eye.

Not only was flax widely grown locally, but "tow"—the coarser fibre—was brought by rail from considerable distances to feed the factory machines and looms.

One truckload from Lincolnshire in 1872 arrived "smouldering from over heating in transit", and was the subject of a long lawsuit, Costerton v. G.E.R.

Sheaves of flax arrived at Eye and Scole, to be steeped in the "Retting ponds", or River Waveney, so softening the outer stem to allow the extraction of fibres. After drying came "scutching", a process by which the fibres were graded for various uses—the coarser for ropes and sacking the finer for twine.

Efforts to encourage flax production in the 1860s were aided by a serious outbreak of Rinderpest which persisted through 1865-6, when tens of thousands of cattle died or were slaughtered.

Flax was then substituted for the root crops no longer in demand. In the following years of "frightful crises in agriculture", no single year gave even an average crop of corn, and flax was widely tried in the hope of buoying up flagging fortunes. At that time, too, cheap corn from the New World came pouring in to peg down home prices.

But fire bedevilled the factories at both Eye and Scole. The former was completely burnt out in 1864 and Sir Edward Kerrison erected the Reading Room as a working men's club on the site.

The Scole factory survived five severe outbreaks of fire, each resulting from sparks caused by grit impingeing on the metal spikes of the "scutchers". The conflagration of 1871 brought near-disaster. "Niagara" arrived late from Diss, and only by stripping sections of roofing and tearing down buildings was the fire prevented from reaching the looms.

Time passed . . . . for various reasons farmers ceased to grow flax . . . supplies of fibre diminished . . . production became intermittent, and finally ceased.

An attempt to revive the factory's fortunes under "The British Flax and Paper Co."—still a Costerton concern—was only temporarily successful and the factory closed in 1881. Machinery was removed, and buildings dismantled, though the great chimney was the last to fall, in 1895.

Some may have wondered how the name "Flax Farm" originated, but many alive today had some connection with the factory.

Fred Thrower and Fred Nunn, for instance, remember the crash of the chimney—Pal Flatman (now 92) remembers his oldest brother (born 1855) trekking daily to the factory in the 1870s. William Murray—grandfather of many Nunns and Murrays in Diss today—came from Belfast as a skilled flax worker, to be foreman for Costerton. George Buckenham (born 1875) remembers entering the factory after its closure, and seeing the metal-studded drums of the scutching machines.

Part of Eye is still "The Rettery"—some buildings are still there, though the retting ponds are choked with bullrushes.

Charles Costerton, who passed his later years at Scole House, died in 1891 at the age of 67 after a life-time of public service, having made a valiant effort to alleviate the tragedy of rural unemployment.

Diss corsets

(PUBLISHED SEPTEMBER 1963)

A BROCHURE, *Picture of Diss*, 1849, noted that stay-making formerly employed many of the town's inhabitants, adding that "The stays were of stout leather for the humbler classes, and of whalebone canvass and jean for ladies—almost equally pistol-proof and rigid, and happily well-nigh obsolete."

Many changes of fashion have occurred since 1849, but I was recently shown a pair of the leather stays referred to. They repose in the Strangers' Hall at Norwich, and are as hard and tough and inflexible as thick papier-maché.

Miss Rachel Young, the curator, gave this description: "They are of the same design as the more common fabric ones used in the 18th century. The bottom edge is tongued to spread over the hips. Fastening is at the back with a single lace. They are lined with canvas, which also covers the front panel, and are higher at the back than at the front, 14 inches down the back, 11 inches down the front."

These were by no means the earliest "garments" used to support the figure and accentuate the female waist. Even in ancient times close-fitting bodices and girdles were worn to constrict the figure and create a wasp-like waist, and in medieval England "kirtles" were used to the same ends.

Willett, an authority on the history of clothes, states: "There is no evidence that the 'exquisites' of Tudor and Jacobean England constricted their waists with corsets, but it is more than suggested in these satirical lines by Bishop Hall (1598):

"*But when I looke and cast mine eyes below,*
What monster meets mine eyes in human shew.
So slender waist, with such an Abbot's loyne,
Did never sober nature sure conjoyne."

Willett—referring to costumes in Elizabethan drama—mentions that corsets consisting of "underbodice made in two parts, so called a pair of bodyes" were in use, stiffened with busks of wood or whalebone inserted into casings in the "bodyes". Busks were usually plain, flat strips inserted and concealed in the corset or corsage.

But there was a rural custom of presenting carved stay-busks as love tokens, sometimes engraved with love messages such as "When this you see, Pray think on me. Tho' many miles we distant be. Altho we are a great way apart, I wish you well with all my heart." Or, "As a ring is round and hath no end, So is my love to thee, my friend."

These ornamental, sentimental busks were proudly displayed in little pockets in the fronts of bodices or sewn on through small holes drilled in the busks.

A Book of Customs (**1631**) speaks of "Bodies for women and children, of whalebone or leather"—scornfully described by a male writer as "privie coats by art made strong with bones and steels and suchlike ware".

By the mid-17th century "pairs of bodies" and "leather stays" appear to have been in general use. I found among the parish records of St. Nicholas, Ipswich, that Simona Smyth, a poor child, was apprenticed to William Fairchild, of St. Stephen's, "upper-bodys maker", in **1676**.

At that time "bodyes" were also being made in Diss, for the overseers' accounts for **1685** record that "Sarey Eastoll and Dayes Girl" were each given "2½ yds. Wolsey, canvis, buckram, thread, and 4d. of bone" to make "a pair of bodyes". When worn, these parts were laced together to the correct tension to form a stiff bodice.

Many references to these garments occur in our parish accounts. For instance: "**1693**. To old ffolgers wiffe, for Matthew Turners girll, a pr. of bodyes and an apron, 3s. 2d." And, in 1704: "ffor Scotts girle, a pair of forstayes and bodyes, 3s. 6d."; and at Gissing in **1733**: "A pair of shoes for Rose Gooch, 1s. 10d., and a pair of Bodyes for her Girll, 1s. 6d."

By the 18th century the names of several leather staymakers appear—among them Sam Sandy, John Reeve, John Clark, William Stebbings, Charles Harper, William Bird, Isaac Ayton, Thomas and John Gudgeon, John Thain, John Chamberlaine and Jeremiah Howe, all master craftsmen, training sons and apprentices. The Reeves, Aytons, Gudgeons and Sandys followed the craft for well over a century. An old diary—quite authentic, I believe—mentions that Tom Paine, the celebrated revolutionary, served part of his early apprenticeship with the Gudgeons on the Terrace near the old "Beehive" Inn as a staymaker—before joining the Excise service, from which he was dismissed for agitating for an increase in Excisemen's pay.

The making of leather stays continued through the 18th century. John Reeve, who learned his trade with Sam Sandy, took Thomas Stebbings, a poor child, in 1762, for the full term of seven years, to instruct him "in the trade and mystery of a Cordwainer and leather Staymaker".

Nineteen years later, in 1781, Reeve took another "poor" apprentice, William Bird, to instruct him in the same trade. The actual indentures of both these apprenticeships have survived, since they were signed by the churchwardens, overseers and two Justices and put away for safety in the parish chest.

The indenture of John Thain 1787, also remains. But by now fashions were changing—the stout, rigid bullet-proof garments were being replaced by more supple bone stays.

John Thain, of Diss, was apprenticed to Richard Thain, of North Walsham, whose advertisement in the *Norfolk Chronicle* of March 7th, 1789, ran thus: "To the ladies—Richard Thain returns his grateful acknowledgements for the very great encouragement he has been honoured with by them, and hopes to merit their further favors by his utmost exertions to oblige. He begs leave to inform them that he has returned from London with the newest fashions of French, and Italian Corsets and Riding Stays."

Thereafter, the services of the cordwainer were dispensed with, as leather stays became obsolete. In the early 19th century the craft passed into the hands of the old masters' wives and widows. Fabric only was used and the deft fingers of women were better fitted for the stitching and insertion of bone or steel.

The salons of widows Reeve, Wharton, Hague and Garrod were opened in various parts of Diss. Widow Hague's daughters practised on Market Hill, later moved to Mount Street (now Mr. Sinclair's, opposite the "Saracen's Head") and then to a cottage adjoining the Rectory garden further up the same street. Many old friends remember the Misses Hague as "corsetieres" and as staunch supporters of the church.

But a great revival came in 1888, when a stay factory was opened in Heywood Road, in premises later known as the "Imps' Hut", which remains to this day. Here, some 60-70 female "hands" were employed by this subsidiary of an Ipswich firm—first under a male manager, Mr. Green and later under Mrs. Cocksedge, who continued until she was over 70. A male engineer attended the Singer machines and the oil engine that provided power for the overhead driving shafts.

The girls faced each other in two long lines the length of the building. Two of the earliest employees were Miss May Cann and Mrs. Kitty Martin (née Cutting), both now well in their 80s. Several of their contemporaries survive, too, and I have a long list of those who worked in the factory in later years containing many familiar names.

The 'parts' were guillotined in the parent factory at Ipswich, and arrived in Diss in bundles of "busks, fronts, backs, gores and hips" to be assembled by "stitchers, strappers and double strappers". Then, after inspection, they were returned to be "trimmed, bound, eyeletted, laced and boned (or steeled)".

The old hands say work was "pretty regular", though there were slack times when some were stood off. It was then that many girls engaged in private repair work. But there were peak times of rush, too, when work was taken home to complete urgent orders on time, and the firm encouraged employees to purchase their own machines by instalments to meet such emergencies. Such machines proved a good investment in slack times—and later, when the factory closed.

Several of these machines are still in working order after 70 years of use—May Cann has one of them.

Bertha Frost (later Mrs. Potter) joined the staff in 1906 and worked there until 1921, when the factory closed, helping to train the novices. She recalls that it was difficult to earn 10s. a week at the piece rates prevailing—so that much private work was undertaken.

Bertha and her sister-in-law, Frances Frost (née Bailey) speak of the pleasant and co-operative spirit among the girls, and of their attractive uniforms of "pink blouses and white embroidered pinafores", hair securely tied back.

All employees paid a penny a week into a "pool" for the weekly scrubbing-out of the factory—an operation performed by rota in pairs with the "pool" as a reward.

Maude Sparling, now 71, joined the staff in 1905 when $13\frac{1}{2}$ years of age, as a "stitcher and assembler". She remembers assembling corsets with 18-inch waists, for those elegant figures some of us recall in the first decade of this century. She (and of course others) remembers the impact of the First World War, when work was switched to the war effort and machines put to making Army shirts, canvas jackets for the hospitals, and pyjamas for the wounded.

Full employment reigned—a skilled worker could earn 5s. 6d. a day by stitching up a dozen shirts (excluding button holes and buttons). Earnings were doubled or trebled due to the tragedy of war.

Albert Frost—still in khaki in May 1919 and waiting to go to the Middle East—remembers an awkward moment not long before the factory closed. He had gone to meet his fiancée Frances, then an assistant overseer. She invited him in to wait until work ceased, and the entrance of a man in khaki caused 70 pairs of bright eyes to be focused suddenly upon Albert (to his temporary embarrassment)—an occasion he recalls 44 years later.

The war ended, back to corsets ! Somehow the old drive had gone. Stitching which passed muster during the war was no longer accepted in the competitive post-war period, and there were more rejects and fewer orders.

The parent firm was involved in a financial crisis and closure came in 1921. The old building has been used for a variety of purposes since. It is to many the Scouts' H.Q., but to the large band of former staymakers it is still "The old stay factory in Heywood Road."

Bertha Potter (née Frost) was one who acquired a skilled knowledge of all the processes of cutting out, assembling and finishing. She developed her own private practice "making to measure" for a local clientele, until 1935. She thus has the honour of being the last of the Diss staymakers—a survivor of an industry carried on in Diss for at least two centuries.

Diss Lace Association

(PUBLISHED MAY 1964)

THE Diss lace industry was started in 1901 and wound-up in 1941. In its comparatively short life it performed a useful social service, produced things of beauty, and achieved a degree of fame.

It was on the initiative of Mrs. Slack, a bank manager's wife —who left Diss in 1911—that a provisional committee was called together in the Church Hall on May 10th, 1901, to consider the introduction of pillow-lace in the district. But clearly some unofficial activity and discussion had gone on before this meeting, since Mrs. Slack and others came to it armed with a good deal of information and even some practical experience.

Mrs. Manning, the Rector's wife, presided. She said she felt that a cottage industry would meet a need, and that the making of pillow-lace was easy, clean and remunerative. Mrs. Slack said that in the course of visiting in the district she had met a number of women who would be glad to supplement their income by "homework"; but, more than this, she reported that she had visited Miss Barnes, Gold Medallist at the Women's Exhibition at Earls Court, and had taken some lessons in lace-making. Apparently the demand for pillow-lace was far greater than the supply.

Also (evidently before this first recorded meeting) Miss Barnes had come to Diss and met a group of ladies with whom she agreed to give a course of six lessons for a fee of ten guineas, plus travel expenses. On the strength of this experience, Mrs. Slack asked at the meeting if it would be desirable to engage Miss Barnes for a course of lessons at individual fees of 10s. 6d. to a guinea, with 7s. 6d. for the whole course for "poorer neighbours".

It was determined that the industry should be self-supporting, but an initial outlay of £16 would be necessary (in addition to Miss Barnes's fees ? This is not stated) after which the expenses would be very small, as the thread was cheap. Presumably the provisional committee provided this starting-money; details are not available, but the industry certainly came into being.

At this first reported meeting it was pointed out that active young girls who would normally go into service were not to be encouraged to get a living by lace-making. There were young married women with time on their hands, and there were invalids, and there were cottage homes where additional income without expense on plant or machinery would be welcome. It was possible for a skilful worker to earn 4s. to 10s. a week by lace-making.

Mrs. Downton, commenting on the undesirability of attracting active young girls away from "service", said the work would be a great blessing to those not strong enough for "service". Looking back today, we can bear in mind that delicate young girls were a commonplace in cottage homes, where inadequate diet and crowded, stuffy conditions led to anaemia and consumption. The boys were more fortunate because their work took them into the open air.

Mrs. Downton also remarked that there would be no hindrance to ladies selling their own work if they cared to; but some modification of this was found necessary when the Diss Lace Association was finally set up and furnished with a set of rules.

On July 5th, 1901, the *Diss Express* reported the formation of a class of 33 members, and a first lesson from the Gold Medallist, Miss Barnes. This took place at Mrs. Slack's house.

The committee took final form in August, 1901, at The Nunnery, where Mrs. Hanbury Frere was then living. The names were: Mrs. Manning, president; Mrs. Murray Downton and Mrs. John Tudor Frere, vice-presidents; Mrs. Fenn, Miss Howe, Mrs. Firth, Mrs. Hanbury Frere; with Mrs. Slack as hon. secretary.

Subsequently Abbott's, printers, of Diss, printed the rules of the Diss Lace Association. These rules were comprehensive, strict and practical. Membership was gained by sufficient training in the craft, followed by signing the book of rules. The secretary received orders for lace and gave the work out at the committee's discretion. The Association took 1d. in the shilling of all money paid for lace, whether in fulfilment of private orders or by sale in the open market. The individual lace-maker received, through the secretary, the payment for the lace she made (less the commission) within one month of the customer's payment to the Association.

No member was allowed to teach lace-making "on the side", and no member was allowed to sell work privately. The Association provided materials and patterns. Patterns were very important; some were designed by members themselves—presumably by those ladies who had taken lessons at the start—and were marked "Exclusive"; some were worked from photographs of old lace belonging to members. Workers were under an obligation not to impart these patterns to outsiders. The whole set-up is rather like that of a medieval Guild, with its trade secrets, and one can see why. A high-class product depends on exclusiveness, and could be sabotaged unless those engaged on it were perfectly loyal.

Workers not trained by the Diss Association could be admitted, on a test of proficiency, by payment of 12s. 6d. Children under the age of 14, parents permitting, could enter on payment of half a crown if they satisfied the Committee as to their ability. 1901 closed with the completion of the Association's first order, three large collars of Honiton type. Sixty workers had been trained, many of whom, says the *Diss Express* of that date, had shown exceptional ability. The Association had a balance in hand after paying all expenses, and had reason to be greatly encouraged by the results of its first six months' work.

In the early years of this century, the farm worker's wage was only 12s. a week, so a woman living at home thought herself quite well paid if she earned from four to ten shillings by lace-making. We have no complete list of Diss lace-makers, but those names which do crop up show a good cross-section of social status.

Mrs. Francis Taylor made lace; Miss Cox, of a Wortham agricultural family, bicycled from the Long Green every week for lessons. Far away from Diss, 300 Indian girls were taught the art by Miss Grace Borrett (now aged 90), who had learnt it from Mrs. Slack.

Mrs. Mauro, a daughter of Mrs. Slack, gives a picture of the actual process: "I have sat for hours with my big round pillow in front of me and 40 to 60 bobbins wound with 100 to 150 linen thread, fine as gossamer, tossing them backward and forward weaving the fine web of the lace. We made it on special brown card patterns pricked with the design, and used very fine pins . . . It was very soothing and fascinating work."

The capable and public-spirited Mrs. Slack left the town when her husband retired in 1911; soon after, she wrote a short account of the Association's progress thus far. A bad outbreak of scarlet fever had disrupted the work for a time; Miss Alice Savory, of Palgrave, helped out as secretary while Mrs. Slack was out of action, and subsequently took over the management of the Association.

It was in the early days that a Chalice Veil was made for Diss Church, and a first prize gained at a competitive exhibition at Aldeburgh. Queen Alexandra bought some Diss lace at an exhibition at the Albert Hall. 1912 was a good year, with work on view at six exhibitions (London, Norwich, Felixstowe, etc.) and plenty of orders, especially towards Christmas. After that, there was a real burst of glory in 1913.

But by that time the constitution of the Lace Association had changed. When Mrs. Slack departed, the Committee dissolved itself, feeling that the work of establishment had been safely accomplished. By 1913, Miss Savory was the sole official, assisted by Mrs. Johnson (née Nice), one of the original workers, a Blue Star and Gold Star winner.

The 1913 successes started in January, when, as reported in *The Times* of the 14th, the Queen requested that a box of lace be sent to York Cottage, and bought several pieces, including a double fichu of appliqué from an original design belonging to the Association.

On March 7th, there was an exhibition at the Mansion House at which Diss work was again admired by Her Majesty. *The Times* and *The Queen* both had a lot to say about this exhibition, with special mention of Diss items.

In May Diss took part in an Arts and Crafts show at Yarmouth; this brought forth a whole article in *The Queen* on "A Norfolk Cottage Industry".

In June, the Association had a stall at the Home Arts and Industries exhibition at the Albert Hall, and gained three Gold Stars, six Blue Stars and two Red Stars. Queen Alexandra made several purchases including a fan, some black lace (the work of a girl of 15) which had won a Gold Star, and a jabot with a raised rose design. Simultaneously the Association was exhibiting at an International show in Ghent, so the London pieces were by no means its entire output.

In August, the Association had a stall at the Town Hall, Eye, where workers demonstrated the making and mending of lace.

Evil days followed. The 1914 war crippled the industry. No doubt the able-bodied workers found other things to do, and the minds of rich purchasers did not run on luxury and adornment just then. The number of workers fell from about 50 to half a dozen. Miss Savory and Mrs. Johnson kept it ticking over, and after the war it revived, though not to its former strength.

However, in 1922 a wedding gift—a handkerchief—was made for Princess Mary, who, in giving her permission (one cannot just send presents to Royalty out of the blue) referred to the "invalid cottage workers" of the Diss Lace Association; which seems to suggest that most of the remaining workers were in that category.

Undoubtedly one of the reasons for the falling-off was that the pay of the workers had not risen. By the 1920s, fourpence an hour (attained by a really quick worker) was by no means what it had been in 1901, and could only be of value to an invalid who had no other way of earning money.

The 1939 war finally put an end to the Association. Miss Savory died, and when her estate was cleared up, very little money was found in the Association's fund.

Her sister, Mrs. Macdonald, at the end of 1941, sent £2 each to the surviving workers, of whom there could not have been many, since there was some money over to donate to "good causes", including the provision of comforts for the soldiers.

None of the accounts of the Association have come to light; no doubt in the course of more than 20 years they have gone into limbo with the rest of Miss Savory's papers. It would have been interesting to know whether a cottage industry, started for philanthropic reasons, was fully solvent after repaying the original outlay made by its sponsors, and all running-expenses. Did the penny commission in the shilling really meet all this ? If private purchasers and luxury shops paid pretty highly for the lovely cobwebs made in Diss, as they ought, this might be so; but the facts are lacking. It is sad to think that clever machines and changes of fashion have put a craft, which sometimes reached a peak of creative art, out of business.

Indentured apprentices

(PUBLISHED MARCH 1963)

IN a directory of 1790, Diss was described as "a flourishing town, its market well stored with yarn and linen cloth, its manufactures including hempen cloth, hose, and making of stays." And when the woolstapler, John Leech, of Market Hill, died in 1842, Diss was said "to have been esteemed a great manufactory of hosiery, one of the chief in Norfolk and Suffolk."

These facts were certainly true, but they afford only a limited idea of the many trades and skills practised in Diss and district. For greater detail one must delve into "Indentures of Apprenticeship", "Examinations for Settlement" and the hundreds of other "papers" which accumulated mainly between 1600 and 1850 through the day-to-day working of the old Poor Law System.

Though indentures of apprenticeship were made even in the 15th century, it was not until the Statute of Artificers in 1563 that an attempt was made to harness the nation's latent skill by a compulsory system of apprenticeship. It was contended that "until a man grow into 23 years he is for the most part wild, without judgment and not of sufficient experience to govern himself". After 24, having served his apprenticeship, he was at liberty to marry, become a journeyman for hire, or set up on his own.

Many actual indentures of those days have survived, particularly those for poor children, who, because of the poverty of their parents, were indentured by the churchwardens and overseers at the expense of the parish. Such agreements were signed by the contracting parties in the presence of witnesses who, in turn, testified before a Justice as to the validity of the signatures.

Bressingham still has some of the earliest indentures (1629) and Dickleburgh the latest (1891), but Diss, Gissing, Denton, Starston and Needham all have a fine assortment.

Between them they represent well over 100 occupations—the usual ones of husbandmen, bricklayers, carpenters, cordwainers, blacksmiths, weavers, drovers, etc.; and the less usual, hecklers or hatchelers, hot pressers, brickstrikers, mantuamakers, woolcombers, bone and leather staymakers, and even an oyster dredger.

Apprenticeships were normally for seven years, until the age of 21 or 24 was reached. Some began at a very early age, especially if the Parish Officers saw the opportunity of putting a child out for good and so save the parish rate the continued cost of its maintenance.

In 1713 Edward Oadham, the father of the male child of Rebecca Wharton, of Diss, was ordered to pay "18d weekely untill the childe attaine ye age of 8 yeares, and then to pay £5 towards bindeing it out an Apprentice".

Even earlier, a Michaell Carsey died at Dickleburgh in 1682 leaving a 9-years-old orphan daughter, Mary, for the parish to maintain, but of the "goodes and chattells of the sd. Michaell, the Inhabitants of Dickleburgh raysed the sum of £5 wch they paid to John Ludbrooke, of Ubberstone, Suff., to take maintaine and keep the sd. Mary dureing the time and terme of 8 yeares with sufficient clothing meate drinke washing and lodgeing suitable and necessary for her".

Mary, at the tender age of nine, was removed from Dickleburgh and placed at the mercy of her master, in domestic service, to which most "poore girls" went.

For boys the terms of indenture were tightly drawn. Thus, in 1629, Thomas Keen, of Bressingham, a "poore boy" was apprenticed to ffrancys Harrison "to serve him untill the sd. Thomas shall accomplishe ye full age of XXIIII yeares, dueringe wch tyme the sd. ffrancys will fynd sufficient meate drinke and apparrell and other things necessary, and at thend of the sd. terme give him double apparrell".

Later other conditions were added as part of the indenture. When, in 1710, Samuel Manneing was apprenticed to Thomas Okly, "Lening Weaver", to be instructed "in ye trade or mistery of a Lening weaver for the terme of 7 yeares", it was agreed that Samuel was "not to do damage to his sd. Master, nor see it to be done by others; not to wast his master's goods nor lend them unlawfully; not to commit fornication nor contract matrimony within the sd. terme; not to play at cards, dice or any unlawfull game; not to absente himselfe day or night from his masters service without his leave; nor haunt Alehouses, taverns or playhouses . . . "

—all these in return for "sufficient meat, drinke, lodgeing, washing and shurts befittinge an apprentice with all other wareing things and apparel (shifts only excepted)". There is little doubt that long hours of work and irksome restrictions prompted many an unhappy apprentice to run away, only to be caught by a constable and returned to drudgery.

Constables' accounts record many such cases. Having paid the premium with the indenture, the Parish Officers expected to be rid of further obligation, especially of the boy who was something of a delinquent.

The Bressingham officers placed one Thomas Chamberlain as an apprentice in West Mersey, Essex, through the good offices of the boy's brother-in-law. When Thomas arrived, the brother-in-law wrote, saying: "The lad is now at my house and I am using my best endeavours to get him bound as cheap as I possiblely can, as he was almost naked". He sent a bill for "shirts, breches, coat, shoes, stockings and wast coat", and an account for £2 14s. 10d. for "enrolling indentures and inrollin". Thomas was apprenticed to an "oyster-dredger". On the bill was a note, "You have got red of a loose, idle youth".

Of course, if master and apprentice were completely ill-suited, the apprenticeship could be dissolved by a Justice—so "Wm Banks of Bressingham dislike woolcombing and is freed from his Indenture"—by a Justice.

In the great majority of cases apprenticeships were served locally, so that Parish Officers could verify that conditions were observed.

In **1723** Robert Baxter was apprenticed in Diss to Edward Archer "to larne the trade and misstery of a wollcomber", Diss then being an important woolcombing centre. Edmund Smith was apprenticed to John Sands, miller, of Diss, in **1742** "until the age of four and twenty in the arte and Trade of a Miller", and Thomas Stebbing to John Reeve, of Diss, in **1761**, for seven years "to learn the Trade and mystery of a Cordwainer and leather Staymaker".

For some trades, however, boys were sent further afield.

In **1749** Robert Newby was apprenticed to Thomas Hendley, of Shoreditch, Middlesex, for seven years "in the art mistery and occupation of chimney sweep and Fire Defender"—and so began his escapades in the London chimneys, far from the ken of the Diss Parish Officers.

In **1773** Richard Lord, of Diss, was apprenticed "until the full age of 24 years to Robt. Smith, of Old Buckenham, in the trade of a worstead weaver which he now useth".

The earliest surviving indenture in Diss dates from 1714, when "John Hunt, in consideration of the sum of £3 was appr. to Henry Gooderham, of Shotisham, for and dureing the full end and term of 7 yeares in the Arte and Trade of a Bricklayer".

An unsual indenture (1783) records that "Benjamin Mully, of Diss, a poore child of 13 years, was appr. to Elizabeth Liveing, of Harwich, fisherwoman, in the art and skill or employ of a Fisherman, until he shall accomplish the full age of 21 years". With him was paid £1 10s. "in full for taking the sd. Benjamin and fitting him out for the sea service".

Gissing has 26 indentures, mostly for husbandry—though one boy went to Wymondham for worsted weaving in 1753, and another to Norwich in 1778 (like William Burdett of Diss in 1742) to be taught "the trade of a hot-presser".

All but one of Denton's 'six' were trained locally—he was apprenticed at Redenhall as a "Brazier and Coppersmith from 15 until 21 years of age".

Dickleburgh has a fine run of 25 indentures. In 1693 Henery Andrewes was apprenticed to Edward Ruddleditch "to learn the mistery and occupation of a worsted weaver until ffouer and twenty years", while in 1746 John Kempe was apprenticed "at Shottisham as a plummer and glazier".

Robert Newby—apprenticed at Shoreditch as a sweep in 1749, later settled in Dickleburgh, where in 1798 his son Henry, also a sweep, accepted "John Herbert, aged 9, a poore child of Eye, as an apprentice for the full term of 7 years, in consideration of 2£ of lawfull money to him in hand paid by the Visitor and Guardians of the Poor of Eye".

What became of John Herbert is not known, but Newby was taken into the Workhouse in 1803.

An Act of 1816 to regulate the binding of parish apprentices attempted to improve conditions by demanding an authentic certificate of the master's humanity and trustworthiness. So, when, in 1818, James Shibley, a poor Dickleburgh boy, was apprenticed as a manservant to George Lee, of that parish, a Justice, two of his fellow-Justices declared Lee to be "a fit and proper person to whom J. Shibley may be bound".

The most recent document preserved was the apprenticeship

of James Randle, of Dickleburgh, to Albert George Draper in 1891, for the space of five years "to learn the business of a baker and confectioner". The boy was to receive 2s. per week in his 2nd year, 3s. per week in the 3rd, 4s. in the 4th, and 5s. per week in the last year, together with food for six days per week throughout".

On the satisfactory completion of the apprenticeship, the Trustees of "Mrs. Mathison's Gift for poor boys" were to pay Albert Draper the sum of £10. This "gift"—by a former Rector's wife—was one of many such bequests to help in the training and equipment of "poore children".

Now, in 1963, our system of apprenticeship is under review. Exactly 400 years after the Statute of Artificers was passed in 1563, the subject was debated in the House of Lords. As the Elizabethans devised a system of training suited to the 16th century, so it is hoped that a national system in keeping with conditions of the 20th century will be formulated to develop the latent talent in the youth of today.

People— A Diss family

(PUBLISHED DECEMBER 1962)

EVEN a casual visitor to Diss Church cannot fail to notice the name of Manning—on mural or floor tablets, or the Roll of Rectors, or in stained glass windows. For the Manning family rendered distinguished service to Diss through four centuries, providing Churchwardens, Overseers, High Constables, Justices and, finally, four successive Rectors spanning, between them, 128 years.

This unique and completely documented record can be traced from William Manning, born in 1526 when Henry VIII was King and John Skelton, the King's former tutor, was Rector of Diss.

It was a vastly different Diss from that of today. The flourishing Guilds of St. Nicholas and Corpus Christi had erected their own Guildhall (c.1500) near the church, while their Guild Chapel of St. Nicholas dominated Market Hill.

Those carved corner posts, with their religious motifs, still visible on the Diss Publishing Company's and Cramphorn's premises, were only recently carved when William was born.

He lived during the long dispute between Henry and Rome. He witnessed the arbitrary confiscation of the Guild Lands at Framlingham in Edward VI's reign and saw the slow decay of the Guild Chapel and its final demolition by those speculators Croft and Hallyett, who acquired many such buildings in East Anglia.

As a Churchman William knew of the enforced sale of the extensive and beautiful town plate to Henry, Earl of Sussex, for a mere 20 marks, and to his honour he was one of the determined band who resisted the Earl's later overtures to acquire "such porcon more as may be sold at a convenyent price".

His name appears as warden in 1571, while in 1594 he was a leading witness in a tithe dispute—his evidence makes interesting reading.

William married in the year of Queen Elizabeth's accession. His son—another William—born 1564, was a schoolmate of the madrigal composer John Wilbye at the Guildhall Grammar School. Together they survived that distressing year, 1579, when the plague exacted its dreadful toll of 56 Diss lives. Like his father, William served as churchwarden. Later, as constable in the early 17th century, his duties were far less pleasant. They involved "impressinge able men of bodie" to serve King James and collecting arbitrary impositions from unwilling taxpayers—such as "good, dry and sweete oats for His Maties hunting stables at Thetford"; or "expences for watching ye beacons of Haseberough and Waxham" or "2 combe of best pease kyll dried for His Maties hunting horses".

William's sons, Thomas and William, lived through the reigns of James I and Charles I, through the Commonwealth and into Charles II's reign. Their names appear as substantial ratepayers towards the maintenance of Cromwell's armies in Ireland and under "My Lord ffayerfax". The rate demand "for ye some of £23/10/- ffor six months from ye Towne of Dyse" was to be paid "att or beffore the nynth day of May, 1645, to avoyd ye penalties imposed upon ye neglecters thereof".

Thomas's son, Samuel, a linen merchant, shared in the prosperity of the Diss hempen cloth industry. He served successively as overseer, constable and churchwarden—the Town papers testify to his widespread activities.

Probably his greatest service to Diss was in 1691, when, with a few public-spirited colleagues, he frustrated the cunning attempts of an influential local attorney, John Burrough, to impose his own rating system on the town. Much dissension and many lawsuits followed—even the town accounts were not kept as they "ought to have bin".

Samuel died in 1701, to be followed by his son Samuel, who made a great mark in public life. He organised a fund for erecting the west gallery in the church, where "the young men, ladds, and maydes should sitt for their better convenyencye of singing". He was founder-trustee of the Charity School for poor boys (1716) and contributed generously to the cost (£50) of the first Diss fire engine in 1730, one of the earliest in Norfolk.

Samuel's only son died at 21, but the descendants of his brother Thomas, carried on the family tradition. Thomas's son William became Rector of Diss in 1778. As such he presided over the "vestry"—the gathering of leading townsmen who controlled almost every aspect of town life.

He was one who advocated a general—and completely successful—inoculation in the outbreak of smallpox in 1784. As a Justice he shared the unenviable task of "drawing lots for the militia" during the Napoleonic wars, but, to replace the defunct Charity School, he had the satisfaction of organising a "Sunday School", the forerunner of the first "National School" to follow in his son's time.

William and Thomas, his sons, attended the Guildhall Grammar School which had survived from Tudor times. Thomas, a brilliant mathematician, also studied medicine and joined the East India Co. He became a leading Oriental scholar and traveller, the first Englishman to enter Tibet and be received by the Dalai Lama.

William followed his father as Rector in 1810. He lived to see vast changes in Diss—the enclosure of the Commons in 1816; the end of the first Grammar School (1820); the recasting of the bells (1832)—his name is on the tenor bell; the sale and demolition of the Guildhall (1846); the erection of a National school in the corner of the churchyard (1846); and the opening of the railway (1849).

As a Justice he was called upon to adjudicate in many difficult cases—particularly those following the machine wrecking, riots, and incendiarism fomented by the introduction of farm machinery. The records speak of his sympathy and impartiality. A life of great service ended in 1857 at the age of 86.

Charles Robertson Manning succeeded. The new National School in The Entry, whose centenary has just been marked, was largely his inspiration, as was the Heywood Chapel School later.

Untiring in his public duties, he instituted the Reading Room and the then-popular "penny readings"—wholesome, varied entertainment for all ages.

An antiquary of national repute, he produced many learned treatises for the Norfolk Archaeological Society; and as a Justice his integrity was above reproach. He received an ovation from the dense throng around the Magistrates' Room as he left the Court after the hearings of the Roydon Riots case 1893.

No greater tribute could be paid him than that contained in the Board of Health's final resolution as it disbanded to make way for the U.D.C. It recorded its "sense of obligation and thankfulness for his diligence and punctuality, his fairness and impartiality in discussion, his courtesy and consideration to members and officers" throughout his 21 years as chairman.

Charles Upwood Manning became Rector on the death of his

father in 1899 and he continued the family tradition of service until his retirement in 1916.

His daughters rendered devoted V.A.D. service in a local hospital in World War I, while their two brothers were on active service.

Several members of the Manning family still retain their interest in, and contact with Diss. The many who knew them remember with gratitude and affection their service to the town, while the Manning collection in the Norwich Library is a mine of information covering four centuries of Diss history, and the family's share of it, through ten generations.

Bertie Harrison

(PUBLISHED JANUARY 1963)

BERTIE HARRISON needs no introduction in Diss for he is well known in several capacities. Solemn and trim in his verger's robes, dignified and serious in his frock-coat-and-topper as a funeral director; stern as the complete "master ringer" when conducting a treble-bob or as the cheerful decorator, perched high on his ladder. But above all he is one of the sixth generation of a family that has provided St. Mary's, the Parish Church of Diss with sextons, clerks, vergers, choirmen, ringers and pitch-pipers and even the town with its town criers over more than 200 years.

Notes from the family diary, some pencilled scrawling on the door of the vestry cupboard, and the parish registers—with churchwardens' and other accounts, have enabled me to compile the family story.

It began when Robert Parr (born 1743) attended the Diss Charity School at the age of ten. There he learned the three R's, to repeat the Catechsim, and to become familiar with church services. Charity Boys were compelled to attend regularly, under supervision. Later, Robert joined the choir in the gallery and when only 18 became Town Crier.

His deep bass voice boomed through the Market Place to announce the accession of George III in 1760. Later, Robert announced his Coronation and other national events of importance at the time, such as "The great victory gained by the capture of Pondicherry in 1761'.'

Church duties in those days were interesting, varied and at times exacting. Of powerful build, Robert was one of the four burly men paid 1s. each in 1783 "to keep the church quiet at the Bishop's Visitation".

Alone, he performed a similar task in 1786. It may seem strange that it was necessary "to maintain order" in the church, but those were times of bitter friction between the religious sects and services were frequently interrupted.

However, Robert lived to see peace between them, and he was

among the vast congregation to welcome John Wesley to St. Mary's in 1790.

Years before, Robert had wandered through the leafy lanes of Palgrave with Susanna Grey, succumbed to her charms and married her early in 1769.

Before Christmas in that year, a new young Robert had arrived—the first of the nine children Susanna presented him with at regular intervals before she died in 1785.

Robert sought consolation in a second marriage, but dropped out of public life, and after all his service to the town he ended his days in poverty. The Book of Requests at the House shows that he was on poor relief from 1816 until he died in 1824, at the age of 81.

Young Robert helped his father in many ways. He had the family ear for music, and soon learned to churn the handle of the barrel organ placed in the gallery in 1786. Each of its barrels could play ten tunes——psalms or hymns—but it had to be "set" at the correct "snotch", then turned with great dexterity, especially for those sustained passages in the psalms.

Robert was dubbed "The Dumb Organist"—but he received two guineas a year, nevertheless.

He married Hannah Howlett in 1794, and four years later became sexton, as well as "organist". It was then that the pitchpipe came into use. This wooden instrument, like a miniature organ pipe, was fitted with a whistle mouthpiece and an adjustable "slider", so that any note in the scale could be pitched to start a hymn.

As sexton, Robert tolled the bell and then had to descend from the belfry to "grind the organ". To avoid delay in starting the service, Hannah began the first hymn with a note on the pipe—then Robert arrived to take up with the organ in due course. Later his daughter Hannah (born 1796) relieved her mother of pipe duties, even at an early age.

The church was then furnished with high box-pews and a three-decker pulpit. During a long sermon some members of the congregation were wont to "doze off" in the recesses of the pews.

According to a diary of this period, left by Wilton Rix, Robert Parr used to perambulate the aisles silently in sermon time, clad in felt slippers, discreetly prodding with a willow wand those who succumbed to drowsiness.

In the church, on August 11th, 1816, Robert (as Town Crier)

pronounced the completion of the enclosure of the Greens and Commons of Diss, when the Diss Moor, Westbrook and Walcot Greens and Heywood Common disappeared.

He was in charge of the volunteer firemen at a conflagration at Blackthorn Farm on a bitterly cold day of January, 1823. Hundreds of people flocked to the scene. Ponds were frozen and had to be sledge hammered to obtain water for the bucket line to feed the "ingeon". Confusion followed the collapse of a chimney —two of Robert's colleagues were killed, and he sustained one broken leg, the other being frostbitten.

However, Robert continued his wheelwright's business and sexton's duties until old age forced him to retire in 1859, shortly before his death. His son-in-law, Terah Nicholson, noted in the diary: "June 1st, 1860, died my much-respected father-in-law, in the 90th year of his age". So ended a long and happy partnership for Terah, also a wheelwright, had married Hannah Parr in 1823, and had joined her father in business. He became Parish Clerk in 1825, and remained so till 1879, when his daughter Emma wrote: "My dear Father, departed this life August 20th in the 82nd year of his age. His end was peace".

Dignified and imposing, and a clever 'cellist, his photograph still adorns the vestry wall.

Emma Nicholson (1832) was one of Terah's seven daughters. He and his wife had obviously hoped for, but were not blessed with a son—because, when Amelia (No. 7) was born, he wrote: "July 20 was born Amelia, 7th daughter, the last of all".

Emma helped with the pitch-pipe until in 1844 a pedal organ replaced the hurdy-gurdy.

She married James Harrison in 1856 and their son William was fostered in the Church's tradition. At ten he was in the church choir and when the new, 3-manual organ was erected in the Corpus Christi Chapel in 1877, and the chancel furnished with new clergy and choir stalls, young Harrison was in the first procession of the surpliced choir, proudly singing "Who are these like stars appearing?"

William, a skilled cabinet maker and a faithful Churchman, became sexton and verger at the age of 29 in 1896, devotedly filling those offices with dignity and regularity until his retirement in 1943. He died in 1955, aged 88.

William and Bertie, his sons, had been of great help in his

later years, both in Church affairs and in business. William, a chorister, boy and man, for over 50 years, is now removed to Northampton, and assists another choir, and is also custodian of that pitch-pipe, nearly 200 years old. Bertie followed his father in 1943 as verger and sexton.

Now 62—but looking much younger—he has, we hope, many years to run—especially if he is to maintain the family tradition of longevity (Robert Parr I, 81; Robert Parr II, 90; Terah and Hannah Nicholson, 82 and 90; Emma Harrison, 89; W. H. Harrison, 88; Gertrude Harrison, 87).

Bertie has the family flair for cabinet making, and is known wherever bells are rung. His long-suffering wife helps him most assiduously in his duties, and patiently waits Sunday by Sunday as he completes them, while his daughter Kathleen is also an accomplished "ringer" when freedom from domestic duties allows her to indulge.

What a family record of service this is! Little did Robert Parr and Susanna Grey realise what they were setting in motion, they first met nearly 200 years ago.

Horse doctor

(PUBLISHED JULY 1962)

AFTER 50 years in business as a chemist and druggist in Mere Street, Diss, Francis Cupiss, then 76, threatened to retire in 1874. He went with his wife to the "Parson's Entry" to inspect an unoccupied mansion he proposed to acquire.

"What a wilderness," exclaimed his wife, as she surveyed the overgrown garden, straggling hedges and drab paintwork. Cupiss, who knew the possibilities of the place, and was determined to buy it, simply replied, "That's what we'll call it—the Wilderness !"

He did purchase it, and the names of Francis Cupiss and The Wilderness have been linked ever since—spreading far beyond East Anglia, even to distant corners of the Commonwealth.

That Wilderness had been a boarding school for boys for half a century, known for many years as "Dunlop's Academy," it had offered a "Classical or Commercial Education to Young Gentlemen," at modest charges. It had started when the old Guildhall Grammar School ceased in 1830 on the death of the last master—the Rev. Simon Westby. An assistant, William Grear, had bought the mansion in the Parson's Entry, added a spacious schoolroom with dormitory above, and had developed a successful educational establishment, later taken over by Mr. Dunlop, whose wife also had a clientele of young children to educate with her own. Quite abruptly, in 1872, Mr. Dunlop "declined keeping school." His extensive library and school effects were auctioned, and the throbbing life of the Academy was stilled. The unoccupied premises suffered from neglect, and became "The Wilderness" which Mr. Cupiss restored in 1874.

Cupiss, born in 1798, was educated at Huntingdon Grammar School, then apprenticed to a chemist and druggist in London. He attended the Veterinary College, also one of the famous Anatomical Schools (then supplied with bodies for dissection by those clandestine "workers"—the "Resurrection-men). Thereby he acquired an expert knowledge of both humans and animals—being, for a time, a lecturer at the College.

Love of the country brought him, in 1823, to Diss, where he could combine the business of a chemist and druggist with a veterinary practice. An expert horseman and lover of animals, he became a familiar figure in South Norfolk as he performed his rounds on horse-back, his horse always being noted for its immaculate condition. When asked how he maintained such perfection, he would shrug his shoulders and attribute the horses' condition to those "Constitution Balls" he made from his own secret formula—for in 1838 he had won a National Prize for a "Thesis on the liver of a horse." He knew every ailment and how to treat it.

So began the manufacture of a range of proprietary medicines —Constitution Powders, Physic Balls and Cough Medicines—for use in his practice and for general sale, The gallon sized copper in which he brewed those original concoctions over 130 years ago is preserved by the firm still bearing his name. The fame of his products spread far and wide—carried overseas by a stream of East Anglian emigrants who sent home continuous orders.

In 1830 a printer's business was acquired, mainly to print his own circulars and wrappers. The original design of a double panelled label is still used. One panel bears the form of a dejected looking horse, sadly out of condition, with no interest in its provender, and carries the caption "Out of sorts." The other, entitled "All Right" depicts a spirited prancing animal in first rate condition, clamouring for its bait.

All branches of the business flourished. Then, at 76, came the "retirement" from Mere Street to The Wilderness. In those more spacious surroundings there was an upsurge of activity in printing and medicines. But Cupiss wisely delegated responsibility to a former apprentice, Walter Clarke, and to Alfred Rushton who came from the "East Anglian." To them he confided his formulae and the "knowhow" of preparing pills and powders. When he died in 1888, aged 89, he left a prosperous business, which still continues.

The Assistants too have passed on, but Clarke's son and grandson now manage the firm's activities, with Cupiss' great-granddaughter as chairman of directors.

At a "make" or medicine-making session, Cupiss' original recipe book of 1830 is brought out for consultation. It contains directions for making an infinite variety of "preparations," some devised by Cupiss, others made to customers' own requirements.

Turning the pages recently I noticed "Blacking Balls," "Balls for chapped hands," "Harness Paste." "Mr. Ellis' Curry Powder" and "Blist'ring Ointment" among a host of entries in the Cupiss copper-plate hand.

Though horses have declined with the advent of car and tractor, a steady demand for Cupiss' products persists, boosted recently by the popularity of riding. However, 80 per cent goes for export to meet repeated orders from Australia, New Zealand, Pakistan and Ceylon in particular, while products are made under licence in Eire.

Mr. Dunlop's schoolroom is the printing office—printing now forming the major part of the business. The Master's desk is in its old place, the underside of the lid scored deep with many familiar initials and names of a century ago. The school cupboards bulge with printer's materials, while on the interiors of the doors are scrawled well-known names. A proof reader occupies a corner of the old dormitory, and the Usher's cottage is now the company's office.

Several of the oldest inhabitants of Diss actually remember the short, sturdy form of Francis Cupiss, "in his spotless suit of black broadcloth," his "snowy shirt frill, white hair, and coloured spectacles." When they have gone his name will still be linked with that "Wilderness" he made to flourish.

William Betts

(PUBLISHED AUGUST 1962)

WHEN William Betts, of "The Court," Victoria Road, Diss assumed the ownership of Frenze Hall Estate in 1868, he planned to make it a vast market garden, producing fresh vegetables for London, with the General Eastern Railway as link between producer and consumer. His ideas for a self-supporting venture were progressive and practical—with brick, tile and drainpipe works to make his own building materials; sawmill and carpenters' shop for joinery; and the most modern farm machinery for cultivation, including steam ploughs.

But the king-pin of his project was the standard-gauge railway network to traverse the estate, bringing manure from London's thousands of stables direct to the fields, and to carry produce, via Diss Station, to London, without break of bulk.

In May, 1869, permission was granted by the Board of Health for a "tramway" across Sandy Lane. Crossing gates were stipulated, and an annual charge of 5s. imposed.

Work proceeded rapidly. At a workmen's celebration in June, 1869, a barrel of Mr. Cuthbert's best beer was broached to mark the completion of the first section of the track, and the arrival at Sandy Lane of trucks of manure straight from London.

Soon the line extended eastwards to the Frenze river, crossing the Boiler Meadow—so called because of the huge boiler like cylinders sunk there to give a firm foundation—then over the river by a girder bridge, up the long drag to Dark Lane, where it divided into two branches. One turned north towards Frenze Hall near which it forked, one section crossing the stream behind the Hall and terminating near the G.E.R., the other leading further north to a field known as "Scotland" (probably Scott's land, earlier).

The second branch continued east, ending at buffers behind Scole Inn, but sending off "feeders" north and south to Nab Barn, and to a point behind Scole Rectory, thus completing a single track system of seven miles, serving every part of the 400-acre estate.

One brickyard was developed just east of Diss Station, using clay from the enormous pit near the "Jolly Porters". The other was behind Scole Rectory, north of the Bottle Cottages, near Mill, or Miller's Lane, while the tile and drainpipe works were opened near Fisher's Farm, at Scole.

Water, pumped to an elevated tank near the Frenze River, fed the tanker wagons which were moved about the estate when transplanting. Then, in what is now Mission Road, an enormous greenhouse was erected for raising thousands of plants. To complete the picture, there were Gate Houses at Sandy Lane and Dark Lane; Lay's Barn was built for sorting, cleaning and packing produce, with Nab Barn for stores and equipment.

Rolling stock comprised two "locos", 0-6-0 and 0-4-0; 12 tip-wagons for manure; three flat-bottomed trucks for transporting building materials; four railway wagons, four tank wagons, and a mobile crane for emergencies. There were also some 50 horses, a flock of over 500 sheep, many meat stock and swine, four donkeys, a steam threshing tackle, vehicles and implements in great variety. The size and complexity of the undertaking can be appreciated.

Betts, reputed to be a wealthy man with extensive commercial interests, spared nothing to ensure success. By the early 1870's vast quantities of produce—potatoes, cabbages, carrots, onions, etc., were being despatched direct to London from Lay's Barn, and loads of manure from London's stables and the city's street sweepings, poured into Frenze.

One who knew the railway when it was working was Pal Flatman, of Tottington Lane, now 91. His brother worked at Scole flax factory, and Pal remembers walking along the Scole road as a small boy and seeing the trains puffing through the fields on the northern sky-line.

George Buckenham, now 87, lived in a cottage beside the railway near Lay's Barn—his father worked on the Betts estate—and the turn table was behind the house. He saw the whole organisation in full swing—William Betts touring his estate in a wicker cart drawn by a donkey—women and girls planting, thinning and harvesting crops—wooden water butts placed about the fields and filled by lengths of hose from the tankers—truckloads of manure arriving to be transported to every part of the fields, and a considerable labour force bustling to prepare and pack produce. His mother, after shopping at Scole, often rode back on the footplate of the engine with either Short or Vyse, the drivers. So too, did George, and he sometimes picked up a shilling accidentally dropped in some London street before finding its way to Diss in a load of manure.

The Frenze enterprise continued successfully until the mid 1880's, though the owner was heavily and expensively involved in legal disputes with the Railway. He suffered family bereavements and set-backs—his wife died in 1883, his eldest son in 1884. Frustrated and disappointed, he died in June, 1885, aged 74.

George Buckenham witnessed the funeral procession across Hume's fields, down King's Head Lane—and along the riverside path to Frenze Church. The six bearers wore "long black cloaks, hard hats with wide silk bands knotted at the back, and long streamers flowing behind". It was a sweltering day in early July.

Betts affairs proved to be in a tangled state, and came under the jurisdiction of the Chancery Court, by whose authority Thomas William Gaze assumed management of the estate. At a 2-day sale in July, 1887, the farming effects, live and dead stock, and most of the railway equipment were disposed of. The engines fetched £20 each, and were exported to India. Vast quantities of bricks, tiles and pipes, with brickyard equipment came under the hammer later. Then in September Frenze Hall and the Court were offered but withdrawn, to be sold by private treaty later. The Betts empire had been liquidated. Thomas William Gaze became tenant of Frenze Hall in 1888, the remnants of the railway track were cleared for scrap, and the great expanse of market gardens gradually reverted to normal cultivation. Much evidence of this interesting enterprise is visible today. The girders of one river bridge can be seen; two stone pillars in the river bed behind the Hall mark the site of the other. The Gate Houses, the Barns, the Railway cottages in Mission Road, Betts' Terrace at Scole, and Betts' siding are still in use. Signs of the various brickyards are easily discernible, so is the imprint "Betts—Diss" on the bricks of a house in Sunnyside.

As boys in the 1890's Charlie Denny, Fred Nunn and others amused themselves on one of the last trucks to survive and run down to the River, but Pal Flatman and George Buckenham are probably the only survivors to remember Betts enterprise as a going concern.

MATTERS OF GENERAL INTEREST

The "Town Topics" of a century ago . . .

(PUBLISHED NOVEMBER 1962)

IT is interesting to turn back the pages occasionally to assess change and progress over a given period, and this week I'd like to give you a few jottings on the Diss of 1862—at a time when public executions still attracted large crowds in the county towns (but not in Diss) and when more than one tired farm-worker, rumbling along the road in his tumbril at the end of a hard day in the fields, was fined for "failing to have some other person on foot or on horseback to guide the same."

The Board of Health, an elected body, then governed the affairs of Diss—paying its Clerk, Mr. Brook, the princely salary of £20 per annum, while Mr. J. T. Muskett—surely the "Pooh Bah" of the town—received £50 p.a. for fulfilling the combined offices of Surveyor, Inspector of Nuisances, Superintendent of the Fire Brigade and Rate Collector (neither appointment, it should be said, was full-time).

Mr. John Aldrich was then a familiar figure in the town, still remembered by many for his grey, black-banded topper, elastic-sided boots and frock coat. He had purchased "Niagara" for the Board in 1859. It had already become a boon to the district, operated as it was by a trained fire brigade, generously supplied in 1862 with "a spreader, wicker basket for the suction pipe, whipple-trees, ropes and harness, and TWO pairs of boots for the firemen".

The sexton received 2s. for ringing the church bells to alert the brigade—one shudders to think of the delay inherent in such an alarm system.

The big problem of housing Niagara was solved in 1862. So far, it had been temporarily accommodated by Mr. Brook. Mr. Garrett having emphatically refused to have it in his coach-building works, Mr. Moore's offer to keep it at the "King's Head" had been declined; and so the Board decided to erect an engine house on Mere Green (Mere's Mouth). They had even agreed on dimensions, approved plans, and gone to tender when some knowledgeable townsman, insisting on the citizens' ancient rights regarding "Town Lands", pointed out that the concurrence of the major part of the ratepayers was essential, before the Board could proceed.

Counsel's opinion was being sought when Mr. Lyus saved what was developing into a town rift, by offering premises in Chapel Street at £6 a year (Niagara stayed there for 84 years).

The highway rate for 1862 was 10d. in the £, the general district rate 9d. in the £ on houses and buildings, and 5¼d. on "arable, meadow, pasture, woodland, market and nursery ground".

The Board's major expense was £279—chiefly for the purchase of stones for the Norwich to Scole road across what was then still called Diss Common. The Surveyor was empowered to buy all clean stones available, at 1s. 9d. per load of 24 bushels. Some came from Bishop's pit at Roydon, but most from local fields, picked up principally by women who performed the back-aching job of stone-picking for ½d. per bushel. Hundreds of loads were crudely laid on the Common in 1862.

The division of the income from the town's "Framlingham Estate" had been a bone of contention for years. In 1862 the 93-acre farm was let for £240—part of which was given to the church for the maintenance of fabric and bells and part to the town for repair of the streets, in accordance with the wishes of our 15th century forbears who purchased the farm in about 1500.

The Board of Health received £20 in 1862 and purchased Yorkshire Stone Flag to pave the streets "from Half-Moon Inn to the Corn Hall" and "from the King's Head opening to the pavement opposite Mr. Barkham's".

Straying animals frequently roamed the streets in those leisurely days, but John Clarke was officially authorised to impound them in the parish pound—where the Church Hall now is. The fine for the first offence was 2s.; it was 5s. for the second, and up to 40s. for subsequent offences.

The water level of the Mere, too, gave rise to considerable anxiety in 1862, because of an obstruction in the overflow. The Board decided to place "a barrel arch across Park Field Road, to lay a double row of pipes in the overflow ditch, as far as the drain from the Ebenezer Schoolroom (now Messrs. Chitty's Park Road Store), and to place a sluice at the end of the pipes".

The new National School came into use in 1862 "in a quiet corner of the Parson's Entry near the Rectory Grounds. Here the children of the poor assembled under tuition of Mr. and Mrs. Horsfall and pupil teachers, in a building in old English style, with two spacious playgrounds.

Pedestrians in the town centre suffered great inconvenience from cattle indiscriminately herded in Church Street and Market Place for the weekly market. Mr. Chase—butcher and grazier—offered to enclose, with hurdles, the space before the "Dolphin" and "Bell" inns, if market tolls were suspended. No evidence exists of the idea being implemented, but it set people thinking about the properly-organised livestock market which was to come later.

The year 1862 was not an exciting one, but other items I have read included: "Mr. Slack received £1 3s. per lamp per ann. for illuminating the town with gas"; "A new water cart was purchased for spraying the streets in the heat of summer" (shopkeepers complained bitterly of the dust raised by traffic in Mere Street); "Posts were erected at Horne's Entry to keep out wheeled traffic"; and "A tallow chandler's office was erected in "Baptist Chapel Lane" (i.e., the old slaughter house in Croft Lane, now demolished).

Then, I see, "Diss Sessions Fair in the Market Place (formerly of three days' duration in Sept.) was for the first time limited to one day"; "The Board insisted on properly-constructed ashpits at the new Church School premises"; "An offender was prosecuted for conveying night-soil through the streets in an unsuitable cart, dropping, slopping and spilling it"; while the threat of prosecution hung over the heads of "persons using catapults and throwing or discharging stones or other missiles, and for knocking bungs about, or running hoops on public footways".

The Board ended the year with a commendable human touch, by appointing a sub-committee to "go through the rate books for the purpose of reducing or remitting payment of any rate, on account of poverty".

Emigration

(PUBLISHED OCTOBER 1963)

"TWO gallant young people set off for the Bahamas" ran a headline in the *Diss Express* on August 23rd, 1963, announcing the departure of the Rev. John and Mrs. Ruth Bilverstone to work as missionaries in the island of Spanish Wells. They flew from London Airport on August 21st, via New York for Nassau, to complete their journey by sea. Their emigration—for such it was—was a voluntary act; they have left behind the comforts of an affluent Britain to preach the Gospel to coloured and to white people. "It will be an exhausting life, with many problems," said a former missionary.

Two years ago, Miss Audrey Officer, of Scole, left these shores of her own volition to carry the same message to the Araucanian Indians of South Chile.

This year Australia expects 80,000 immigrants from Britain, and recent figures show that nearly 12,000 settlers from Britain arrived in Canada between January and June. We are told, too, that poorer employment prospects for school leavers here are likely to keep Commonwealth Emigration at a record level.

By a strange coincidence, I was rummaging among the contents of an old box in Shelfanger Church on the very day John and Ruth Bilverstone flew out of London. In the overseer's accounts was this item: "This is to certify that Edmund Duffield received the sum of four pounds ten shillings to provide clothes for himself, his wife and seven children, for the purpose of Emigrating to America. Ap. 22 1837 (signed) Edmund Duffield, (witness) Charles Ellis." There was a similar receipt from Dennis Frost for £3, for clothes for himself, his wife and four children, for the same purpose.

This interesting discovery led to further searches and inquiries which have revealed details of emigrations from Lopham, Brockdish, Tivetshall, Gissing and Stradbroke on a considerable scale, but under conditions and for reasons vastly different from those of today.

For in the second quarter of the 19th century families left East

Anglia in their thousands to face the perils of a six weeks' voyage across the Atlantic, and to take a chance of employment on arrival, with no definite future guaranteed.

Some idea of the movement from East Anglia is provided by this paragraph from Mackie's *Norfolk Annals for* 1836: "195 emigrants from villages in the neighbourhood embarked on April 13 at Friar's Fleet, Lynn, on board the ship Anne of 400 tons, bound for Quebec. Mr. Daniel Gurney distributed Bibles and Prayer Books among them".

It continued: "Large numbers of emigrants left the country during the spring. By May 17, 1,625 had sailed from Yarmouth alone. On May 25, the 'Morning Star' sailed from the same port, with 212 emigrants, chiefly labourers from Suffolk, and the 'Brunswick' with 447 agriculturalists from East Norfolk. By July 2, the total number embarked at Yarmouth for Quebec and Port St. Francis on the St. Lawrence was 3,200.

Yarmouth and Lynn were only two of the ports of embarkation, and those 3,200 but a mere fragment of the great stream of emigrants who left these shores to swell the growing population of Canada by some 30,000 a year, and that of the U.S.A. by half-a-million in the decade 1830-1840, and by nearly 1½ millions from 1840-1850.

What were the reasons for these movements ? What prompted a Reepham man, R. Morlege, to drive his covered van containing his wife and seven children to Liverpool—there to embark—with the van—for Baltimore, and thence to proceed in the van about 400 miles up country to settle on the banks of the Ohio ?

And why should more than 100 persons from the Lophams emigrate to the U.S.A. in 1830, prepared to submit to the perils of a 3,000-mile sea voyage and the uncertainties they would encounter on landing ?

Historians have attributed these migrations to many causes First of all there was the decay of traditional rural industries, such as spinning and weaving, with all their attendant crafts and skills Population was increasing rapidly—Shelfanger jumped from 382 in 1801 to 440 in 1821; Stradbroke from 1,215 in 1801 to 1,637 in 1841; Diss from 2,540 in 1811 to 2,934 in 1831. These increases may not appear great to us, but there were just not the jobs available for the increasing numbers.

Enclosures of common land had deprived the ordinary folk of

their grazing rights for geese and cows, which "saw them through" in hard times. Prices fluctuated tremendously—low prices for corn bringing ruin to farmers, high prices bringing misery to the workers. According to Dickleburgh farm accounts, wheat fetched 75s. per coomb in 1817, but only 14s. in 1822. In the season 1815-16 the prices varied from 26s. to 60s.

Low wages, harsh laws and the introduction of agricultural machinery on an increasing scale created unrest and resentment. Machine-wrecking became widespread—a violent outburst occurred at Shimpling and Burston in 1822—and incendiarism of stacks and barns was a symbol of the general malaise.

The use of troops to suppress outbreaks and demonstrations added fuel to the fire of discontent.

David Thomson, now Master of Sidney Sussex College, Cambridge, writing of 1830 in his review of the 19th century, refers to the starving field labourers of the Southern Counties who rioted in support of a demand for a wage of 2s. 6d. per day. Three were hanged and 420 deported to Australia.

Mason's History of Norfolk quotes the Rector of Kilverstone as saying, in 1822, following acute unrest in his area—"This district is heavily enclosed country in the hands of small occupiers generally, and the common people are much neglected".

The opinion of a Norfolk magistrate, Col. Harvey, is also quoted by Mason, on the question of prosecutions for incendiarism and machine-breaking: "It is my duty to say that the great mass of operative labour in this county are ill paid, not kindly treated, too often neglected and insulted, and have been driven to commit acts of violence to obtain by force what they ought to have had without".

Addressing a meeting of 500 landowners and yeomen, Mr. W. E. L. Bulwer, of Heydon Hall, spoke of "The universal distress and degradation of the agricultural poor, a class once contented happy and vigorous, now thankless, listless and unprofitable, unable to earn even the slightest means of support".

This contention was borne out by the rising cost of Poor Law relief in Norfolk, which rose from £170,000 in 1803 to £276,999 in 1829—even then tens of thousands were barely subsisting.

Overseers' accounts, kept very strictly, and inspected annually by the Justices at Quarter Sessions, provided perhaps the most penetrating insight into prevailing conditions of the post-Napoleonic War period.

Consider Brockdish in 1831, with a population of 482. It supported its own workhouse—the inmates referred to always as 'paupers'— (this term was in general use) and also had a list of some 25 persons (also classed as paupers) receiving out-relief regularly.

The parish raised £550 during 1831 to support its permanent poor, and to meet the daily demands of other individuals 'out of work'—'at need'—'for loss of time'—for clothes, fuel, medical help, bedding and the like.

Here are a number of items of parish relief which support the contentions of Mr. Bulwer and Col. Harvey, quoted earlier: "Charles Pretty at need, having no work 2s."; "Robert Rodwell at need, to go and seek work 8s. 6d."; "Jas Knights at need, not being able to work 1s."; "Jas. Cooper's daughter towards a pair of stays at her going to service at Mr. Burgess 3s. 6d."; "Pd. for altering a waistcoat for Boy Welton that was his father's, 6d."; "Wm. Drewmilk, to buy 1 stone meal, the weather not permitting him to work 2s. 7d."; "Ann Warren at need having a lame hand 1s." "Bought an ass for Sam Culham for him to go pedling with, for support of his family, he not being able to walk 10s. 6d."; "altering the biggening breeches for old Drewmilk 4s."; "Relieved a woman on the road, being near her confinement and conveying her and family to Harleston 5s."; "Relieved a man his wife and family on the road to git them out of the parish 6d."; "apprehending old Stannard and carrying him to Harleston for steeling Davy's Turnips 3s."; "Expenses attending funeral of travelling pauper found ded in Mr. Reeves Hayloft 3s. 6d.".

One page of the book consisted of 40 successive items "at need"—these being small sums for those in temporary want, who appealed to the overseers for immediate relief.

Nor were conditions in other parishes one whit better. Stradbroke had a population of just over 1,500 in 1827, 'according to the Overseers' book no less than 125 were receiving a weekly allowance varying from 1s. to 8s. 6d.

In addition there were another 204 in receipt of temporary relief. Both groups were classified as "paupers" and there was an "alphabetical list of paupers" for each. Taking into account the number of children (quoted for each family), it can be seen that between a quarter and a third of the population of the village were dubbed "paupers".

To discourage persons from entering the workhouse the "Select Vestry" of March 25th, 1830, agreed that "linsey Woolsey dresses and yellow stockings shall be worn by all young persons who shall become inmates of the parish house of Stradbroke". This branded them as paupers.

It was against such a background that thousands of East Anglians—'paupers'—braved the Atlantic perils to launch themselves into the unknown of a foreign land to seek a better future there. To quote an announcement April 29th, 1837: " 'The Anne', with 171 emigrants for Quebec, was towed out of Lynn Harbour. They are leaving their native country for another, where they hope their services will be more in request."

The 1830 wagon train for Diss emigrants

(PUBLISHED OCTOBER 1963)

"THE second quarter of the 19th Century was the period in the settlement of Canada, Australia and New Zealand which decided that those lands should be peopled mainly from Britain. The over peopling of Great Britain, and the sorry plight of the English peasantry at home caused the great rural exodus to the Colonies in these years. The tide of emigration also ran strongly to the United States, and might have run there almost to the exclusion of British territories, but for the organised effort of emigration societies, and the occasional assistance of the Government, inspired by the propaganda of Gibbon Wakefield."

So wrote Prof. Trevelyan in his "English Social History". If any corroboration is needed of that sorry plight of the peasantry and the resulting rural exodus, then parish records of East Anglia provide it. The Diss Vestry Minute Book (1818-44) shows that there was so little employment for young people in 1824 that the overseers were instructed "to go round the parish immediately and endeavour to prevail upon the parishioners to hire poor children, offering 40s. from the rates to those who hired a child for a year, half to be paid on the delivery of the child, and the other half at the end of 6 months".

Conditions evidently did not improve, for the Vestry met in January, 1829, "to take into consideration the state of the unemployed poor". Later in that year they met again "to consider and devise the best means of employing the poor". In the following year they were forced to raise the poor rate from 1s. to 2s. in the £ (and later to 2s. 8d.) and they "allowed Wm. Roper ten pound to go to America". (He was the first parish-assisted emigrant). The situation was acute for in November the Vestry again considered the state of the unemployed poor, and decided "to adopt some plan whereby the poor may be enabled to earn their own livelihood, and not be beholden to the Parish for support". Procrastination!

Presumably matters drifted—no 'plan' was mentioned, but on April 1st, 1832, the Vestry met to consider "Emigration". Four days later they called together the principal inhabitants to meet a Yarmouth shipping agent and "the applicants for emigrating" —Yarmouth being the principal East Anglian port of embarkation.

No result of this meeting is recorded—though it may be that emigrants were privately sponsored, or aided by one of the Emigration Societies.

On Easter Monday, 1835, there was yet another meeting—"to determine upon the best means of employing the poor", but not till 1844 were emigrants again in the news. Then, it was agreed that "William Rudd, shoemaker, his wife and four children be sent out as emigrants to Canada at the parish expence". To defray this, £38 was raised as a fund for the Emigration of Poor Persons. Poverty was still widespread in Diss, for the year 1844 ended with an urgent appeal to support "a subscription list for the relief of the necessitous poor".

Diss records are admirable in many respects, but on emigration at this time they are exasperatingly deficient in detail. However, a cutting from a Bury paper lifts the veil on what was just one of many such events. "April 30th, 1830. Seventy-eight men, women and children from Diss, Palgrave and Wortham, and fifty-eight from Winfarthing and Shelfanger, passed through Bury in stage waggons on the way to London to take shipping for America. They were in high spirits".

Fortunately Shelfanger is far more forthcoming about this period simply because a young girl, Alice Holmes, born 1821, was among those who emigrated in 1830 from Shelfanger. In 1888 she published a book of poems and reminiscences under the title of "Lost Vision"—for in later years she lost her sight. In her book she wrote—"Early in 1830, when I was just 9 years old, there was great excitement in Shelfanger in regard to families emigrating to America. My father and two cousins were interested, and affairs were speedily settled. Mr. Early Granger decided to bring his family and come with us, and Mr. John Granger too. He afterwards sent for his wife and family, and settled on Long Island, where his children and grandchildren now reside (1888). A large van was engaged to convey us to London, April 28th was set for our departure from the Fighting Cocks, Winfarthing. We passed through Shelfanger, my happy home for the past 7 years, and there in the main street were gathered many friends and familiar faces to wish us a long and last good-bye". The Rev. Mr. Harrison, Rector of Shelfanger, 1898-1912, in a notebook he left, mentions an old resident of the parish whose memory went back to 1825, and who lived on into Edward VII's reign. This old resident remembered the departure of those emigrants, and of other groups like them. He also described the bad times when he was a boy. Many of his boy friends of the 1830s were sent out all day "shooing" (scaring) birds—having had only barley bread to eat, for wheat flour was 7s. a stone. Their day's allowance was eaten by 9 o'clock For the rest of the day they went hungry.

The two men, Duffield and Frost, mentioned last week as emigrants in April, 1837, were classed as "Paupers" in those days. Their expenses were paid by the parish under the provisions of the Poor Law Act of 1834. This act made it lawful for any parish to raise a sum of money "not exceeding half the average yearly rate for the three preceding years, for defraying the expences of emigration of poor persons, willing to emigrate". Careful selection of emigrants was called for, and the Poor Law Commissioners had to approve them, and the expenditure on them. The nomination form submitted asked for a statement of money paid in relief to paupers in the previous twelve months. Habitual paupers, who were probably unfit for the hard pioneering work of an emigrant, were not considered.

In the 12 months prior to departure Duffield and family had received £13 17s. 5d. in cash, and in addition many items of food, fuel and clothing, while Frost and family had received £13 1s. 1d. in cash, plus other items. The cost of emigration was £12 10s. for a man and wife, £3 2s. 6d. for a child—so the two families would cost approximately £60 and transport to the port. The parish employment situation was eased and the poor rate relieved of the expense of maintenance, perhaps for years.

Gissing papers contain a full record of the emigration of Simond Watling, Robert Palmer, James Morley and George Heavers—all sponsored by the parish with the approval of the Poor Law Commissioners and the Agent General for Emigration. They travelled to London by the Bury, Diss, Norwich and London Stage Waggon at a cost of 7s. per passenger plus 1s. 6d. each for baggage. A summary of the total cost includes "Conveyance of Paupers to London £1—14—0; Expences in London, Provisions, passage and board to America £37—16—0; Overseer's Expences £1—6—0; Cash paid to Paupers £12—10—0" (the last item was "landing money", with which every emigrant had to be provided). On board, emigrants had to supply their own bedding, provisions and even cooking apparatus—so such items as "Tin 'where' 12s " 6d —Beding for men £1—8—0 — Tea, sugar and soap 3s; Knives and forks 1s " 8d; Frying pan 1s " 6d; and 2lb. of Tobaco 8s " appeared among expenses. To meet the total cost the sum of £50 was borrowed from William Carter, Jr., of Gissing, at 5 per cent. interest and repaid the following year from the poor rate.

In Tivetshall events followed a similar pattern. The "Towne Book" shows that at a parish meeting in 1837 it was resolved "to borrow 60£ forthwith for defraying expences of the emigration of poor persons, willing to emigrate". Accordingly Jonathan Thrower (27), Richard Long (20)—both single labourers—and Mary Browne (45), widow, described as a 'chairwoman', and her four children, George (17), Elizabeth (16), Harriet (13) and Charlotte (4), were accompanied by the overseer to Yarmouth from whence they sailed in the "Old Brunswick" for Quebec. These emigrants had collectively cost the parish £22 2s. 6d. in poor relief during the previous year. Now for £60 (plus £3 interest), all repaid the following year by sale of parish property, responsibility for the future support of these "paupers" was over for good.

The emigration season was from April to September—a round trip for a vessel occupied at least three months, so one trip only was possible each year before the St. Lawrence was closed by ice.

Yarmouth "shipping intelligence" contained these items for 1837 in addition to the departure of the Brunswick—"Baltic sailed April 15 with 200 emigrants for America, in a fair wind"—"April 22 The Preston sailed for Quebec with emigrants"—"April 29. The Anne of 400 tons sailed for Quebec with 171 emigrants"—"May 4. The Carron sailed from Gt. Yarmouth with emigrants"—"May 11. The Venus sailed for Quebec".

All returned with "timber and deals".

New World pioneers from Stradbroke

(PUBLISHED OCTOBER 1963)

STRADBROKE, like other parishes, experienced grim times during and after the Napoleonic Wars. Population was rising rapidly, unemployment was rife, and the Parish Vestry (responsible for the affairs of the parish) was conscious of the existence of a potentially inflammatory situation. It met twice in 1825 "to consider a plan for alleviating distress," then formulated its plan of action. The Vestry Records contained full details of the plan, set out in seven long clauses.

Clause 1 provided for the employment of more labour: "Every occupier of land whose assessment to the poor rate was 40£, engaged to employ one 'constant labourer'; if the assessment was 80£, 2 labourers; if 120£, three; and so on in proportion."

Then, "after taking men as aforesaid", the 30 principal inhabitants who subscribed to the plan, agreed to consider "the surplice labourers as classmen". Every occupier who employed his quota of "constant labourers" was entitled to the labour of a number of classmen, who were paid by the overseer according to a scale of maintenance, though every occupier was expected to allow what he thought "reasonable" in addition.

Other clauses made provision for such contingencies as bad weather or a classman's refusal to do his allotted work.

These arrangements ran for a month in the first instance and were then under monthly review by the Vestry Classmen were grouped into 32 "sets", and a complicated list contains their names, the names of occupiers, their assessments, and the number of days' work each classman was to give his allotted master.

But this cleverly-devised scheme proved to be only a temporary alleviation of a worsening situation.

Early in 1828 the Vestry resolved that "in consequence of the number of unemployed labourers in the parish, some further plan be adopted to have such persons employed". They revised Clause I of the earlier plan, so that every occupier whose assessment was £20 (instead of £40) took one labourer, whose assessment was £40, two labourers, and so on. Further, the Town Meeting agreed to allow John Pipe, farmer, of Park Farm, to set up a "treading machine at his own expense and charge", the parish agreeing "to make good all wilfull hurts and damages done to the machine by any man employed to work on it".

A true account of the "quantity of corn thrashed by the machine" was to be given after a year's trial, and the parishioners agreed not "to thrash their corn by any other machine save this Treading machine and the Flail".

This was the period of machine wrecking, hence John Pipe's stipulation about wilful damage.

The Town Meeting also agreed that Mr. Robert Farrow, corn miller, of Battlesey Green, "do make a spinning mechean for the purpose of spinning Hemp for making sacks and tilts or any other article which may be thought of most advantage to the parish".

Thirteen named, substantial householders were to "supretend the said manufactering".

But by April, 1830, conditions in Stradbroke were desperate once more, yet all exchanges and negotiations were conducted in a temperate and constitutional manner, as this petition from the unfortunate workless shows: "We whose names are hereunder subscribed, being persons who belong to the parish of Stradbroke, and desirous to emigrate to N. America, but are unable to bear the Expences and charges of such undertaking, hereby request the assistance of the said Parish to enable us to carry such intention into effect. And whereas the ship called the Preston will sail from Yarmouth in a few days, we request the favour and hope that the parish will be pleased to take such means as may enable us to embrace the offered opportunity of going on board the said ship, or any other, as soon as conveniently may be. We have hereunto set our hands and thereby bind ourselves to carry this Engagement into full effect as soon as the means are provided for so doing."

Seventeen names are appended—all men—of whom 11 "made their marks".

This urgent petition met with spontaneous approval, for the Vestry Book continues—"and we do agree and consent that the officers, churchwardens and overseers of this parish, and others the parishioners, do enter into a Bond to raise a sufficient sum of money for the purpose of enabling a number of poor persons of this parish to emigrate to N. America, that is to say, a sum not exceeding

300£". This was signed by Wm. White, the Vicar, and 18 others. There were 20 in the Vestry.

Yet another resolution was passed, binding the parish officers to pay to "the Capt. or owner of the ship the Emigrants shall go on board of" sums for "landing money" to be paid to each emigrant on arrival at Quebec.

From a series of rough calculations pencilled in the Book, it can be gathered that the cost of passage and maintenance during voyage of a man and wife was £12 10s., of a singleman £6 10s., of a child £3 2s. 6d. Landing money was allowed—for a man or woman £1, for a child 15s., and for each individual 10s. for clothes, and 5s. for "hospital".

In this first exodus from Stradbroke 12 men, 12 women, one singleman, and 18 children sailed in the Preston. A crowded Town Meeting authorised an expenditure of £215 15s., more than 50 townsmen signing their names in approval.

Yet another similar petition was presented in April, 1832, in the names of 15 men (ten of whom 'made their marks'), who described themselves as "poor persons desirous to emigrate to Canada, but unable to bear the costs and charge of such undertaking". They expressed "their earnest desire and intention of emigrating" and bound themselves to "carry out their engagement as soon as the means were provided for so doing".

More pencilled notes provide a list of 11 adults and 30 children who were despatched at a total cost of £199 5s. including £6 "for waggon to Yarmouth", and £1 10s. for the constable who acted as escort.

It was thus that Stradbroke attempted to solve its problems of depression, unemployment and poverty. *White's Directory of Suffolk* for 1855—based on authentic information supplied by responsible persons in Stradbroke—sums up the parish effort in this terse sentence: "The Parish sent about 200 pauper emigrants to America from 1831-1843." In fact, these were among the sturdy adventurous pioneers who helped to lay the foundations of two great modern nations.

Some Norfolk Bread Doles

(PUBLISHED JANUARY 1964)

ONE of my most vivid childhood memories of Redgrave in the early years of this century was the monthly distribution of bread provided under John Hubbard's will of 1727. He laid a charge on "Calkpritts Close" for the purchase of bread "to be given every 4th Sunday to the poorer inhabitants who should be present at Divine service or would have been unless prevented by sickness or infirmity."

A mass of tempting cottage loaves adorned the Altar Table and at the conclusion of the service those eligible received their gifts from the Rector. I recall the line of aged and often bent figures wending their way home across the fields, carrying their precious burdens—many enclosed in knotted red handkerchiefs with large white spots, the kerchiefs of many uses in those days.

These recollections led me to the massive report of the commissioners appointed by Parliament "to inquire concerning the Charities and Education of the Poor" (1815-1839). There it stated that Norfolk has no less than 148 "Bread Charities". The Report described them as they were then administered nearly 150 years ago.

Perusing them all was no mean task—but what struck me most forcibly was that such a simple operation as a "Gift of Bread" could arise in such a variety of ways, or vary so much in the times, methods and conditions of distribution. Time has depreciated the value of money—the penny loaf is no longer realistic, so most of the 148 will have been, by now, adapted to the conditions of 1963.

Some charities provided for monthly allocation, some were fortnightly gifts—many were connected with Christmas, or St. Thomas's day, December 21st—for St. Thomas was associated with charitable distributions to the poor during his journeyings in the Middle East in the First Century. The following are typical cases to illustrate the great variety contained in the Commissioners' report on bread charities.

At Kenninghall in 1832, £4 received from Dorothy Gawdy's

bequest provided bread for 162 poor families, while at Hethersett £3 was derived from Cordy's Charity, originally intended to provide "a threepenny loaf to each individual in the family of the resident poor". But it had to be kept in hand for two years as "the number of poor was so great that the dividends for one year were insufficient to provide a supply".

Almost every one of the charities imposed conditions on the recipient—more often than not they demanded attendance at Church. Thus Rev. Thomas Rogerson, of Denton, left money in 1722 to buy bread to be distributed every first Sunday in the month among "such poor housekeepers as should constantly join in Common Prayer in the Church and frequently receive the Holy Sacrament".

At Redenhall "The Rent of Seymers Pightle, plus 1£ from the Bullock Fair, and 4£ from Bransby's Charity" provided for distribution of bread in which "all the poor partake unless of notoriously bad character". (The Commissioners were not too happy about Redenhall—some of the recipients, it seems, did not really pass the test).

In Diss a number of small bequests were amalgamated to make £29 6s. for the annual "Dole Distribution" which gave "a quarten loaf to every grown up person in a poor family, and half of that for each child, some distinction being made between those of good and those of bad character". The bread was given "to those who apply"—leaving each poor person to assess his own character. (There was no lack of applicants, it should be said).

The Le Neve Charity of Aslacton produced 20s. yearly from a charge on land at "Little Well nigh the Low Common", for "the support of, and to cheer up the most necessitous poor, and not to be applied to the easing of the Parish Rates". In 1839 20s. was expended in bread, from 3d. to 9d. to each family according to number, "persons of bad character being excluded". But who adjudicated on the character test no-one knows.

Oliver Neve left two Closes in Trust at Gt. Witchingham in 1674 to produce £6 5s. 4d. annually for 4s. worth of 1½d. loaves every fortnight "for the poorest who attend service, with 6s. extra on Christmas day in like manner." Here it was the Governor of the Workhouse who made the distribution, and who better to know where poverty existed ? — but he received the rather disproportionate fee of 10s. "for his trouble". This parish also had a covenant with New College, Oxford, to distribute amongst the poor "two seams of peas containing in all 16 Bushels"—presumably for pea soup and peas pudding.

In Aylsham the Constable was entrusted with the annual distribution of 3d. and 6d. loaves under the gift of Robert Marsham. The origin of this charity was unknown, but it seemed a cunning idea to entrust the selection of recipients to the Arm of the Law, as an aid to maintenance of good order. He distributed the bread "according to his discretion" said the Commissioners.

The poor of Little Cressingham were regaled with "14 pecks of good sweet rye where most need should require" under the will of John James 1727. The rye was delivered to a miller by whom it was ground and delivered to the poor about 4lbs. per head.

The oldest bread charity occurs at Northwold where one John Peyrs in 1501 "devised a messuage with 61 acres and liberty of fold course for 300 sheep on condition that the Township should yearly keep an 'obit' for his soul". Every householder received a pennyworth of bread, and each Church reeve two pennyworth of white bread. Northwold possessed another Bread Dole from Carters Charity of 1706 "from the rent of Corne Close"—the people being called to receive it on January 17th by "the tolling of the bell from 8 to 10 o'clock" for which the Clerk received 1s.

The Commissioners found a return of 1786 stating that the Lord of the Manor of Watlington had arbitrarily enclosed 1ac. 8p. of land called Broadcorners which had constantly been used for food for the cattle of the poor. The incensed inhabitants had pulled down the fences, and the Lord then decided to pay 10s. p.ann. to the poor—but refused to sign any agreement. An old parishioner verified that Broadcorners was formerly Common land and that for some time after enclosure the parishioners regularly threw down the fences. After paying £5 for a long period, the Lord ended by admitting "no claim"—and there the matter rested; for there was no deed to establish the claim.

Billingford, near Diss, has a Bread Charity of unknown date or origin—but pre 1786. It was a rent charge of £2 to be laid out in bread at the beginning of each year—"a 6d. loaf in the first instance to each poor man and woman—the remainder to the poor according to the size of families". Older inhabitants have told me how the poor, in picturesque procession, toiled up the track to the Church on the hill, pushing prams and home made hand carts to bring back their bread. From the records I found that in 1932, 38 families received 180 loaves—the highest number distributed —and that two large families actually received 18 loaves each. That certainly explains the need for prams and handcarts.

Some Bread Charities carried unusual provisions. At Thurgaton John Bacon provided for "6 penny loaves to be distributed every Sunday of the year to 6 poor persons considered proper objects of charity, provided that the monuments and grates where his Father and Mother, and those lineally descended from them were buried should not be designedly broken or defaced". Land in Cawston provided the 26s. per. ann. to purchase the loaves.

Dr. Cuthbert Norris, of N. Tuddenham, left a house and land in 1621 to pay for a distribution of "malt and maslin" to the poor on Christmas day, and two pennyworth of bread each Sunday in Lent. But the procedure of many or most of these 148 distributions has been modified in keeping with the social changes of past years. At Redgrave the Rector distributes tickets for "cake, bread or flour"—at Billingford the baker delivers the bread to the selected recipients, on his normal round.

Here and there the ancient ceremony is still transacted exactly as the Founder directed. At Woodbridge, George Carlow, a Sabbatarian, and a tanner by trade, born 1650, was buried at the rear of the Bull Hotel. He willed a charge on the property, to provide bread for the poor, to be distributed from the top of his tomb. The practice has continued since his death in 1736—the bread being given by the Rector of St. Mary's, from the founder's tomb, to the selected beneficiaries. This quaint ceremony is carried out on Candlemas Day, "except when Feb. 2nd falls on a Saturday, when the distribution is made on the Friday before".

A similar ceremony was carried out by the Rev. L. O. Kenyon when Rector of Hull. He distributed bread every Sunday—and once a year over the Founder's Tomb, "a plum pudding" to each of about 20 beneficiaries.

Many Norfolk Charities have lapsed—it is sad to read of a charity at Acle "nothing has been heard of this money for 20 years at least"; or at Weeting where the Commissioners were "unable to find by whom a certain charity was paid or who was then liable to pay". There is much to be said for the present strict Control of Charities exercised by the Commission.

Charity at Christmas in bygone years

(PUBLISHED DECEMBER 1962)

THE early annals of Diss are barren of "all that is momentous," according to White's first directory of Norfolk, published in 1836. Be that as it may, there is no gainsaying the fact that the Christmas spirit of good will has never failed to prompt the more fortunate to perform acts of generosity to enable their poorer brethren to enjoy at least some of the material comforts of the festive season.

Turning back 100 years I find hosts of local references to the Christmas distribution of annual bequests or direct gifts in this district. At Wortham, 7½ tons of coal and 50 blankets; at Diss, scores of blankets ("the winter being early and severe"); ¼lb. of tea to every widow in Kenninghall ("with gratitude to their benefactress and prayers for her long life and happiness"); 38 coats and waistcoats of velveteen, 17 pairs of blankets, 272 yards of sheeting (Harrison bequest at Palgrave); and six greatcoats and 290 yards of flannel to the "deserving poor" (South Lopham Charities).

Looking back still further to the records of a parish not many miles from Diss, there is evidence that "Att Christmas, 1667, Sir Robert — did give a ffatt cowe to ye poore of ye parish in lieu of ye 40s formerly given, wch was distributed by me according to the manner and forme of these bills; witnesse my hande C— P—, Churchwarden".

The following year, Sir Robert —, still solicitous for the welfare of the poor, distributed 40s. at Christmas—again through C— P— and his colleague—"amongst ye poorer sorte of ye towne on ye 23 day of Decebr".

In 1670, the local harvest having been much below average, Sir Robert purchased 40s. worth of corn which was "given out to ye poore against Christmas, yt is to saye, foure combe and a bushell". The list of recipients is given—"Widowe Baulie and John Baulie —three pecks"; "Anthonye Baldrie, half a bushell and halfe a pecke"; and so on.

We can even share C— P—'s anxiety, as he watched the queue

shrinking and his supply diminishing, as to whether the allotted quantity would suffice to meet demands. It did suffice, and as he ticked the last name he must have heaved a sigh of relief, for he wrote at the end—"ffower combe and A bushell—just".

We have no other details of those proceedings, but it is easy to imagine that such gifts, in their day, were generous and brought comfort to many a needy family in that parish.

One of the most interesting bequests of more recent times was at Roydon—made possible by the Susanna Frere Warm Clothing Charity. By her will of December 21st, 1814, Miss Frere gave £400 "to be invested upon Trust, the interest thereof to be paid to the resident Minister for the time being, who shall lay out half the same in blankets or warm clothing for any of the poor married inhabitants of Roydon, at his discretion, on Christmas Day, or the Sunday preceding or following".

The other half of the interest was for church furniture, books, and hangings.

The earliest records of the annual distribution have not survived but complete lists exist from 1870, when the Rev. T. C. Hose became rector of the parish and supervised the charity.

There were then 18 recipients and in our mind's eye we can see the old widows, widowers, or couples, happily leaving the Rectory with their bundles of "6 yds. of flannel, 6 yds. of calico, 2 prs. stockings" (The flannel was for shirts or petticoats, the calico for "tops".).

Here was something to bring outer warmth, at least, with which to face bitter weather.

Mr. Hose's son Ernest was born in 1872 and has been associated with Roydon ever since—he still lives there, and is in his 91st year. Recently we joined in perusing the annual list of recipients of "warm clothing" and his amazing memory enabled him to pass a few biographical remarks about most of them.

He remembered where they lived, their work and for whom they worked, and even the names and careers of their children !

This was no mean feat, especially when the same surname appeared in a list several times, with only the words Fen, Barracks, Green, Freezen Hill or widow, in brackets, to distinguish it.

The grand old man recalled, too, the annual distribution as carried out in his father's lifetime. His mother purchased huge rolls of red and grey flannel and of calico, together with bundles of blankets, some shawls and a few knitted jackets at the special request of some of the old ladies.

On the appointed day widows and others attended the Rectory. There in the spacious kitchen, after a homely chat and cup of tea or mug of beer the lengths of material were cut off by Mrs. Hose, and the happy recipients departed with feelings of gratitude for the one who made the gift possible, and to those who administered it with such good grace.

Time, however, brought changes. Income remained the same, but decreased in purchasing power. Where, in 1870, 142 yards of flannel and calico, with 24 pairs of stockings, could be bought with the proceeds, 50 years later such quantities were impossible. So the less personal, less intimate, less picturesque—and even less valuable—gift of a 5s. "clothing order" replaced the procedure of earlier years.

Today the Warm Clothing Fund still exists and just a few deserving old people receive a Christmas gift of coal.

I know many alive today who remember the early years of this century, and even toddled with their parents through that delightful avenue of lime trees to the Rectory to receive a warm welcome and their Christmas gift from Mrs. Hose. That avenue appropriately symbolised the Christmas message of peace, for it was planted just before Susanna Frere died, to celebrate the return of peace after the wars with Napoleon—wars which had produced much acute poverty in South Norfolk.

A Diss petty constable's diary of 1649

(PUBLISHED JANUARY 1963)

A FAMILIAR sight today is the police constable, note book in hand, interrogating an offending motorist or the eye witness of an accident. The accuracy of his on-the-spot record may decide the issue in a subsequent Court case, so the details in his diary of duty are of vital importance.

Even 300 years ago the petty constables of Diss and elsewhere compiled their diaries. A faded, tattered and well-thumbed hand-stitched notebook of 18 closely-written pages is among the documents in the Diss Parish Chest.

It contains the constables' notes for 1649 and 1650 and provides an interesting insight into the day-to-day work of the forerunners of our modern police force.

I am told there are few of these books in Norfolk. Entries are in ink, written up after a spell of duty and not on the spot, as today.

The roll of constables for Diss is complete from 1611. It shows they were nominated annually at the Town Vestry, to be approved and sworn-in by the Justices at Long Stratton Sessions. They were usually farmers, businessmen, and even "gentlemen". But the ordinary routine of daily duty was delegated to "petty constables"—burly and tough, with little or no education, yet capable of dealing with awkward situations and refractory "customers".

In the extracts which follow, spellings are exactly as they appear in the book.

Repeated references to "drincking" run through the notes for 1649. "Gooch of Shulfunger topling at Scotts" and "John West at Hinnry Turners with others". That was mild, for "Willi Culum" over-indulged, and was "dronck in the stret", while "Thomas Oldin was so diskempred with drincking that he could not goe but by stagrang and reling".

When, on June 27th—"being friday at 10 of the clock at night"—the constable met "Tetsalls wife going to petits for bear" he found her "veri ffre in words". These, of course, were days of

247

strict puritan rule, when efforts were made to suppress gambling of all sorts. We can imagine the constable on his nightly prowl peering into lofts, outhouses, and dark alleys, then coming across "Benjam Payns and Rogar Spinck playing at cards in lofte behind Whit Hors" and calling "Henry Kett wattchman, wettness" to give supporting evidence to the justice, if needed.

In 1649 there were many "passengers" (or refugees) on the move—some, fleeing from a fighting zone during the Civil War; some, peaceful citizens, returning to their place of settlement to claim poor relief; some, wounded soldiers wending their way home; and others who were rogues, vagrants and vagabonds. All came under the keen eye and scrutiny of the constable.

Philip Fetturby was a beggar; "Tack vagrant at Diss and ponished according to the law". Actually, he was stripped to the waist, secured to the whipping post and publicly whipped in the Market Place, then handed over to the constable of Palgrave to be passed from "Constable to Constable the straight way to St. Allbons", where he belonged.

"Twoe travellers that come from Ridd in Kent goeing to Linn" received 2d. for sustenance en route; a genuine refugee from Ireland was "Franccs Doer, who come out of Eiarland, and left her meanes, to seeke her friends". She, too, received 2d; and "Two lame soulgers that came from Yorrkshire paseing to the Ile of wit" had the same.

But Mary Goslin's arrival aroused suspicion. The constable put her in the lock-up near the old "Bell" Inn and "Edmond Browne" was paid 1s. "for watching with Mary Goslin 2 nites". Mary was later taken on horseback to the Bridewell at Wymondham—the book states, "for a horse to rid to the bridewell 1s.".

Ann Mann, too, went to Bridewell, for the constable "Payd Sur Robt Kemp for a warrant for manes daaughter to carri her to bridewell 6d" and "for a lofe for her 1d"—to eat en route. Ann presumably behaved well on the way for the constable "layd out for her, 10d" at the Bridewell, probably a tip to the doorkeeper to treat her leniently.

John Block, a thief, was quickly dealt with. "Layd out that day I went to Justis with John Block 2d; a lofe for him when he went to the gayle 1d; 1 horse heyar for to carre John Block to the gayle 6d.".

One of the most exacting duties was "Raising the Hue and

Cry" when information about a theft, or an escaped prisoner, was brought by a messenger on foot or on horseback from an adjoining parish. All able-bodied men then joined in the hunt for the offender, whether for larceny, housebreaking or gaol-breaking.

Some of the descriptions in these "Hue & Cry" entries are most picturesque and apt. Here is the gaol-breaker "Recd, a heuig cri after Marmaduke Russell, a yong man, blackhared, in a white peticott, and Robt. Jannar, a brod man, a mark on his nose lick a cut, both seamen, for brecking out of the Castell of Norwich".

Then the housebreaker: "Rec. a Hew and Crey after Cherestoper Waller of Loddon for steling 60£ ffrom Anndrew Wallar of Norton, the sd. Cherstpor a brod sett man, gray bard". This information was to be passed "Thru the commonwelth of England".

There were many horse thieves—"Rec. a Hew cri after persons unknowen for steling of 2 horses, one with dark blackish coler, whight hares on his head and neck, a natrull ambler; the other a rond coler, a long thick freseld mane, a sore on his throt not yet cured, and a troter, stolen from the pastuer of Robt Willson of Cromer".

Such were the "cases" these petty constables had to cope with in an age without telephones, radio or cars, or even bicycles. Though vagrants, rogues, and vagabonds no longer throng our highways, the other types of offenders still have their modern counterparts, even in our affluent society.

The petty constable, having made his entries, took his book to the Harleston "Swan" to submit it to the Justices for perusal. On his return he entered, "waited all day at Harlston to gitt the book sinid. Spent 8d for my horse mett (i.e., meat) and my own mett", with a final note that the book contained a "trew note of layeings ought in Anno 1649".

The duties of a 17th century petty constable

(PUBLISHED JANUARY 1963)

PARISH records rarely contain a complete constable's notebook such as the Diss Book mentioned in the previous article, but many constables' accounts exist with details of their "layings-out" during their spell of office. These provide real insight into the varied, arduous and thankless duties involved in their unpaid work—though certain fees and out of pocket expenses were allowed.

The following examples, reproduced in the original spelling and, occasionally crude language, are taken from records in South Norfolk. The constable, nominated by the Parish Vestry, had to be first approved and sworn by the Justices in session, so his "bill of Constableship" usually began with "ffor my owth att the Cort 4d" or "ffor gooing twis to Stratton to ye Justis sitten 1s 2d".

His duties then began, perhaps with a "Hue and Cry". For his time and effort in rousing the parish "ffor a Hue and Cry" he claimed 6d. and "ffor Passing a hue and cry after a lewd band a Souldier", another 6d.

Constant vigilance was necessary in seeking out and watching strangers or suspects. From this constable's account, reading between the lines, we can reconstruct what happened when one Bird arrived in the village:

"Pd. two watchers for Bird 1s"—"Pd. 3 men when we took Bird 1s 6d"—"pd. to Larrance Tarna for gooing along with me to the Justis with Bard, 2s"—"my jarney to Sir Ed. Bacons with Bard 1s,"—Pd Robt. Virgo for attendance along with Bard 2 days and one night 2s 6d"—"ffor my time 2s 6d". Bird was eventually committed to the "Castle Jayle".

So, too, was Tho. Blome, an itinerant pickpocket who arrived at Gissing Fair to prey upon the unwary. He appears in the constable's account thus: "Spent at the faier when we took the thefe 6d,"—"pd. to Mr. Kidman for his carte to cary awaye the Roge and a fellow goen with me, 3d"—"layd out for carien Tho.

Blome before the Justis 1s"—"pd for keepinge of the Roge one night 1s". Blome was then carried off to join "Bard" in the gaol, with the inevitable charge for "horse hire and horse meat".

Another duty of the constable was to maintain the stocks and whipping-post in good order. "A bill of worke for the Towne for Irons for the Stocks, boltes and lock and Irons for the wiping poost 7s" appeared in one account, with "Charges when the prissoners were in the stokes 2s 6d". An old whipping-post is preserved at New Buckenham, and stocks at Bressingham.

I knew the Rev. Edmund Farrer, who died in 1934 and who in his younger days was curate at Bressingham in the 1880s. He said that the then Parish Clerk remembered (as a boy) pelting with rotten eggs a "vagrant" put in those very stocks—so they were still used well into the 19th century.

One parish constable records "laying out 8d to the Clarke of the Market at Disse for his maties procklimasions about the rate for shipmoney" (1637, Charles I). The County of Norfolk was assessed to raise £7,800 to provide a vessel of war. Each Hundred and each town and village were then apportioned their shares—to Diss Hundred it was £191 3s. 2d., to Diss itself £33 19s. 7d.—for the constables to collect.

Diss paid this unpopular tax in full, though Sir Francis Astley, Sheriff of Norfolk and finally responsible for the county assessment, stated despairingly: "From divers Hundreds I have not received a penny". Winfarthing Towne Book expresses the general resentment against shipmoney in an entry: "Pay'd for the towne land for that unlawful tax of shipmoney 9s 10d".

The 17th century was one of internal strife in Great Britain and of external threats from the French and Dutch. Hence the constant demands on every parish for manpower and equipment for armed forces—the men being drawn from those irregular "trained-bands", who were far from efficient.

In Queen Elizabeth's reign Diss provided "3 Pikemen and 6 muskets" for an expedition to Cadiz (1596)—the Pikemen "to be appointed with their armour suited and furnished—their coats of strong cloth and colour red, guarded with white.

"They were to carry with them 2 shirts, 2 prs. stockings, and 2 prs. shoes, and to be mustered and delivered at Chapel Field, Norwich, on 12 July 1596, then with all expedition to be shipped at Yarmouth to be transported to Plymouth." It was the constable's province to deal with these matters of men, training, equipment. To us, in this atomic age, the equipment sounds primitive—but here are items from an early 17th century constable's accounts:

"Layd out for Kipenge of the Towne coselete (i.e. corselet) 2s 4d"; "To Stiven Dunman for makin the buttes 1s"; "for repayre of hangers for ye towne sword 1s"; "for mendinge the Towne muskete 2s"; "Pd for a bolyte bagg for the Towne muskete, 4d"; "quarter of pouder and a yard of mach 5d"; "for two pownde of bulletes, 4d"; "layd out to the Towne soulger for trayning at Haywood grene 1s"; "my joraye thither 1s".

Items of parish armour of this period are preserved at Palgrave and at other East Anglian villages—usually in the church, where in former times they were kept in readiness in the porch or the chamber above.

Internal disputes—civil and religious, impressing men and calling them for service, brought distress to many. Maimed soldiers, wrecked mariners, refugees and vagrants constantly tramped the rough roads and tracks.

The constable "relieved" the genuine and needy—"three men that lost their shippe on the boarders of Scotland, for ther Dyet one night and ther brekfast in the morninge 16d, and money I gave them 3d". Or, "Eighteene poor Eiarish" who received 18d; while "18 Egeptianes (gipsies) received 1s to move on".

But Hanna Gosling and her two children, natives of Gissing, had fallen on bad times in Boston, Lincolnshire. A Justice had "examined" Hannah, and declared her true settlement to be at Gissing whence she was ordered to be removed. The constable arranged it, and the almost inhuman and degrading treatment to which the poor were then subjected, is reflected in the constables charges:

"To 2 Horses hird to convey them at 12s, £1 4s"—"to the constable for conducting them 9s,"—"Expences on the Road being about 70 miles, £1 10s"—"For 2 crates to put the children in and 2 cords to fasten the Crates 2s 2d". The Gissing officers paid the account February 2nd, 1739.

To the constable were addressed many "precepts" for raising frequent and arbitrary imposts and taxes. Here is one (1607): "To require and charge you to collecte within your towne 20d towards ye repayeringe of Earleham Bridge and to paye ye same at Tivetteshall". It concluded: "Herof fayle you not at your perills—yr lovinge ffrind Charles Woodward" (High Constable). Other orders required the constable "to summon the Butchers to appear before the Justices to become bound with suertyes not to kill dresse or utter any ffleshe in the tyme of Lent" (1624)—and each year "to be at the Kinges Hd. in Disse before H.M. Seasors (Assessors) to deliver in wrytinge what alteracon is within your towne synce last year".

This enabled those responsible for taxation to keep in touch with local changes and movements of people.

The constable collected "Bridge money"—and at Starston paid 1s "for mending the stile to Pulham", and 17s 6d "ffor mending the Bridg, tower steps and the Causey". Testing weights and measures, binding apprentices, restoring fugitive apprentices, and even inquests came within his scope. At Starston in 1697 he "pd the Coroner for sitting of the child found at Milmount Mote, 10s,"—and 2s "for Buring this child and my hors to warn the Jewry".

With all these and many other duties thrust upon him, one is hardly surprised when the Starston constable, claiming his expenses for attending the rate-fixing meeting in 1691, wrote: "Spent att the Towne meeting when the Rat was mad, 2s 3d".

Probably, at the end of his year of duty, he felt rather like the 'Rat'.

In the days of the Press Gangs

(PUBLISHED APRIL 1964)

AMONG the most interesting of old papers locked away in parish chests are bundles of "Examinations for settlement" —concise life histories of those who, for one reason or another, had to "go on the parish" in former times. Before relief was granted, the applicant was taken before a Justice for interrogation or "Examination." On the evidence given (and it was taken down in writing) the Justice decided in which parish the applicant had a settlement—and that parish was bound by law to afford relief in money, or in the "Town House."

Over 220 of these "Examinations" have survived in Diss alone—Denton has 130, Winfarthing 33, and I have recently transcribed 24 from Tibenham. Many parishes have none—they have probably been thrown out as useless lumber by some well intentioned incumbent, or parish official. But where they do exist, they provide fascinating details of occupations, hirings, wages, conditions of employment, rents, movement of people, and above all the work of parish Vestries from about 1660 to 1850.

In these "Examinations" I have found frequent references to the work of "Press Gangs". There was the case of John Smith, of Denton, labourer, who stated—"In 1790 at Haddiscoe I let myself to James Elliott, Blacksmith, for one whole year. I continued for two further years, then went to Yarmouth and went apprentice to go to sea for 3 years. But after serving about 18 months I was pressed into H.M.'s Service". This means simply that a Press Gang with an official warrant descended on the merchant ship in which Elliott served, and bundled him away to serve in the Navy, irrespective of whether he wished to go, or not. There was no appeal.

Press Gangs had operated for centuries—for in medieval times the "Crown" claimed the power to "impress" able bodied subjects for the Defence of the Realm. As early as the mid 14th century complaints were voiced against the excessive use of this power. So great were the needs of the fleet in Elizabeth's reign that a "Vagrancy Act" was passed rendering "all disreputable persons liable for impressment for the Fleet". Sheriffs and Mayors were bound, upon warrant, to provide the men required by the Press Gangs—so that under that Vagrancy Act the jails were cleared of tough characters who were drafted to ships' companies —causing constant complaints from Naval officers about the quality of men supplied to them.

The law remained unaltered through the 17th and 18th centuries —and to quote one authority "even at the height of Britain's maritime power 1780-1815, the Press Gang was the chief means of recruitment for the Fleet". Malcontents and agitators were handed over to the 'Gangs' who hustled them off to guard ships stationed round the coast, ready for drafting into the Navy. This "bad element" was said to be a contributory factor in the Mutiny of 1797.

Our local examples of "pressing"—for both Army and Navy —span over three centuries, but to give a general picture of the operations of Press Gangs—here are some items from old Norfolk Journals.

June 2nd, 1741: "This morning, very early, there was a general Impress for Seamen in the River (Thames) and in a few hours the several lieutenants with their Gangs, got upwards of 1400 able Seamen for the service of H.M. The Press was so general that they took all hands (Capts. and Chief Mates only excepted) from on board all vessels, Colliers and coasters included".

On August 22nd the same year: "Wed. night last there was a terrible fray in St. Katharines between a Man o' war's Gang and the Mobb, about pressing a seaman, who was so sorely wounded, 'tis feared he cannot live. That night there was a general sweep along the river, and abundance of sailors were pressed. A smart skirmish occurred on Tower Hill between another "Press Gang" and some coopers of the Victualling Office, who, having more liquor than Brains in their Pates, obstructed the Officer from carrying off a seaman he had pressed, which so justly exasperated him, he hauled away 2 of them, and clapped them on board the Tender to bite their thumbs and repent their folly".

The Norfolk Journal of 1770 had many items like this of February 5th: "This morning several ships in the river were again stripped of all their men by the Press Gangs, in consequence of a search warrant granted by the Lord Mayor. Twenty-six persons taken up in Chick Lane were delivered to the Lieutenants for the King's Service. The Press was very hot last night in Westminster and met with great success amongst the disorderly houses many of which were emptied".

Press Gang methods can be gauged from this report of November 3rd, 1770: "At 11 o'clock on Thursday the several Constables of Westminster received their Press Warrants in the Guild Hall, after which they went to divers public houses and nighthouses and picked up a great number of idle persons for H.M. Fleet. The Lord Mayor 'backed' the warrants granted by the Lords of the Admiralty for impressing seamen in the City of London, after which one warrant was sent to a constable of each City-ward. All the public houses (Around Cripple Gate) open after 12 o'clock were searched by the City Marshall and Ward Constables, attended by a Press Gang, when they secured a number of useful hands who were carried on board a tender lying off Temple Stairs."

Again, in 1770: "Last night a great number of Press Warrants were issued, in consequence of which over 1500 men were pressed below London Bridge from all ships, vessels and boats they could meet with. 'Press Gangs' consist of long boats each carrying 7 men armed with bludgeons. Upwards of 10 press gangs were now operating in parts of the Town exclusive of those on the river. It is computed that not less than 4000 men have been forced on board men of war, Press warrants having been sent to every port in the Kingdom".

Ugly incidents were not uncommon. In September, 1770, "a Press Gang in their Long Boat ordered a Merchant Ship near Deptford 'to bring to', when one of the crew gave the Lieutenant very 'ill language'; upon which he ordered the gang alongside the vessel, and promised the merchant men he would not press one of them, if they would give up the man who abused him. They agreed. He went aboard and laid hold of the sailor, who desired he might fetch his things from the hold. This was consented to, but he soon returned with a brace of pistols, swearing that the first man to touch him he would shoot through the head, which, the Lieutenant endeavouring to do, the sailor shot him dead on the spot."

Press gangs generally operated in and around ports, but sometimes extended their activities inland, with unexpected results. The "Speedwell", sloop, lay off Newhaven in October, 1770, with "commission to press". Its gangs were very busy on shore, pressing several industrious persons and carrying them on board. A member of one gang, venturing further afield, attacked a shepherd tending his flock on the Downs. But the shepherd "had recourse to his crook, which he applied so lustily that the Tar was glad to sheer off with a hearty drubbing".

In Shakespeare's "Henry IV", Falstaff describing his experiences with "Pressed-men" declares: "I have misused the King's press damnably. I have got, in exchange of a hundred and fifty soldiers, three hundred odd pounds." Later he adds: "I pressed me none but such toasts-and-butter, with hearts in their bellies no bigger than pins' heads, and they have 'bought out' their services" —"No eye hath seen such scarecrows. I'll not march through Coventry with them, for the villains march wide betwixt the legs, as if they have gyves on: for indeed I had most of them out of prison." That was c. 1400.

Tobias Smollett in his novel "Roderick Random" (1748) gives probably the best description of the workings of a press gang —he himself was 'Pressed': "As I crossed Tower Wharf, on my way towards Wapping, a squat Tawney fellow with a hanger by his side and a cudgel in his hand, came up to me, calling, 'Yo ho! Brother. You must come along with me'. As I did not like his appearance I quickened my pace, hoping to rid myself of his company; upon which he whistled aloud, and immediately another sailor appeared before me, who laid hold of me by the collar and began to drag me along. Not being of a humour to relish such treatment, I disengaged myself of the assailant, and with one blow of my cudgel, laid him motionless on the ground; and perceiving myself surrounded in a trice by 10 or a dozen more, exerted myself with such dexterity and success, that some of my opponents were fain to attack me with drawn cutlasses; after an obstinate engagement, in which I received a large wound on the head, I was disarmed, taken prisoner, and carried on board a pressing tender, where, after being pinioned like a malefactor, I was thrust into the hold among a parcel of miserable wretches the sight of whom well nigh distracted me." That was Smollett's introduction to the Navy.

Strangers in the Gallery

(PUBLISHED NOVEMBER 1963)

AN Exhibition entitled "The Church Gallery Minstrels" recently held at "All Hallows", London Wall, initiated considerable correspondence in the press. All letters lamented the increasing scarcity of church organists, and several suggested a revival of village orchestras such as those found accompanying the singing in parish churches in the later 18th and early 19th century. Other letters pointed out that the real reason for the disappearance of the church orchestra was the inability to muster a regular complement of instruments Sunday by Sunday. Hence the organ, a complete orchestra in itself, but requiring only one performer, became justifiably popular in the 19th century.

Today the difficulty of obtaining competent organists—and regular choristers too—is widespread. Fortunate indeed is the church with a regular organist and a choir which trains and attends with regularity.

In the case of our own parish of Diss, the varying fortunes of church music in the past three centuries can be traced from a mass of papers preserved in the church chest.

Churchwardens' accounts contain this entry for September 8th, 1700, among "Disbursments of Wm. Burton one of the Church wardens given to the Towne att Easter 1701"—"pd Tho. ffisher by the order of the Towne towards ye gaallery in the Church £08-00-00." This was of course the "Singers' Gallery" at the west end of the church—typical of such galleries in most churches at that time. Few, however, remain.

A loose paper dated July 18th, 1713, reveals: "That the Gallery att the west end of the parrish church of Disse was att the charge of some or most of us built by contribucon money raysed amongst us to the intent the Batchelors Youngmen and Ladds who would or were willing to learn to sing, should sitt apart and by themselves for their better conveniencye of singing of Psalms and hymes."

Here then was the first choir—an all male one—to sing the

"metrical psalms" then in use—psalms sung as hymns are sung today (the 23rd Psalm sung to Crimond is in this style, so too is "O God, our help in ages past"). This was not the first music to be sung in Diss Church. It was a "revival" after the Puritan suppression of the more elaborate choral music of the 16th and early 17th centuries. There is irrefutable authority for stating that the Chapel of Corpus Christi (where the present organ stands) was formerly divided by a floor halfway up. In pre-Reformation times a small organ was situated in the upper part.

The Puritans, while not disliking music in general—for Oliver Cromwell was a music-lover and even had his own private organ and organist—disapproved of music as an aid to worship. So in the 17th century organs and choirs largely disappeared—until after the Restoration of 1660.

There was then a rebirth of church music in Diss in 1700, with a male choir to sing those metrical psalms, first published by Sternhold and Hopkins 1562, which appeared in a new version by Tate and Brady in 1696. The two versions held sway, side by side, until modern hymn books replaced them in the 19th century. Shelfanger Church has a metrical psalm book among its interesting documents. It gives the 'air' and also a bass accompaniment for a bass viol, or cello, or even for a serpent or vamp horn—instruments then in use.

But the "Gaallery in Disse Church" appears to have been invaded by female intruders who seriously distracted the "young men and Batchelors." A petition signed by several influential parishioners states: "It is our intent and desire that the said Gallery and the seates there shall be still kept up and used in the same way first designed, and the singing men, young men and ladds shall soe continue their sitting free from the women maydes and Girlls or any other persons who do or shall make disturbance or hindrance to the singing men and Ladds there."

No further interruptions are on record, and there is nothing to suggest that any church band or orchestra accompanied the singers. But we do know they were "given the note" from a "pitch-pipe," for that instrument still survives. It was a small wooden organ pipe of square section about 18" long, with a whistle-mouthpiece and a wooden stopper that could be pushed in or out to set the pitch. Pitch-pipes are known to have been in use at about 1700. Handel's own instrument still exists. The old Diss pitch-pipe eventually came into the hands of Robert Parr (1769-1860) and finally to his descendants, the Harrisons. Now, quite 250 years old, it is in the possession of Mr. W. Harrison of Northampton.

Palgrave Church accounts record this item "pd for a pitch-pipe 5s ,, 9d.," in 1749.

For many years the Gallery Minstrels took their note from the pitch-pipe—then an interesting item appears in 1786. "Pd. for making ye curtains for ye organ 1s " 4d " —followed by many expenses for tuning, repair, and "Robert Parr his organ salary £2—2—0". The organ installed about 1785 was a "Barrel Organ" working on the barrel and pin mechanism. Messrs. Flight of London (later Flight and Robson) were making such organs from 1772. After a trial it was thought desirable to "screen" Robt. Parr as he churned his hurdy gurdy with his sleeves rolled up—hence the curtains. Robt. received 2 gns. per year for many years. White's Directory of 1836 lists him as "Sexton and Organist". His annual bills submitted to the Parish have been preserved, including "surplus washing at 3/6". Only the priest wore a surplice at that time. Joseph Hart (organ builder of Redgrave) submitted an amusing bill in 1820. "For a new Barrell to the Church Organ with 12 Psalm Tunes to Do. £6—6—0. Caridge from and to Diss, with brass Handles etc. 10s".

This barrel organ had five interchangeable barrels, each with ten tunes for metrical psalms—but unaccompanied singing was often started by Hannah Parr with the pitchpipe. Then Hannah married Terah Nicholson, and he provided 'cello' accompaniment as a diversion.

Incidentally, Bressingham Church still possesses a barrel organ, which Mr. Pearce the churchwarden plays very competently. And Mr. Boggis too has one, purchased from the Unitarian Chapel a few years ago. This also plays extremely well, in its quaint way.

However—there were definite restrictions and limitations with a barrel organ. So in 1844 a subscription list was opened for the purchase of a "finger organ". The response was excellent—and £210 10s was soon paid into the Diss Bank of "Oakes, Fincham, Bevan and Moor", and enquiries made for a suitable instrument.

Gallery singers and musicians

(PUBLISHED JANUARY 1964)

FEW Rectors, can have amassed as much historical detail concerning their parishes as the Rev. W. R. Harrison did about Shelfanger after he became Rector in 1898. His researches took him to the British Museum, the Record Office, and the Bodleian Library, while he delved into Norfolk records and into the mass of papers in his own parish chest, with great effect.

But for details of the 19th century he chatted with the old folk of the village, whose memories carried them back to the early years of the century, while "what their parents had told them" probed well into the 18th century. His notes on Shelfanger run to hundreds of foolscap pages.

Several of Mr. Harrison's parishioners remembered Thomas Brooke Morris, Rector from 1803-1863. They described him as a man of "commanding presence" and held him "in wholesome awe". But Alice Holmes, the girl of nine who emigrated in 1850, wrote in her book "Lost Vision" that she remembered "the dear old Rector with his pleasant face and kindly manners, winning the hearts of the children, and when arrayed in his sacerdotal robes, well becoming his hallowed calling".

It was Mr. Morris who introduced a new version of Tate and Brady's Metrical Psalms in 1805. There was at that time a Singers' Gallery in the S.W. corner of the nave of Shelfanger Church—a lofty structure between the tower arch and the south wall—reached by stairs on the north side, and furnished with three benches, facing east. At first, Mr. Morris gave the "starting note" on a pitch pipe, but soon purchased a "base-fiddle", round which the singers grouped themselves. Later a violin was added—and so Shelfanger had the typical set up for church music of the 18th and 19th centuries. It was simple, possibly effective and wholehearted—yet one of Mr. Harrisson's venerable friends remarked that "The music warn't much at that time".

Mr. Morris remained Rector until he reached 91 and was followed by the Rev. Clement Ogle Smith (who later changed his name to Blakelock). He inherited considerable wealth, and his father, a Sheffield solicitor, is said to have offered to build him a new Rectory, or to pay for the restoration of the church. He chose the latter. He made extensive changes—and, sad to relate, dismembered the Singers' Gallery as well as the quaint old 3 decker pulpit. The "base-fiddle" and violin were discarded, a harmonium installed in the chancel, and a mixed choir led the singing. Later "the femine element" was excluded, when a surpliced choir then held sway.

Thus it remained until March 1906 when Mr. Harrison generously supported by the parish, purchased "a pipe organ with five stops and pedals" offered by Messrs. Howlett of Norwich "delivered, erected, tuned and warranted for five years"—all for £35. However, it was agreed "not to part with the harmonium"—for organs were an "unknown quantity" in Shelfanger, however well guaranteed.

At North Lopham the Churchwardens' accounts provide an insight into the musical side of church services from 1813 onwards. Here too was a Singers' Gallery, for William Beales was paid £1 8s for "altering gallery and painting"—when a barrel organ was installed. But the first indication was in July 1813 when six "Read and made Easey" were bought for 3s. This peculiar entry was elucidated later when this item appeared "6 Reading made Easy" at 6d . . . 3s.—for Wm. Gathercole was then conducting a Parish "Sunday School" for 4 guineas per year—teaching a few children each Sunday to read, write and do elementary arithmetic. It was then the custom for children of all ages to work throughout the week—picking stones, scaring birds, dropping corn etc.—and a smattering of education was received for an hour or so on Sundays.

Lopham's accounts for 1818 are a curious hotch-potch. Mixed up with "a lock for the stocks 1s"—"paid for sparrows and hedgehogs £2—2—7$\frac{3}{4}$"—"1 pr. hand cuffs and lock, 3s—2d"—etc., appeared, "allowed the singers 6s" and "expence of the violincello 1£". Later followed "a new Violin cello for the use of the church"—for 3 guineas, and in 1830, "pd 1/3 part of 25s. to redeem the Base Viol from G. Kemp 8s ,, 4d." (One can visualise a glorious dispute over the ownership of this viol.).

Items followed—"Books for the Singers"—"Pd the Church Singers 1 year 1£"—"pd for Violin cello strings 3s " 6d"—"New Bag for the violin cello 4s — 9d."—which show that N. Lopham followed the usual practice—a mixed body of singers in the Gallery clustering round a band of "strings", to lead the singing.

So it continued until 1859 when, one imagines, it proved impossible to provide a cellist or violinist for the band—for in that year came an expence of £22 "pd for orgern". This proved to be a "barrel organ" and R. Leeder (the Clerk) commenced receiving an extra £1 "for playing organ" (i.e. churning the hurdy-gurdy). Lopham had fallen back on this mechanical accompaniment—such as Diss had discarded in 1844. One can appreciate the difficulty —nay, the impossibility of sustaining a note on the barrel organ for the long recitative passages in the psalms. It may be that R. Leeder was not adept at manipulating the instrument—but Mr. Buckenham presented a harmonium in 1868, and the Singers' Gallery was vacated. Then a surpliced choir came into being for the first time.

When searching the parish chest of Swardeston last July an old exercise book was discovered, containing "Articles belonging to the Company of Singers in Swardeston 1783". It reveals the zeal of the Gallery Songsters and their readiness to accept strict discipline. Here are some of the nine rules: "1st That the Teacher of the Company do regular attend twice a week viz. on Sundays and Tuesday nights at 7 o'clock to practise, or forfeit 6d. without a lawful excuse for his neglect". Clauses 2 and 3 stipulated similar conditions for singers. The 4th prescribed fines for "introducing idle talk or swearing on oath during practise". 5th, a forfeit of 1d "if any person laugh or make dirision of another for his being Awkward, or not altogether so apt as some". No. 6 decreed "that no member shall be offended at the master for his freedom or taking the liberty of reproving of them when they are going wrong". No. 7 required every member "to pay the Teacher 2d per wk for his instruction", and No. 8 "appointed James Buck to receive forfeits which were to be attributed to what use the majority of the Company shall think proper". The last, No. 9, laid down that "no Excuse shall be lawful unless the person be sick or about any particular business, and if any refuse to pay their forfeits they shall be excluded". The names of the 16 all-male company were appended, of whom three "made their marks".

It is interesting to speculate on the reactions of most church choirs of today to such a set of conditions.

From hurdy-gurdy to finger organ

(PUBLISHED DECEMBER 1963)

ON May 8th, 1844, the Vestry Committee met to hear the results of Mr. Farrow's enquiries concerning a finger organ to replace the "hurdy-gurdy" in the Singer's Gallery of Diss Church. Profuse thanks were afforded Mr. Farrow "for the trouble he had taken in procuring information respecting organs." Amongst the organs offered was one from the Redgrave organ-builder, Mr. Hart, at a price of £245 (though several very desirable extras were suggested—an octave of German pedals and pipes). The others, ranging from 160 guineas to £280 were from London firms.

It fell to Mr. Bates, of Ludgate Hill, to provide the one manual finger organ in solid oak case, with gilt 'shew-pipe' front, etc. Mr. Farrow had taken the precaution of having this instrument 'vetted' by a Mr. Austin in London. To him it appeared "perfectly sound and sufficiently calculated for service in Church or Chapel".

Adjustments were made to the gallery to receive the organ, and it was arranged that Mr. Reeve's "waggon and team of 6 horses" should fetch it from London at a cost of £9, and that Mr. Bates's son and his assistant should travel by coach to fix and adjust. Mr. Farrow had discreetly enquired the lowest price Mr. Bates would accept but the latter kept to his quoted price, which was "very cheap at 168£".

Mr. Harrison—a forbear of 'Bertie's', provided "a sett of oak Pannel'd Pillars with spiral ornamented Tops and Oak Rods, 4 scarlet moreen curtains with gold colour silk lace Trimming etc. for £2-10-0," (from which Mr. Farrow in his persuasive way effected a deduction of £1 for the organ fund).

The official opening of the new organ came on Thursday, June 27th. Mr. Warne, organist of St. Nicholas, Great Yarmouth, was invited to preside at the organ. His acceptance was in courteous terms—"I shall be happy to preside on the 27th inst. My terms, for time and all incidental expences will be £3-3-0, and I shall be glad to know what music will be sung—if possible".

The Rev. Richard Cobbold, Rector of Wortham and of

Margaret Catchpole' fame, "was solicited to preach". He also gladly accepted (and incidentally bought the Barrel Organ for £15) —and preached with such effect to a crowded congregation that the collection amounted to £25 5s. 5d. It was a happy and unique occasion—a new 'finger organ' after an interval of 300 years.

But there remained the great problem—who was to be the permanent organist ? A Mr. Long and his daughter were invited to fill the office, 'on approval' and at no fixed remuneration. The supreme caution of Mr. Farrow during these testing months was really admirable. The subscribers to the organ fund expected a competent performer, and such a person must be found.

Mr. and Miss Long, however, failed to fulfil expectations. Criticisms of their playing increased, until "murmurs grew to mighty rumblings". Mr. Farrow sent out urgent notices on November 16th calling his committee together for the evening of that same day. It was unanimously resolved that "Mr. and Miss Long should discontinue playing the organ, and that an organist should be elected". To Mr. Farrow fell the unenviable task of writing to Mr. Long to break the news of his suspension. He wrote—"I am deputed to the unpleasant duty of acquainting you that the performances of yourself and Miss Long on the organ, are not satisfactory to the subscribers and the congregation generally, and that at a meeting of the principal subscribers it was resolved to proceed to the election of a competent performer or organist, and that for the services of yourself and Miss Long the sum of 10£ shall be paid."

Mr. Long accepted his dismissal and the implications of -incompetence, with good grace and unusual humility—"I beg to say we have done all in our power to give satisfaction, and are sorry we have not succeeded."

Meanwhile, the importunate Mr. Horton, of Wattisfield had been keenly angling for the post— but the bumptious tone of his enquiries raised suspicions in the mind of the wily Mr. Farrow. Mr. Horton wrote— "I should have no objection to undertake the duties of organist for 20£ p. ann., leaving it to the discretion and generosity of the congregation to increase the sum if they should deem my services worthy of it. Having filled a similar appointment before for 7 years I flatter myself this circumstance will have some weight in recommending me. In addition I am furnished by nature with a very good tenor voice, which, I apprehend, would be found a considerable acquisition to the choir. I have a little girl (14 yrs of age) possessing a very excellent and powerful voice, whose services would be found very effective in assisting the trebles."

Mr. Horton concluded, condescendingly—"Should my proposition be accepted I should take up my residence in Diss after a time, but having an annuity which renders me independent of music as a profession, it is a matter of indifference to me where I reside."

In spite of Mr. Horton's overpowering self-esteem, Mr. Farrow did not accept him, on his own assessment, but invited him to 'submit testimonials' or 'to play for one Sunday'—adding a cautious note, "that a strong feeling exists to elect no one who is not in every way well qualified and competent". Mr. Horton appears to have been cold-shouldered after that, especially when he came to Diss in person. The red carpet wasn't out, and the deflated gentleman dropped out of the contest.

Meanwhile Mr. Farrow had been engaged in other enquiries concerning the salaries paid to organists in other places comparable with Diss. From Framlingham he elicited that £15 p. ann. was paid, with £1 to the blower. East Dereham paid 20 gns. p. ann.; Harleston 30 gns. "for only part of the day on Sundays—morning and afternoon alternately". Beccles paid "about 43£ p. ann. out of which the choir and Tunist were paid about 5£ each, and the Blower two more". Swaffham gave £30 p. ann., and a further £5 for tuning and repairing the organ—the organist being a good mechanic and tunist". Bungay topped the list with a salary of £38.

Armed with this information Churchwarden Farrow wrote rather guardedly to Mr. F. W. Gray, of Grantham, who had previously been very highly recommended for the organist's post at Swaffham, but submitted his application too late. "I am requested," wrote Mr. Farrow, "to apply for your terms to undertake the playing of the organ here. We have already an offer from a Gent. to take the situation at 20£ a year. I have written to him (i.e. Mr. Horton) for testimonials, and if they are not satisfactory, you may stand a chance of the appointment if your terms are acceptable."

Mr. Gray replied—"I think 20£ is a small salary for one who understands his profession. Nevertheless, I do not object to that sum, but leave it to you, as it is only a secondary consideration.

Should I succeed in the appointment, it will be my study to fulfil the situation with satisfaction, and, as far as is consistent render the organ service amusing."

The post was offered to Mr. Gray. He accepted in gracious terms the £25 p. ann. stated—"I shall be most happy to accept and hope to prove my capability of holding the situation and of returning my sincere thanks for the favour conferred upon me. Mr. Gray also agreed to the conditions prescribed—"Practices from 4—5 p.m. on Tuesdays and Thursdays"—"choir to be selected according to their 'abilitys' to sing"—"perfect understanding to exist between organist and clerk as to tunes to be sung, likewise Psalms"; soon there was a choir of 30, 16 girls and 14 boys (6 Head Girls at 2s. 6d. p. ann.—Junior boys at 6d. each—remainder at 1s. each). Familiar Diss names Cooper, Moye, Whiting, Batley, Cory, Leathers, Crick, Leeder, Studd, Anness and Lusher appear among the choir lists.

The Blower—"William peake" submitted his account for "blowing the orgin 20—4 weeks at 6 pence per wk. 12s recd. William X peake his mark".

Mr. Gray became a musical force in the town until 1862 when his salary reached £35. He officiated at the organ in the Corn Hall when it was opened in 1854. His temporary successor in 1863 was Mr. Caseley, who filled the gap until Arthur Hemstock commenced his long reign from 1864 to 1916. He it was who saw the installation of a new 3-manual organ in the Guild Chapel of Corpus Christi in 1877, the removal of the Singers' Gallery (now called a cumbrous and unsightly object), the elimination of girls from the choir, and the inauguration of a surpliced choir on All Saints Day, November 1st, 1877.

Processing in their immaculate new and spotless surplices, they sang "Who are these like stars appearing?" and "Who are these in dazzling brightness?", much to the amusement, I believe, of one of the young choirboys—William Harrison—then a boy of 10, but later to serve as Sexton and Clerk for many many years —a post now held by his son.

Parish Registers — Some unusual entries

(PUBLISHED JANUARY 1964)

PARISH Registers have been kept for well over 400 years, for a 1538 mandate ordered every parson, vicar or curate to enter in a book every wedding, christening and burial in his parish, with the names of the parties. The parish was ordered to provide a "sure-coffer" with two locks, the parson having the custody of one key, the wardens of the other. Entries were to be made each Sunday, after service, in the presence of one of the wardens.

"Old" Registers, of blank sheets of paper or parchment, gave the imaginative parson (or Parish Clerk, who often made up the Register) plenty of scope to add a variety of details of all sorts, if he so wished, to relieve the rather monotonous sequence of names. Some took the opportunity in full measure—others entered only the minimum requirements. The following are just a few "oddities", interesting though often tragic, noted recently in some Parochial Registers in South Norfolk.

In one very tiny parish, where baptisms, weddings and funerals were very infrequent, the Rector was called upon in 1619 to christen two children and to bury two of his parishioners in the space of four days. Such a sudden spate of official duties prompted this note in his Register: "Two Christenings and two burrialls in this small parish in 4 days time never so hapned since any man can remember".

It was the clerk of the same parish who entered this account of the baptism in 1641 of "Marye Weavers the Daughter of James Weavers and Mary his wyff the viiith of ffebruary. They wear walking people (beggars) and the woman came into Plombers barne (in the use of Thomas ffuller). They sayd the child was borne under a tree, abroad nyer unto the sayd barne but in what place or field or pastur close they would not tell".

The year 1697 saw another very curious baptismal entry —"Henery the son of Wildgoose Wanderer and To and Fro his wife, being laide under the window of widdow Barker living in the gravel pit house the 19th day of ffeb. in the midnight in bitter cold, was put out to be kept by the Town and was Bapt. the 12 day of March following". One can only assume that the parents' names were fictitious, as they were "vagrants"—but the incident is a sad reflection on conditions at the time.

A most unusual and irregular note had appeared in 1669. A certain marriage was recorded thus—"Mr. Daniel W— was married to Mrs. Jane U - - - the 2d Day of ffebruary. She was a widdow and came from Lin". It would appear that the partnership was not an amicable one—Jane proved to be a termagant—for in a space over the word "married" was inserted "to his much ruine".

Two more rather quaint but quite graphic notes were added in 1670—"ffebruary the 27 died Richard Huels and was buried the 28. He wash kild by ye overthrowing of a cart in wch he was it was not loaden and in the close called Hayhil or Common hill this hard acident befell him". A few days earlier—"Eliz. Reeder widdow died on ffriday ffeb. 17th and was buried on Sunday folowing carried to church by 4 own cousins of hers John Web and Richard Web of this parish and by Robert Web and Richard Web of Tacolston they were all of them above 50 years of age but none of them 60, and none of them took tobacco. This I set down because I believe the like will scarce happen in any age again".

The Rev. Edward Chappelow, Rector of Roydon and Curate of Diss for many years in the 18th century, was responsible for a host of revealing details in the registers of each parish. One from Roydon, August 10th, 1750, read thus: "Burial. Robt. Bulling 20. He was murdered at Yarmouth by John Banham a sailor about 19 yrs of age who was executed for the same crime on Wed. 26 Sept 1750 and then hung in chains at Yarmouth". Equally tragic was another note of 1750: "May 30. Burial. Wm Mason 41 who was killed on the Gravel Pits of Roydon. He had hold of a pole with which they were picking or pulling down a huge mass or vast quantity of Gravel which fell upon and broke the pole and occasion'd the end which he had in his hand to fly up and dash his brain out".

It fell to Mr. Chappelow to write up the Diss Registers, and in his enormous but very clear hand is recorded the last public execution in Diss—thus "Burial Nov. 19. 1741. Mary Frost who was poyson'd by Robert Carlton, Tayler, of Diss, for which crime and for sodomy he was condemned at the Assizes at Thetford viz. 20 March 1741, and executed the 5 April 1742. at Diss and afterwards hanged in chains on a gibbet upon Diss Common" (The 'year' then commenced at Easter, so March and April were actually consecutive months of 1742).

On September 24, 1766, buried "Sarah Foulger. 32. Her husband Wm. Foulger cut her throat in the most barbarous manner imaginable, having first offered to kiss her, then he instantly committed the horrid crime. She survived about an hour. In the interim he went and hanged himself and was bury'd without Christian Burial".

It seems to have been Mr. Chappelow's lot to record tragedy, for in Diss, 1748, he baptized "Honour the daughter of Honour Tipple, widdow." whose husband Thomas "was choked with eating a piece of beef and dyed in less than a quarter of an hour's time, and was buried March 1st, 1747". The next must have been a merciful release: "Buried Oct. 22. 1747. Robert the son of John and Elizabeth Syer who was born with a shorn lip without hands arms legs and thighs."

Nor did the unfaithful wife escape Mr. Chappelow's notice: "Bapt Ap. 20. 1751. Elizabeth daughter of Mary Barkaway the wife of James Barkaway who has been absent from his wife 2 years last past." But Elizabeth died, and at her burial in July, 1753, the entry ran: "Buried. Elizabeth. d. of Mary Barkaway whose husband James has been absent from his wife above 3 years. See Baptisms Ap. 20. 1751."

Following the baptism at Redenhall of "Elizabeth Bedinfield, daughter of Giles Bedingfield, and Marie his wife the 10 day of Februarie 1604" came this strange paragraph—"footnote—Giles B. and his pretended wyfe Marie Skeete were maried in a prohibited tyme wtout licence in an unlawfull place by an unlawfull minister viz. one Nicholas —, a Taylor, The woman being great wt. childe as wtin one monthe of her delivery."

Occasionally a well merited tribute may be implied in an entry as on "Oct. 31. 1766. Buriel of Martha, the wife of John Miller,—a noted midwife. aged 78." but more frequent are entries recording tragic deaths—"1650 John Norton buried May 3. fell from his horse and never spake word till died."—1651 "Henery Bell'd buried Aug 12. fell from house and brake his neck."—1762 "Henry Bullock 48, who fell into a pond and was drowned."

Following Lord Hardwicke's Marriage Act 1755, records of banns and marriages were required to be entered in registers of a prescribed and standard form, and from 1813 baptisms and burials were also recorded in standard form, with no recognized space for extra remarks like those already quoted.

But even then some rectors contrived to add interesting and informative marginal notes. Thus—1827. "Burial of George D —, in sight and in understanding blind from his birth, aged 24 years."—'1831 Buriel of David N —, accidentally drowned in the Mere when swimming 20 July. aged 16 yrs."

The bare fact that "Lorina Gooderham aged 46 was buried on 17 May 1829" was amplified thus—"found murdered in a lane near the Roydon Road called Broom Lane." Lorina Gooderham was none other than Louie Bryant, whose murder caused such consternation in Diss, and in spite of weeks of enquiry and examination—the mystery of her death remained unsolved.

Whipping and burning in Merrie England

(PUBLISHED FEBRUARY 1964)

ON January 21st, 1964, the Governor of Delaware, U.S.A. declared he would do all in his power to prevent the "public whipping" of a prisoner sentenced to receive ten lashes for a four dollar robbery. Delaware, it seems, is the last and only state in the Union to use the whipping post as a method of punishment. Lashes may be imposed for more than twenty crimes, including robbery and wife-beating—and the Governor thinks it is high time his state "should move ahead and abandon this practice."

I have recently spent many hours transcribing the "Tibenham Constables' Book"—quite a rarity, covering the years 1693-1756. It contains references to whipping, for which the Constable received a prescribed fee. Thus "Aug. 27th. 1750. To an order to whip Girl Baldra, and Expencis", for which Jacob Towler claimed his fee of 2s. 6d. Then in 1753 John Francis included in his "Disbursments"—"Expencis after Stephen Smith and going to Justices with him 10s."—"To Thos. Bolden 2s, and 1s. to James Abbet, for gard."—"Expencis at the Bell at Aslacton 1s ,, 6d"—"To whiping and expencis and corn for two Horses at Wymondham 2s ,, 10d." So far the story is clear—but what crime had Smith committed? The following items give the clue—"A lock for the Town Chist and mending the Church Door 1s ,, 2d."

Our Diss accounts for 1686 contain a disbursement by William Camell, Churchwarden "To the Rogue that was whipt at Sir John Castletons 6d." Sir John lived at Stuston—and the Diss constable whipped the rogue in his presence.

Gissing Accounts for 1732 include "for ye stocks and wipping post and a Church Stool £1-5-0" and "a bill of work for the towne, for irons for the stocks, boltes and lock and Irons for the wiping poost 7s-0d".

Whipping was for centuries a regular form of punishment. A 14th century theological dictionary, preserved in the British

Museum, states that according to Canon Law "a man may chastise his wife and beat her by way of correction for she forms part of his household; he, the master, may chastise that which is his". This was the view of "cultured ecclesiastics of the period."— Chaucer's England !

In an attempt to reduce the number of wandering beggars—an Act of 1388 ordered "all sturdy vagabonds and valiant beggars" to remain where they were at the passing of the Act, or to return to their place of birth, under penalty of "whipping" for the first offence, "loss of ears" for the second, and "hanging" for the third —if they flouted the Act.

Nearly two centuries later, in Tudor times, Henry Machyn described some of the revolting scenes he witnessed in London, of which city he was a "Citizen and Merchant Taylor".

1552 "The XIII day of January was put upon the pelore (pillory) a woman for she wold have poyssoned her husband and XIIII day she was wyped nakyd upward, and the XVIII day folowhyng she was agayne apone the pelere for slanderyng". Then in 1555 "The XVIII day of May was nodur lad wypyd at the same post in Cheap (side) for loytrying and rouning abowt as a vacabond".

At this same period a hired or retained servant who absconded from his employer without a parish testimonial, could be imprisoned or whipped unless some good natured soul would undertake to hire him.

An Act of 1575 imposed punishment for illegitimacy—and a typical illustration has survived among Denton papers. There in 1593 "Agnes Dey singlewoman was delivered of a manchild borne out of lawfull matrimony". It appeared, upon examination by two Justices "that ffrancys Everard was the indubitate reputed ffather". After ordering that Agnes Dey "shal not only as an naturall mother gyve milke unto ye said child" and that "the said ffrancys shall paie twelve pence of lawfull mony of Englond wekelie during the space of seaven whole yeares" - - - - - - then it was decreed "that Agnes Day shall att ye appoyntment and Discrecon of John Porter, minister, Robt Tyte, yeoman, and Richard Buninnge and ye two then Constables of ye towne of Denton, be whipped eyther publykely or privately within ye said Towne for her lewde offence".

That was Merrie England of Elizabeth I, which by another Act of 1572 had provided that all "rogues, vagabonds or sturdy beggars convicted of a roguish or vagabond trade of life" should be "grievously whipped and burnt through the gristle of the right ear with a hot iron of the compass of an inch abowt"—unless some honest person should take the offender into a year's service.

Even these drastic and brutal measures failed to reduce the number of vagrants, for yet another Act of 1598 ordained that "Every rogue, vagrant or sturdy beggar, taken begging, shall be stripped naked from the middle upwards, and openly whipped until his or her body be bloody, then forthwith sent from parish to parish the next streight way to the parish where he was born, there to labour for one whole year".

Among our Diss archives we have a beautifully written and preserved record of a public whipping in the Market Place at Eye in 1649. It reads "Eye: fforasmuch as John Neale, aged ffiftie yeares or thereabouts, beeinge a lusty stout man with browne beard, hath been taken vagrant within the Towne, and here openly whipped, Hee is therefore assigned to passe from Constable to Constable the next streight way to March in the Isle of Eleymeere Wisbitch where he was borne, and where he ys limited to bee within Tenn Dayes, at his perill. Given under our handes and seales beinge Bayliffes and Justices of the peece of the Town of Eye, Tho: Deye and John Throwge XXI ffeb: 1649." Similar warrants refer to the whipping of Phelep ffeturby and Thomas Jones "tacken vagrant at Disse" the same year.

A curious Act of 1697 provided that "Every 'pauper' (in receipt of parish relief), his wife and children should wear on the shoulder of the right sleeve of the uppermost garment in open and visible manner a large Roman P, together with the first letter of the name of the parish, in red or blue cloth". Any pauper defaulting was to forfeit his relief or be sent to a House of Correction, there to be whipped and set to hard labour for three weeks. Diss accounts show that 2s 8d was expended on "20 Badgges for ye poore" in 1709.

Whipping continued through the 18th century. The Norfolk Chronicle teems with examples—1741 "John C—— to be whipped for stealing a scythe and a spade"—"Philip H—— for stealing irons"—"Sarah Pooley for stealing a silver spoon, and to be burnt on the Hand."—1770 a woman "to be whipped in the Mkt. Place at Norwich for stealing a loin of lamb"—1776 "Nfk. Sessions —George Lyng for stealing a spade, to be publickly whipped in

Mkt. Place of E. Harling". An unusually degrading incident occurred in Norwich in August, 1776, when "Thomas Manclark was sentenced to be publickly whipped round the Mkt Place by the Common Hangman, for theft of yarn". It was intended that this method would be more salutary and ignominious than usual. But the intention was defeated "by the executioner being so far intoxicated as to be incapable of carrying out the sentence with any degree of propriety". For his "offence" the hangman was convicted of drunkenness, fined 5s, and "discharged from his office of public executioner".

As long as the Elizabethan laws remained in force, Justices not only had the power to order vagabonds to be whipped—but the duty to see it was done. Then in 1792 women were excused the indignity of being whipped by the passing of an Act stating "no female vagrant may be whipped for any reason whatever".

Whipping for men remained on the Statute book—though used less and less as the 19th century progressed, until it remained only as a disciplinary prison punishment for recalcitrant inmates. Not however till 1948, by an Act in the reign of George VI, were "penal servitude, hard labour and the sentence of whipping, abolished". The Act stated that "no person shall be sentenced by a Court to whipping, and as far as any enactment confers on a court to pass a sentence of whipping, it shall cease to have effect".

Now sixteen years later Governor Carvel of Delaware is trying to abolish whipping from the Statute book of his state, as Britain did in 1948. Soon, we hope, the whipping posts of Delaware will be just souvenirs of the past, or grim reminders of a harsher age, like the whipping post supporting the 17th century Market House at New Buckenham.

Corruption in high places
300 years ago

(PUBLISHED MAY 1963)

RATES, Revaluation and Assessments are much in the headlines these days and give rise to much controversy, both locally and nationally. Nearly 300 years ago—in February, 1689—a revaluation took place in Diss which caused deep dissensions and led to four years of continuous bickering and litigation. A sheaf of papers running to over 47 foolscap pages, containing petitions, rating lists, and Court evidence, covers the whole episode.

In those days the main rate was the poor rate, levied by the annual town (vestry) meeting on an assessment "agreed by the Townesmen among themselves for above 50 yeares, without differences". The overseers collected it, and relieved the poor under the direction of the church wardens.

It was said in evidence that "according to antient and constant usage time out of memory of man, the valuation of the town came to 2570£ which at 12d. in ye pound raysed without any manner of hardshipp opression or inequalitye such a yearely sume as was sufficient for ye reliefe of ye poore unless contageous distempers or great accidents befell".

John Burrough, an attorney, had recently come into the town—according to many, "to rule and order ye whole affaires of ye Towne, causing great contentions and disturbances by an arbitrary way of rating who and what he thought fitt".

Burrough was not well disposed towards the new King. William III, who had succeeded James II in 1688. Like many leading people in the district he was a Jacobite, and "because of his indecent and other demeanours and discourses against the new Government he was turned out of his Leifetennants place in the Militia".

But by intrigue, and "to set himself right against these miscarriages", he procured himself to be nominated a Commissioner of

Taxes under two Acts of Parliament—"one for a grant to their Maties of 2s. in the £ for one yeare, and the other for an additionall ayde of 1s in the £ for one year". As Commissioner, he nominated the assessors and "caused those persons to be returned assessors who were his own Croanyes".

Burrough produced his list of assessments in February, 1689, with 47 land and property owners and businessmen on it. It raised the town valuation to £8,500 by adding the value of business stocks to real estate.

This was to be the basis of the two grants to the King, and also of the new poor rate to be fixed at the Easter Vestry, 1689. It was particularly noticeable that Burrough—reputed to be "a great moneyed man worth above 3000£"—appeared on the list with no assessment against his name. He was ruthless, too—for "appeals" had to be heard "within tenn dayes before 3 Commissioners, according to the Act".

But Burrough was the only Commissioner within the Hundred, thus "many unjustly lost ye benefitt of appeale". An attempt was made to persuade Sir John Holland, of Quidenham, to complete the panel, but "being so indisposed, he could not travel so far".

By now Diss was seething with discontent, but worse was to come. Burrough and his "croanyes" (Heyward and Smyth, the churchwardens, and Ffoulser, a former overseer) schemed to re-elect themselves to make and levy the poor rate. Here are events as the documents relate them:

"On Easter Monday, 1689, Burrough having declared he would have his owne way and minde, and rate the Stocks, he took Heyward and Smyth, ye two old Churchwardens, with him from Church to ye Taverne (the 'White Horse') and there sett up all night, and there prevailed with Heyward and Smyth to hold Churchwardens for the yeare following, and that those two Churchwardens, Burrough himselfe, and Sam ffoulser, would be ye four overseers.

"Ffoulser should collect all rates, and pay all to ye poore ye whole yeare round, and Burrough would allow him for his trouble 5£ for his yeares sallery.

"According to this proposall (made over ye wine), they went early Tuesday morning from ye Taverne to ye Church againe, and there caused their names to be entred in ye Towne Book in ye absence of ye cheife Inhabitants, whereas there alwayes hath been chosen at the Publique Towne assembly two Churchwardens and four Overseers who provided for ye poore, and ye overseers executed their office each man his quarter, without charging the Towne anything.

"Burrough being an Attorney ought and always was excused from all offices, and his puttinge himselfe forward in this could be noe other than a piece of practice to sett ye Towne at variance."

Diss was now in a ferment. A petition by the leading townsmen was presented to the Justices at Stratton, asking them to annul the appointments of wardens and overseers, and order the four conspirators to hand over the books and the town stock (wool, hemp etc.) to the former officers, who agreed to serve a further year. The Justices also ordered the poor rate to be levied as before, on the old assessments.

Burrough, however, was still Commissioner and swore that as such he would "sowce" the tradesmen that opposed his being overseer; and he refused to pay his own poor rate.

The townsmen then appointed William Amys, a Woollen draper, "to reteyne such Councell, Attorneys, Agents and Sollicitors for the defence and preservation of antient rights and priviledges to prevent the altering of the poores rate".

Meanwhile, many others—under duress from Burrough and because of the confusion caused by the blunt refusal of Ffoulser to hand over his books, refused to pay their rates.

The big battle between the rival parties eventually took place at Quarter Sessions in April, 1690, when the evidence concerning Burrough's arbitrary action went overwhelmingly against him. The Court accepted the contention that his "new way of Asseasseing must create uncertaynty and intollerable trouble through the constant alteration in tradesmen's stocks", but compromised by ordering "every 100£ of such stock to be laid and rated equivalent to 5£ in land".

Further trouble ensued between "occupyers of land" and tradesmen—the former complaining that their share of supporting the poor was out of proportion. The Court appointed arbitrators —William Amys and William Camell, a "beere brewer"—and the townsmen agreed to abide by their assessments.

Two years later, in 1692, another conspiracy developed round one Samuel Kidman, a wealthy maltster, who, with others "being in confederacy", refused to pay rates, because their stocks were assessed too high.

Kidman was "a substantiall Tradesman with a dwelling house, maulting office and land, and 800 combe of barley. His daughter had a shop and traded in linning clothe and silkes. He was also a great Scrivener and Clark to several Justices which added to his ability at least 30£ p.ann. He had one sonne and he a fellow of a Colledge in Cambridge and another daughter sett up as a linnen Draper in Harleston - - ".

Like the others in his "confederacy", he claimed he ought not be rated for his trading stock, for he was "indebted as much and more than the same amount to". He lost his case at Stratton and on appeal at Norwich Quarter Sessions. So ended the rating dispute in 1693, after four years of constant quarrelling.

It should be added that John Burrough and his friends attended the official Town Meeting at the Church at Easter, 1693—at first still refusing to deliver up the Towne Booke. However, after Burrough had indulged in "very rough and rude language, and had taken some private noates and markes from the accounts", the book passed into the hands of the true churchwarden.

It is not surprising to find this entry in April, 1693: "These accounts have not for some time past bin stated in this booke in particulars as they ought to have bin (occasioned by some difference that happened amongst ye townsmen), but now we shall endeavour to put them into a right method."

The Diss Home Guard of 1640

(PUBLISHED MAY 1963)

WHEN German bombs fell near Canterbury on May 9th, 1940, and German glider-borne troops helped in the invasion of the Low Countries on the following day, the imminence of an invasion of Britain could not be discounted; and on May 14th, Mr. Eden, Minister of War, appealed by radio for Local Defence Volunteers "to deal with enemy parachutists by whatever ruses they came."

The response was overwhelming. There were queues of volunteers at Yarmouth; Norwich was "inundated"; a "rush" took place at Dereham; and at Diss one volunteer even applied to join while Mr. Eden was still broadcasting!

By the end of May more than a million men were organised in nightly patrols covering the whole country. Later they became the Home Guard.

Time and again Britain has been threatened with invasion. Time and again all able-bodied men have been called upon for local and national defence.

Four centuries ago, when the Spaniards threatened Queen Elizabeth's England, Henry Machyn, the London diarist, described how "The Lord mare dyd warne all the craftes (i.e. guilds) to bryng in ther men in harnes to Leydynghall with pykes and gones and bowes and bylles in bluw clokes gardyd with red and to muster in Morefield".

At the same time the men of Diss and Depwade Hundreds were mustered for training on "Buck'nam Comon" or "Cockstret Grene". These were the "Train(ed)-Band"—similar in function and in constitution to the Home Guard, but consisting of "ablemen, smythes, laborers, Pioners, whelewrites and Trayn'd persons".

Some of the last-named were armed with "bills or halberds" six feet long, terminating in a spike and fitted with a chopper-like curved blade. Others were equipped with lances or ragged staffs —knotted blugeons—while some even carried bows and arrows.

All wore "morions" (steel headpieces—forerunners of "tin-hats") and "corslets" (body armour). Pieces from this period have been preserved at Palgrave.

Firing power consisted of the light portable gun, the "caliver", the heavier "arquebuse" firing a ball of nearly 2ozs., and the musket.

Bressingham accounts contain such items as these for this period:

"Payde Thomas Gyffer for mendinge the town calyvere, 4d; payed one of the cunstables for poulder and shot, XVId.; payd for watche of beacons, XVId.; Byll of money laid out for the Towne, ffyrste for a pyke, iiiis " iiiid.; Itm. for a dagger, xxiid.; Itm. for scowring the furniture with a new scoorer for the Kalyver, xxd.".

In 1577 the Lord Lieutenant assumed control of the military forces of each county. They appointed officers and assessed the number of men each Hundred and each parish should provide for any contingency.

But the train bands were notoriously incompetent in rural areas—irregular in training, and undisciplined. Small wonder the Lord Lieut. of Norfolk ordered "more training and disciplining —the replacement of calivers by muskets, and the enrolment of able persons from 16 to 60" in the early 17th century.

For a muster in 1609, "Phillipe Gawdye, Captayne of the ffotmen within the Half Hundred of Diss", addressed this warrant to each parish constable: "These are to require and charge you to give warninge to all traynED persons nowe dwellinge in yr towne, and to every other person wch have been charged with armour yt they be wth ye same, furnished in serviceable manor, together with yr towne armor, before ye said Captayne at Disse upon XXI day of this instant monith by viii of ye clocke in ye forenoon, and to pay at ye time and place aforesaid vs " vid. for William Curson, Muster Master".

Picture the motley assortment of "irregulars", with their town arms and armour, converging on Cock Street Green for muster and manoeuvres, accompanied by parish constables, whose duty it was to ensure their attendance—for any order directed to constables concluded with this threat: "Hereof fayle not at yor uttermost perills". But no constable ever failed to submit his bill of expences "for kipenge of the Towne coselete iis " 1111d—for mendinge the muskete viiid.—for my diner at the muster vid".

France and Spain threatened England in the early 17th century, and when our local trained-bands gathered on Buckenham Common in 1621, they received orders "to defeat any foreign force that might attempt invasion of the Norfolk coast".

How like Mr. Eden's appeal of 1940!

But in 1640 a threat loomed up from a different quarter—for the Scots invaded northern England.

The actual "Commission of Array", dated September 3rd, 1640, directing the Lord Lieutenant of Norfolk to warn the trained bands to hold themselves in readiness to defend their own locality, is preserved in the House of Lords' library.

It reads: "Since certain rebels of our kingdom have hostilely attacked England with great strength, we dispose and ordain you to array a sufficient number of able pioneers and good carts with men and horses for carriage and draught, and a sufficient number of spades, shovels, pickaxes and all tools necessary for making defensive works in these perilous times; also take care that the county magazine is well stored with powder, shot, and match, and every musketeer of the trained bands for his particular use, and lastly, that the beacons be presently made ready and duly watched".

On September 11th certain Lords Lieutenant inquired; "Who is to pay for the Trained-Bands?" On September 24th—King Charles being at York—it was decided to summon a Parliament to vote money to buy off the aggressive Scots. The Lord Keeper of the Great Seal instructed the Clerk of the Crown to "issue orders to the Clerks of the Petty Bag, and to such others who may be useful for quick despatch of the business to make ready writs for Parliamt. which the King has appointed shall be held 3 Nov. next at Westminster".

On October 14th Sir John Holland, D.L., of Quidenham, ordered Matthew Gossling, Constable of the Diss Hundred, to alert local trained bands. The original warrant, signed by Matthew Gossling and directed to the Constable of Fersfield, still exists. It reads thus:

"These are to require you fforthwith to give warning to all the trained band within yor towne to be completely armed and ffurneshed in 24 howers warning with all necesseres for march and serves, and that you charg them to appear beffore Sir John Holland att Brissingham greene upon Monday next by eight of the clock in the morning with sufficient pouder and mach ffor that dayes serves, and that you cause supply men to be thear in readiness to searve iff ocasion shall requier; and that you cause to be beffore him one abell man of body to be Inrouled for a piner, to be provided with a shoulff spad, pickaxe, hachet or bille and the like ffor the making of workes of offence and deffence. More you are to provid one cart horse to carey the ameneshon with the traincd band and allso he requier the names and dwelling places of those piners you are to pressent beffore him in a lest ffairly written. Your loving ffrind, Matth. Gossling, Dysse, 14 Oct. 1640."

But those trained bands did not muster after all. Parliament met in November, refused to provide any money, then parleyed with the Scots to make a settlement finally declaring any mustering under the "Commission of Array" to be illegal.

In fact, Sir John Holland, a staunch Parliamentarian, was actually deputed to suppress all action under the very warrant he himself had issued in October, 1640.

> (Incidentally—the Home Guard of 1940 was for many months little better equipped than its forerunners, the trained bands of 1640.)

"*Old Grog's*" *victory*

(PUBLISHED JUNE 1963)

WHEN Charles Punchard presented his Churchwarden's accounts to the Diss Vestry in April 19th, 1742 "for the year last past"—they included this strange item—"Paid the ringers for ringing in NOT takeing Cartegine, 10s. 6d." This was followed by "paid Henn. Climance for ye ringers 1*l* 0s. 0d." and "paid to Catchpole for beere and for the Ringers 2*li* 8s. 0d."

As a barrel of beer then cost 24s., the consumption of about three barrels must have signified the celebration of an event of unusual importance, and "ringing" of considerable duration. What was this event ?

Britain was at war with Spain. In 1739 Capt. Edward Vernon had made violent attacks in Parliament, criticizing the Government's prosecution of the war, and had urged a firmer and more vigorous attitude to Spain. This had cost him promotion to Flag Rank—but he was unexpectedly appointed Vice-Admiral to take command of the West Indies Station. A man of great ability, though lacking in tact, he was rightly regarded as the best officer for the task of "destroying Spanish settlements in the West Indies and of distressing Spanish ships by any means whatsoever". Such were his instructions.

Vernon arrived off Porto Bello in Central America with six ships of the line. By February 12th, 1740, the Spanish forts guarding the narrow harbour entrance were silenced, and the British force captured the town. News of this victory sent England mad with excitement. Vernon was thanked by Parliament, awarded the Freedom of the City of London, medals bearing his portrait were struck, and many inns adopted his name, and his "likeness' as an inn sign.

In March, 1740, Vernon bombarded Cartagena—a Spanish stronghold on the north-west coast of South America, to force the Spanish fleet to put to sea—they refused to stir. A further assault was postponed until reinforcements arrived in January, 1741, when Vernon's naval forces were strengthened, and 8,000 troops arrived under Brigadier Wentworth, a man of "small ability and much deceit—lacking in tact and self confidence". No love was lost between the two commanders—a situation which later led to most unfortunate results.

Operations against Cartagena opened on March 9th, 1741. Four days later Vernon's naval force "cut the boom", and entered the harbour. On April 1st he sent home a despatch announcing this initial success, and expressing the hope that Cartagena would soon fall—the final assault on the forts being left to Wentworth's men.

That despatch of April 1st arrived in England in May.

News of victory spread rapidly—sparking off great rejoicings and jubilant celebrations throughout the country. A contemporary account describes the excitement when the news reached Diss on May 24th: "Bells were rung and Flaggs display'd on the steeple. In about two hours the town was turned into a Grove. Rich garlands hung in the streets. The soldiers under arms fir'd many vollies. In the afternoon the principal inhabitants met at the "King's Head", and spent the remainder of the day in drinking loyal healths. The Revd. Mr. Bosworth, the worthy Rector, also Mr. Coggeshall, Mr. Shreeve and Mr. Charles Simpson gave, each of them, a barrel of ale to the poor.

"In the evening the town was finely illuminated and a general joy appeared in all sorts of people. Next morning the Soldiers were again under arms, and fir'd several vollies at all the principal Gentlemen's Doors, with three Huzzas. No part of Norfolk could express greater satisfaction on so joyful an occasion, to the great credit of those publick spirited Gentlemen who were the conductors thereof. There were the greatest rejoicings and illuminations that were ever known all over the country—particularly at Diss."

In Norwich the news that the "ever victorious Vernon had made himself master of the forts at Cartagena and the glorious prospect he had of a compleat Conquest of the place, evoked the utmost demonstrations of Joy and Loyalty, including bonfires and illuminations at night, greater than any seen for many years. The Mayor and Principal Citizens drank loyal toasts with loudest acclamations, while beer was given to the populace and poor prisoners to drink His Majesty's health, and success to Admiral Vernon".

Meanwhile, as these very celebrations were proceeding, events at Cartagena had taken an humiliating turn. After Admiral Vernon's early success in forcing the boom, catastrophe had overtaken the subsequent operations. Wentworth, lacking powers of decision, delayed his military assault on the inner forts, and suffered an overwhelming reverse. Half his force of nearly 7,000 men were killed or dying—only a straggling remnant was re-embarked. the attack on Cartagena had failed. Edward Vernon was blamed —and reference books today describe him as "a British sailor in command of the disastrous Cartagena Expedition of 1741".

Diss had celebrated the primary success. It was later when news of the subsequent disaster filtered through that the ringers were paid for ringing in "NOT takeing Cartegine"—a peale of thanksgiving for the escape of that remnant of Wentworth's force.

Vernon returned to England in 1742, became M.P. for Ipswich, then returned to sea during the 1745 Rebellion, only to be struck off the list of Flag Officers in 1746 for publishing forthright criticisms of which the Admiralty did not approve. He died suddenly at Nacton, near Ipswich, in 1757.

But Admiral Vernon achieved lasting fame (or notoriety?) by adding a new word to our language—"Grog". In 1740, while awaiting reinforcements for his operations against Cartagena, he sent his Captains a memo drawing their attention to the danger of issuing neat rum to sailors—a practice "attended with many fatal effects, impaired health, and ruined morals, which made them slaves to every brutish passion".

Sailors serving on the West or East Indies stations had each received daily "$\frac{1}{2}$ pt. of Rum or Arrack served neat a little before noon". Vernon's order—a "Station" order only—stipulated that in future "1 quart of water was to be added to each $\frac{1}{2}$ pint of rum —the same to be issued in two servings at 11 a.m. and 5 p.m.". The practice commended itself to other officers, and it was quickly adopted throughout the Service.

This innovation at first gave great offence to the men, and caused Vernon to be very unpopular. He was nicknamed "Old Grog" at that time because he wore a distinctive cloak made of "grogram", a coarse fabric of silk and mohair and wool, stiffened with gum. The name "GROG" was disparagingly given to the diluted liquor he directed to be issued to his men—a name by which it has been known throughout the Senior Service ever since.

(Graphic details of the attack on Cartagena are given in

Ch. XXXIII of "Roderick Random" by Tobias Smollett, who was serving as a ship's surgeon on board H.M.S. Thunder.)

(Footnote: Serving in Vernon's Expedition against the Spaniards was Lawrence Washington, half brother of George, first President of the U.S.A. His admiration for Vernon was so great that when he inherited an estate at Hunting Creek near the Potomac River, he renamed it Mount Vernon in honour of the Admiral under whom he served. Mount Vernon became the Washington family home.)

Devastating storms of yesteryear

(PUBLISHED JULY 1963)

"A WIND approaching hurricane force, combined with hailstones as big as hen's eggs, created havoc in Diss and district on Wednesday evening. Greenhouses were wrecked, windows smashed and corn flattened by a storm which was without doubt the severest in living memory. At Palgrave greenhouses were shattered by hailstones, as were those in Frenze Road, 500 to 600 panes being broken. Fruit crops suffered considerably and branches of trees were cut off as if with a gigantic knife."

That was a report of a violent and destructive storm many of us remember all too well—on July 16th, 1947. It caused great devastation to crops at Frenze Hall, where "a blanket of hailstones as big as pennies" completely ruined corn and sugar beet crops. As that storm approached, through Suffolk, "geese were battered to death by a whirl-wind of hailstones the size of small apples."

Hailstorms are not uncommon in England, but periodically one of unusual intensity like that of 1947 has made headlines and established itself as worthy of record as an historic event.

Holinshed, in his chronicle of the year 1298, wrote: "On St. Margaret's even, that is the 9 day of Julie, fell a woonderfull tempest of haile that the like had not beene seene nor heard by any man then living. After that there insued such continual raine, so distempering the ground that corne waxed verie deare. Whereas wheate was sold before at 3d. a bushell, the market so rose by little and little that it was sold for 2s. a bushell

Another famous chronicler, Froissart, described the dramatic effect of a hailstorm on King Edward III, who in 1360 was waging war in France. French emissaries had tried persistently to negotiate peace terms, but Edward was stubbornly evasive. Then, in Froissart's own words: "A violent storm of thunder and haile fell upon the English army. It seemed as if the world were come to an end. The hailstones killed both man and beast, even the boldest were frightened by the storm. The King himself was quite overcome by it, and turning to the Church of our Lady at

Chartres, vowed to the Virgin that he would conclude a peace, and so he did."

Two centuries later, a Norwich historian recorded that in 1580 there arose in Norfolk "a great Tempest of Thunder, Lightning, Whirlwind and Rain. The Hailstones accompanying this storm were fashioned like the Rowels of Spurs, two or three inches about. They beat the corn flat to the ground, tore up trees by the roots, and shivered them in pieces."

In the Scole Parish Register I discovered one of the most apt descriptions of a hailstorm, entered as "Memorandum, 1604". (The storm was probably just a local one—a freak—for no mention of it appears in the records of neighbouring parishes.) It runs: "1604 Greate Haile. Uppon the 6 of June in the said yeere, and about 5 of the clock in the afternoone, there was a mightie greatt and fearefull haile, the stones about the bignes of walnuts and rugged like nut galls, clere as glasse, wherein was great hurt in corne, hempe and fruite. John Smith parson there."

Some 50 years later John Evelyn made this entry in his diary for June 1652: "After a drought of near four months there fell so violent a tempest of hail, rain, wind, thunder and lightning as no man had seen the like in his age, the hail being in some places four or five inches about. It brake all glass about London, especially at Deptford, and more at Greenwich."

Again, at Norwich on July 20th, 1656, "there happened a great temptest of Thunder and lightning very terrible with a storm of Hail—the Hailstones as big as pullets eggs, and fire ran upon the earth".

In his *Norfolk Annals* of the 19th century Mackie recorded a severe hailstorm in West Norfolk in 1817, when "hailstones measuring six inches in circumference caused much damage, and killed many rooks". And another severe thunder storm on July 4th, 1819, was accompanied by "a tremendous hailstorm and a heavy rain which washed away hundreds of acres of turnips and did much damage to wheat and barley". In a storm widespread through Norfolk in 1837, "barley and wheat were completely beaten out by hailstones, which lay six inches deep in places. Pieces of ice as big as walnuts, cut turnips to shreds, and lay under the hedges next morning in their original size."

Probably the most spectacular, destructive and violent hail storm ever recorded in Norfolk occurred on August 9th. 1843.

Approaching from the west, it struck Cambridge at 4.30 p.m. Thetford between 6 and 7 p.m. and then, travelling in a track five miles wide, burst on Norwich at 7.30 p.m. In its path entire fields of wheat and barley were reduced to straw by hailstones one to six inches in circumference.

Between 6 and 7 p.m. "hailstones descended in torrents at Thetford, pulverising the windows facing the hurricane. Many of the hailstones, or rather pieces of ice, were upwards of $1\frac{1}{2}$ inches square; they killed more than 100 sparrows, and vast numbers of rabbits on the heath. Shops and warehouses in Bridge Street were inundated to a depth of two feet, and when the Lynn coach passed through the street, the horses were up to their chests in water."

At Norwich old men could remember nothing like it. "Hail stones, or rather morsels of ice two inches and more in diameter, descended in such profusion that objects could not be discerned through the falling mass, which accumulated in many places to a depth of four to five inches. The crash of windows was heard on every side like a volley of fire arms, made more horrifying by the rush and roar of a mighty wind.'

Yet another storm of unusual severity descended upon Diss on Wednesday, June 16th, 1860. This description of it, from an old diary, brings to mind the "Scole Memo. of 1604 ':

"In a great tempest of hails, most of the stones were as big as walnuts which could be taken up the Friday following by handfuls wasted to the bigness of hazell nuts many of the stones the length of a man's finger, bent and rugged. Their force was so great as to break the glass windows of houses, beate downe the leaves of trees and to shore down the wheat and hemp to a very great quantitie."

We in Diss remarked on the size of the hailstones that fell on Tuesday, June 18th, 1963, but they were pigmies compared with those "fashioned like rowels of spurs" at Norwich 400 years ago—or those "rugged like nut galls clere as glasse" which fell at Scole in 1604. Those of 1963 failed to make headlines and were reported in an obscure corner of our daily paper, merely as "half inch hail".

In the dead of night . . .

(PUBLISHED APRIL 1963)

MOST of our East Anglian towns have experienced disastrous fires and other calamities in the past four centuries, but it was in the late 16th century and throughout the 17th that a whole series of catastrophes befell them.

Diss and Norwich suffered severely from the plague of 1597; Dereham was almost obliterated by fire in 1581; Beccles lost 80 dwellings and the woodwork of its church was gutted by fire in 1586; and Bury suffered £60,000 loss by fire in 1608, when 160 houses were destroyed.

Then the plague came in 1636, when "grass grew in the streets and 400 families were sick". In March 1645 Lowestoft was devastated by fire, after recovering from a similar affliction in 1546 and the ravages of the plague in 1603 which caused 316 deaths.

It was in April, 1645, that Diss experienced the most calamitous fire in its history—mercifully without loss of life. It is not surprising that fire spread rapidly through the old thatched and timbered dwellings of those days especially if fanned by strong winds for the only fire fighting equipment was "bucketts and cromes". Diss had not even a "squirt". There was no "fire ingeon" in East Anglia at all until 1690, when St. Peter Mancroft Parish acquired one of the earliest variety. Rows of "bucketts" or "tankards", and long-handled "cromes" or "crooms", hung in the church porch ready for an emergency.

Though the Civil War was raging in 1645, and many weary bedraggled "passengers" wandered from place to place begging for relief, the war did not unduly disturb this part of East Anglia.

Certain ministers were relieved of their livings for refusing to subscribe to the "Solemn League and Covenant", and men were "impressed" for army service. Special taxes too were imposed to pay for the Parliamentary forces, as old rating lists show, while troops of the Diss Hundred trained regularly on Cock Street, Heywood and Bressingham Greens—but otherwise life in Diss was fairly normal.

April 23rd, 1645, had drawn to a close without any excitement. After the day's training on the Green local troops had spent a convivial hour at the "Sign of the Ship" before dispersing to their respective villages.

Thomas Baylye, Jr., of "Nicolas St.", and Robt. Lancester, of "Coxstret", the Town Constables, had completed their rounds. The night watchmen, Henry Kett, of "Nicolas Strett", and Rogar Spinck, of "Markett Stret", were making their final check on the town too when, from the Market Place, they saw flames leaping high into the night sky from the vicinity of the "Ship".

The alarm bell on the "Dolphin" was rung, Spinck hurried to fetch Edmund Tolver, the Sexton, from "Smyth Street" to clash the five church bells and arouse the town, while Kett, armed with a "crome" from the church porch, rushed to the scene of the fire —a group of thatched cottages behind the "Ship".

Soon the whole town congregated at the spot, Reygnould Shuckforth and Thomas Burton, the churchwardens, directed the fire fighting, tearing away burning thatch with cromes, and organising a chain of buckets from the Mere.

In spite of their collective efforts the fire raged for four hours before the last flames were extinguished. A scene of desolation was revealed at sunrise on April 24th. with Temes St. and Mere Green cluttered with the household effects of the 21 homeless families.

The overseers arranged for immediate relief and emergency accommodation for the victims and the Town Vestry met to discuss the course of action. Thomas Colman, Gent., of Temes St., Henry Roper, Carpenter, and Robert Burdith, Mason, were appointed to survey and assess the damage. Their estimate was £2,090, which at 1963 figures would represent nearly £100,000.

This staggering loss seemed more than the town itself could bear, so the Vestry decided to petition for a "brief". The original parchment of this is preserved, entitled "The Humble Petition of the Suffering Inhabitants of the Towne of Dysse". Here is a part of it:

"The 24th Aprill 1645 (in the dead time of night) it pleased

God to visitt your petitioners with a great losse occasioned by a lamentable ffire (which by accident happened) that in the space of four houres burnt and consumed the habitations of your petidioners to the number of one and twentie ffamilies the whole losse whereof amounted to 2090£ as by the severall oathes of workemen and others imployed to veiwe the same by the certificate hereunto annexed may appear. And whereas ye petitioners before this sad accident were both able and willing to contribute to all good occasions both of publique and private concernment, which they more espetially manifested in their exceeding forwardness to be helpfull to advance the cause of God and the Kingdome, to which they are not only disabled to continue their assistance, but are become miserable of povertie and misery, that without the Charity of Godly disposed people, with their wives and children are exposed to utter ruine. They dispaire of meanes of subsistence unless assisted by the Corporate almes of a generall Collection".

The petition ended with a heartfelt appeal for a "brief" for which, if granted, "ye petitioners and their ffamilies would be ever bound to pray for their Lordships".

Parliament did consider it, and noted the undertakings that none of the money collected would be diverted into wrong channels. In a lengthy "Brief" of some thousand words they authorised "a generall Collection throughout the Citties, Townes, Villages, Hamletts, Libertyes, Priviledge Places and all places under the pervew of Parliamt. within the Counties of Middlesex, Kent, Essex, Suffolke, Norfolke and Cambridge, for the reliefe of the Towne of Disse".

Sad it is to have to relate that in spite of all the elaborate petitioning and administrative arrangements, not one single penny was received in Diss. Careful search in the records of dozens of churches, and many enquiries further afield, have failed to reveal even one contribution to the brief. This was not for lack of sympathy or to unwillingness to help the distressed, but to the confusion occasioned by the strife between King Charles and Parliament.

The Long Parliament (in session since 1640) had actually "inhibited collection upon brief under the Great Seal", because the proceeds of such could be (and had been) diverted from their intended use, to support the King against Parliament. This brief for Diss was authorised by the "Lords and Commons", NOT under the Great Seal. Suspicion, however, was attached to all

Briefs at this time, particularly in E. Anglia where loyalties were divided between King and Parliament.

So Diss was left to repair its own losses without outside help. And, by a stroke of bad fortune, exactly the same area near the "Sign of the Ship" was gutted by another disastrous fire on April 27th, 1847.

The great fire of Diss

(PUBLISHED AUGUST 1962)

THE siren wails and within seconds, it seems, the Diss fire engine is manned and on its merciful errand. Modern communications and equipment have reduced the time-lag which formerly allowed many fires to burn out before organised fire-fighting could be effective.

The first great fire recorded in Diss was in 1645, when "in the dead tyme of an April night there happened a great and lamentable fyer" which, in four hours, consumed 20 homes and caused losses of £2,090—a considerable sum in those days.

Leading townsmen, backed by the County Justices, petitioned Parliament for help. "The Lords and Commons in Parliament assembled" ordered a Brief (collection) throughout Eastern England, for the "suffering inhabitants of Dysse".

Alas ! The Long Parliament had already imposed heavy rates to support its forces against King Charles and not one single response to that Brief can be traced.

Only "leather bucketts" and long-handled "cromes" were available to fight that terrifying fire near the "Ship". Even with abundant Mere water nearby, such equipment was useless.

But better appliances were being devised. Experimental engines were produced by a Scot (1650) and a German (1657), yet at the Fire of London (1666) only "squirts, bucketts ladders and cromes" were used. However, that great disaster encouraged Van der Heid to persevere and produce the first reliable engine in 1672—the forerunner of all manuals.

The primitive equipment at Diss was retained until 1728, when the leading citizens organised a subscription list (still extant) to purchase a town engine. Lady Holland, of Quidenham, was paid £50 for it and £9 was expended on "2 doz. ½ of leather bucketts."

Little is known of that Newsham engine except that it was frequently "play'd," or exercised, and that lashings of beer were consumed at each turn-out. "Beer to the men that play'd the engin"—"cleaning and oyleing the pipes and bucketts"—"taking ye Engin apeices and putting together" are phrases that frequently appeared in the expenses.

That engine was replaced in 1774 by an improved "Sun" engine—like that in the Castle Museum—a manual with solid wheels, requiring "8-aside" for maximum pumping. Its range was limited, but it operated at many fires.

In August, 1813, a messenger from Frenze rode into Diss at 3.30 a.m. to awaken the sexton, who clanged the church bells to arouse the firemen. By 4 a.m. the engine was in operation, attacking a fire from a heated haystack with water carried from the river by "two ranks of rich and poor indiscriminately mixed." A vast crowd assembled, and witnessed many "elegant Diss ladies at their bucket stations" for eight hours in succession.

Another challenge came in May, 1847, when fire gutted the "Ship" Inn and adjoining property at 2 a.m. Bells were rung but there seems to have been little confidence in the ageing "Sun," because the Eye Boro' Engine was also summoned.

The wind was violent; for hours efforts to fight the flames seemed fruitless, and not before nine tradesmen had lost their entire effects, and 40 people were homeless, was control gained.

"Sun" had failed, and only "their superior engine and the help of the Townspeople of Eye" saved Diss from an even worse disaster.

But the City Fathers postponed replacing "Sun"—as usual, on a question of expense. With help from the insurance companies they eventually purchased an almost new engine for £100 in 1859. John Aldrich, remembered by many over 70, went to Birmingham to buy it and in August "Niagara" came to Diss.

What a name for a fire extinguisher ! A fire brigade was formed of men of such names as Buttley, Sussames, Lusher, Crick, Chenery, Buckle, Cobb and Easto—trained by an officer of the N.U.F.O. Brigade.

Niagara was fitted with shafts, for single or double draught. She was heavy even for two horses, but "Nigger," the massive Council horse of later years, is said to have "laughed" at having to haul her.

Niagara's career was long and honourable. For 70 years she attended fire after fire and was associated with many amusing incidents.

In 1869 a barn caught fire at Palgrave. The owner was "in the hay," so his agitated wife "sent a boy to fetch the engine."

By mistake he went to Scole. When Niagara eventually arrived the barn and contents were in ashes.

In August, 1871, grit in the machinery of the Scole Flax Mill caused sparks to ignite inflammable fibre. The alarm whistle was sounded, but "for some reason was not understood in Diss." So —while the factory burned, a messenger hastened to Diss on foot. Mr. Humphrey of the Railway Tavern, seeing him pass, and hearing him shout "Fire ! Fire !, then galloped to commission the engine. 'Tis said that only eight minutes passed between "bellringing and turnout."

George Rackham, John Markwell, Flim Rice, Bob Licence and Dorner Saunders can recount many amusing stories of Niagara. Beer was brought from the "Dick" in buckets for the thirsty pumpers after the Butts Fire on Wortham Ling in 1897. Thirty-two men pumped Waveney water to quell a fire of blazing bushes that broke out on the Mound, while the Volunteers were shooting.

At a Thrandeston fire Bertie Ward drove Niagara down the Gassocks Hill at Palgrave, drawn by a horse and a donkey. She gained such momentum that the donkey was lifted off its feet, and rode down the hill seated in the curve of the cross-bar.

A "bathfull" of beer was brought out on this occasion . . . .

Bob Licence remembers helping to drag Niagara to a fire in the Devil House at the Factory. Almost exhausted when they reached the Market Place, they "impressed" two horses from a passing van to haul the engine to Shelfanger Road. The fire over, "everyone with his hand on the handle" received 2s. 6d. from Ben Barber.

Derek Kitchen, going to school one day, heard Niagara rumbling through Church Street. So, too, did the horse in the milk-float standing unattended in the Market Place. But the clatter of hooves was too much—he pricked up his ears and dashed off to follow Niagara up Mount Street— scattering churns and lids to clatter across the street.

With great presence of mind, Kenneth Nunn, then a small boy, ran alongside the float, gathered up the trailing reins and brought the horse to a halt.

However, Niagara had had her day. In 1929 she gave way to a trailer-pump. The brigade then contained seven Rices—veteran "George" with sons Stanley, Reggie and Harry, and "Barney" Rice with sons Bert and Jack—an amazing example of family public service. Niagara was not present at Aldrich's fire of 1938 —outside brigades were called to help from Ipswich and Norwich. Final retirement came with the arrival of the Albion-Drysdale, then in 1946 Niagara was sold for scrap. En route for Rickinghall she "play'd" at New Waters in one final defiant gesture. Her brass pump was sold, her gig lamps and "Niagara" nameplate went to the museum of a "Fire Insignia Antiquarian" in Ipswich, while her mahogany "box" was converted into furniture for use at Walsingham's.

In a sense it was a sad end to a great public servant, but memories of Niagara will live on, and her name is in a place of honour among those museum exhibits—for ever.